The Deepening Crisis

POSSIBLE FUTURES SERIES

Series Editor: Craig Calhoun

In 2008, the World Public Forum convened a group of researchers and statesmen in Vienna to take stock of major global challenges. The magnitude of the global financial crisis was only just becoming clear, but the neoliberalism and market fundamentalism of the post-Cold War years had already taken a toll of their own.

Austrian Prime Minister Alfred Gusenbauer opened the meeting with a call to make sure the urgent attention the financial crisis demanded was not just short-term and superficial but included consideration of deeper geopolitical issues and governance challenges facing the global community.

In this spirit, several of the researchers present envisioned a project to bring together the analyses of leading scholars from a range of different countries, assessing not only the financial crisis but shifts in relations among major powers, trends in political economy, and the possible futures these opened. The group sought insight into emerging issues; it did not indulge the fantasy that the future could be predicted in detail.

The World Public Forum, created to facilitate a dialogue of civilizations rather than a clash, saw value in bringing high quality research to bear on public issues and possible futures. It provided financial support to the project including opportunities for many of the researchers to gather at its annual meetings on the island of Rhodes. This initial support was crucial to inaugurating the present important series of books.

VOLUME I

Business as Usual: The Roots of the Global Financial Meltdown

Edited by Craig Calhoun and Georgi Derluguian

VOLUME II

The Deepening Crisis: Governance Challenges after Neoliberalism

Edited by Craig Calhoun and Georgi Derluguian

VOLUME III

Aftermath: A New Global Economic Order?

Edited by Craig Calhoun and Georgi Derluguian

ALSO IN THE POSSIBLE FUTURES SERIES

Russia: The Challenges of Transformation

Edited by Piotr Dutkiewicz and Dmitri Trenin

The Deepening Crisis

Governance Challenges After Neoliberalism

Edited by Craig Calhoun and Georgi Derluguian

A joint publication of the Social Science Research Council
and New York University Press

NEW YORK UNIVERSITY PRESS

New York and London

www.nyupress.org

Text Design: Debra Yoo

Library of Congress Cataloging-in-Publication Data

The deepening crisis : governance challenges after neoliberalism / edited by Craig Calhoun and Georgi Derluguian.

    p. cm. -- (Possible futures series ; v. 2)

"A co publication with the Social Science Research Council."

Includes bibliographical references and index.

  ISBN 978-0-8147-7280-5 (cl : alk. paper) -- ISBN 978-0-8147-7281-2 (pb : alk. paper) -- ISBN 978-0-8147-7282-9 (e-book : alk. paper) 1. Global Financial Crisis, 2008-2009. 2. Neoliberalism. 3. Economic policy. I. Calhoun, Craig J., 1952- II. Derluguian, Georgi M.

HB3722.D44 2011

330.9--dc22   2010052310

New York University Press books are printed on acid-free paper, and their binding materials are chosen for strength and durability.

Printed in the United States of America

c 10 9 8 7 6 5 4 3 2 1

p 10 9 8 7 6 5 4 3 2 1

Contents

Introduction

Craig Calhoun and Georgi Derluguian

In much of the world, one can simply say "the crisis," and what is under-stood is the financial crisis centered on New York, London, and other major markets for capital and debt. This is so even though there are other serious social problems. Some of these—like the degradation of the environment and global climate change—are arguably more momentous. As important as it is to understand the crisis in global finance, it is also important to recognize that the financial crisis is only one dimension of a larger cluster of crises that coincide to produce turbulence and turmoil in global affairs. The current crisis thus includes a deep—though not fatal—disruption of financial markets and capital accumulation globally. But it also includes severe environmental challenges, wars and other security threats, and disarray in global governance. The economic issues raised by financial crisis are necessarily entangled in politics, large-scale social change, and basic issues of cultures and civilizations. Indeed, the struggle to cope with financial crisis reveals problems in politics and global gov-ernance and threatens to derail action on environmental concerns. While volume 1 in the Possible Futures series focused on the financial crisis itself, volume 2 focuses on these entanglements.

In this regard, the current concatenating crises remind us of some-thing we should have known all along. Economics is always entwined with politics; both are also always matters of social organization and culture. It is only under ideological influence—and through mental habits encouraged by the divisions of academic disciplines—that we ever forget this. If neoliberalism reinforced the idea that "the economy" was properly separate from government interference, the financial crisis reveals this to be nonsense. The crisis is not merely financial, not confined to markets, and not just an aberration within otherwise smooth capitalist growth. Market meltdown coincided with two major wars and the insecurities produced by terrorism and insurgency. It came on the heels of two decades of massive Chinese accumulation of Western, especially US, debt, and recovery from it is shaped by shifts in global economic power. And the crisis and the response to it both reflect intensified globalization and boom markets—each of which was influenced by the fall of Communism, the process of European unification, and a global fashion for deregulation and privatization.

Not only to understand the crisis but also to understand what futures are possible in such a troubled world, it is important both to bring forward new analyses and to situate new developments in historical context. The financial crisis is part of a larger historical process restructuring relations among countries, regions, and civilizations. This was furthered by the end of the Cold War and the rise of neoliberalism with its celebration of minimally regulated private accumulation. Yet major new economic powers like China have succeeded partly by insisting on state-led strategies of economic development. It is important to see how both the nature of the crisis and the possible paths out of it are shaped by wars, the decline of American hegemony, the rise of China and other powers, and shifting geopolitics stretching back to the end of the Soviet Union and beyond. Likewise, both China and Russia are acutely conscious of the importance of geopolitics, even though this was marginalized in much Western academic discussion for many years. At the same time, it is also important to see what possibilities are opened by innovations in global governance institutions—and what possibilities may be foreclosed by the increasing severity of environmental degradation and potentially destabilizing climate change.

The possibilities are informed by new technologies that not only remake markets but remake global social movements. They are informed by geopolitical realignments that may eventually produce a new, multilateral world but in the meantime have produced new security threats and diplomatic challenges. And they are informed by new religious mobilizations and solidarities—linked on some occasions to terrorist attacks and on others to dialogues among the world's civilizations.

Our multiple crises—finance and much more—are crucially crises of governance but also crises of imagination. We struggle to develop the categories and ideas, even the vocabularies, with which to grasp how both global conflict and cooperation are shaped by religion, by regional integration and power struggles, by new media, and by transnational flows of people and money, as well as by efforts at transnational governance.

Meeting these new challenges is partly a matter of governance, within states, in collaboration among states, and in both old and new nonstate organizations, as David Held and Kevin Young lay out in chapter 1. Complexity and risks have escalated across several domains. In each—especially finance, environment, and security—there are a series of deficiencies. These are more than mere short-term failures, and though they are influenced by ideological distortions, they have broader and more basic sources. Held and Young approach these in terms of capacity and responsibility. As problematic and limited as recent efforts to achieve improved financial governance in the wake of the crisis are, they nonetheless point to the possibility that political attention can be focused on needed reform. This is urgent because problems are growing in both their potential impact and the extent to which they are interlinked. But institutional means for addressing them are severely underdeveloped.

Thus, one of the limits to the idea that a new Keynesianism coupled with modest financial regulation can be a sufficient response to global financial crisis is simply that the old governance institutions are inadequate to the new policy needs. This is clear inside individual states: think of the governance challenges posed by massive stimulus spending, much of it based on untested public-private partnerships with inadequate provisions for effective contracting or oversight.[1] It is an issue posed for the European Union, whether one considers it an interstate federation or a sort of superstate—and it has proved a very difficult issue as some member states seek aid and others seek more financial autonomy (see chapter 6 by Della Sala). And the issue appears as both an incentive for the development of other regional organizations (ASEAN, SAARC, AU, OAS, etc.) and a challenge to their efficacy. The issue is equally challenging at a global level. It is an issue not just for the IMF or the WTO but also for the host of organizations set up among private corporations, often within industries, to help govern and stabilize their relations with each other. As Held and Young point out, in every domain there are numerous actors but weak structures of authority among them and thus weak capacity for concerted collective action. Considerable inertia complements active efforts to retain existing institutions—which of course serve some interests, even if not the broadest global interests.

Held and Young hope for a world coalition of liberal, social democratic, and progressive reformers; nongovernmental organizations; "elements of geopolitically resurgent states, such as Brazil, India, China, and Russia; and finally, those diverse economic forces that desire a more stable global economic order," all inspired by the idea of cosmopolitanism. It is worthwhile to connect this discussion to three of the chapters in volume 1 of the Possible Futures series. Immanuel Wallerstein predicts something similar—a search for middle ground between the enlightened wing of Davos's World Economic Forum and the more hierarchical wing of Porto Alegre's World Social Forum.[2] Wallerstein is perhaps less sanguine than Held and Young about the prospects for such a coalition, let alone successful global institutions built on it. It is also important to ask (in the spirit of Nancy Fraser's chapter in volume 1) in what proportion this would shift to global governance the ambiguity of national welfare states that administer social support in often conservative rather than emancipatory ways.[3] And we may ask (in the spirit of Manuel Castells's chapter in volume 1) whether new governance capacities will be exercised to shore up the old economy or to create a facilitating context for creativity and the new economy.[4] Of course, still more questions remain: Will world powers learn to work together to create a new world order, or will they be locked in new patterns of global conflict? How strong will attempts to create international regulatory systems be? How readily will nation-states evade them? Can the numerous other actors be more effectively organized?

The pursuit of stable and effective governance, like the pursuit of stable economic growth, runs into a variety of specific complications in contending with different sets of issues, each also basic to human life and global affairs. Environmental degradation poses many of the most basic and most challenging. It appears in the entanglements of politics, economics, ordinary social life, and troubled ecologies in various localities from the Niger Delta to Brazilian rainforests to Lake Baku.

In chapter 3, Michael Watts takes up this theme with special attention to the wave of famines, droughts, and partially climate-shaped wars in Africa. He lays out the impact neoliberalism has had in Africa—weakened states, subjection to global markets with relatively weak local institutions—but though Africa is in many ways an extreme case, the issues appear on every continent. Africa is, among other things, a sort of laboratory for the invention and circulation of development ideas and practice—and for ideas about how to deal with environmental challenges. So while Watts's chapter focuses on environments in Africa, it informs us more generally about the issues shaping the prospects for sustainable development worldwide. These are issues of governance, as Held and Young suggest, but also of governmentality, the generation of rationalized regimes for constituting the relationship between material conditions and human life. Under both colonial rule and postcolonial structures of unequal exchange and continued domination, Africa exemplified the relationship among development (or its lack), population growth, hunger, and conflict. The lessons have often been bleak, but they do not have to be, and significantly there are signs of both growth and effective reform in parts of Africa even during the ostensible global crisis. Moreover, hidden in the stories of conflict and rapacious rulers there are also lessons about resilience. It would be a mistake simply to predict Africa's future as an extension of its past, and in any case, as Watts reminds us, we should be conscious of the limits to predictive modeling as we think about the contemporary crisis as a complex of potential tipping points.

The challenges of managing natural resources well are played out very visibly—and worryingly—on an African stage. But they are also global challenges, and they intersect with global environmental concerns. This is not just a matter of fossil fuels and minerals but of arable land and clean water. And the competition involves not just rapacity of the world's rich and overconsuming countries, like the United States, but the desire of many poorer countries, like China and India—and for that matter South Africa—to grow and the desire of others that have one major resource, like Arab oil producers, to trade it for a range of others.

As if resource competition and the actual or potential devastation of various ecologies were not challenging enough, there is also the global problem of climate change. In addition to those who deny the increasing scientific consensus that climate change is happening, there are many who cling to hopes that some technological solution will appear and perhaps even more who simply can't bear to focus on an issue with such dire implications and so few promising nondisruptive lines of action. Yet as William Barnes and Nils Gilman suggest in chapter 2, climate change may be even more powerful than capitalist crises in bringing the modern era to a point where the choice is starkly one of transformative change or a descent into barbarism.

The potential for global warming (and the range of extreme weather-related conditions that may be associated with it) is finally being discussed. But it is discussed mainly as a matter of technology to mitigate it and economic measures to reduce it. The latter amount mostly to a variety of incentive systems like carbon trading, each designed to reduce the production and emission of environmentally damaging chemicals. The economic crisis has made many of these measures seem long-term and therefore optional, a matter for future attention, whereas efforts to restore growth demand immediate focus. But there is also a deep disproportion between the proposed mitigating measures and the potential for damage from climate change. As Barnes and Gilman summarize, "The human carrying capacity of the planet may decline by an order of magnitude. Short of thermonuclear war, modern civilization has never faced a more dire existential threat."

What Barnes and Gilman seek to explain is the absence of political will to face this threat. They describe the failure of the Copenhagen summit, held under the shadow of financial crisis, and they reveal the surprising faith of many environmental activists in financial measures like "cap and trade." This reflects the desire to mobilize the existing economic structure to meet the environmental challenge, and thus it incorporates the irony that cap and trade would involve the creation of new financial instruments and markets largely under the auspices of the bankers and traders widely held responsible for the financial crisis. Even many radical Greens seem captive to the economic orthodoxies of finance capitalism. But coming to terms with climate change requires a shaking of economic orthodoxies and renewal of political will similar to those needed to address financial crisis itself. And there is a further shared problem: the difficulty of imagining the decline of existing forms of production as desirable—and the still greater difficulty of acting politically on the basis of such an understanding. Barnes and Gilman find historical inspiration—and tempered optimism—in progressive forms of populism from the nineteenth century, what they call "producerist republicanism," and hope something like this may become part of a more forward-looking, environmentally focused social democracy. As they note, however, moving away from wishful thinking toward realism is, in this domain as in many others, "terrifically challenging."

The issues of security and conflict are also sharply challenging. The financial crisis has been exacerbated by the massive cost of the two wars that the United States mounted in response to the 9/11 terrorist attacks. Whether this was a well-considered response or not, and whether or not the wars have been well conducted, they have had two extremely important consequences: they have enormously increased US debt, and they have severely limited US political options—with regard to both domestic and international policy. There is here an echo of the Vietnam War, shaping conflict of an earlier generation and crucial component of the 1970s crisis. As Mary Kaldor notes in chapter 5, it was against the background of its Vietnamese engagement that the United States first ran an external trade deficit in 1971 and that the system of fixed exchange rates tied to gold was abandoned.

Addressing the relationship of war to economic crisis, Kaldor goes on to show other linkages between the "war sector"—organized for destruction—and the more productive economy. Each has a role in shaping technological transformation, for example, as the military funds technologies of potentially large civilian importance, like the Internet. Kaldor argues, though, that continued dominance of an older organizational style in the military (despite expensive technologies) is holding back an overall economic-technological transition. She connects this to the long cycles of neo-Schumpeterian theory (discussed in volume 1) but also to the many other faces of war in the contemporary era, including the "new wars" conducted partly by means of spectacular violence and the problems of governing chronically insecure spaces.[5] Kaldor ends on a note of hope about a transition "from a war paradigm to a law paradigm" that would transform world militaries into forces for peacekeeping, policing, and humanitarian action. This of course raises the full range of questions about the transformations of geopolitics that might make for more attractive futures.

Economic crises have often become occasions for exacerbated ethnopolitical conflicts. Even without overt violence, there are often new resentments of alleged outsiders—as indeed there are among some on the populist Right in Europe and America. But taking up the relationship of economic crisis to politicized ethnicity, in chapter 4, Rogers Brubaker offers the encouraging report that "nationalist and ethnopolitical responses to the [current] crisis have so far been surprisingly muted." This is a surprise because, of course, there are numerous historical examples to the contrary. Still, Brubaker is cautious about assuming that the peaceful pattern will continue. The many examples of exclusionary nationalist responses to the current crisis are worrying, even if so far they have occasioned only minimal violence.

Brubaker's account of why this should be so centers on political factors (institutions, idioms, opportunities, and struggles). These have given nationalist and ethnic concerns other forms of political expression besides violence. In addition, they have made overall political systems more supple and responsive. This is particularly a welcome development in central and eastern Europe, where memory of the 1930s worries many. Of course, nationalism and politicized ethnicity are broader global concerns, significant elsewhere in the European Union and in the former USSR, on China's frontiers, in India and around Southeast Asia, in Africa, in the Middle East, and certainly in North America itself, where the crisis has exacerbated conflict over immigration and national identity. Since the 1990s, there has been much academic hope that identity-driven conflicts would fade, but this isn't yet an evident trend.

Religious solidarities both overlap and crosscut ethnic and national ones. They offer some of the largest and most effective nexuses of global interconnections and examples of actually existing cosmopolitanism. At the same time, religious identity is often mobilized for violence, for attempts to dominate, and in attempts to produce doctrinal or cultural conformity. Religion is harnessed to state politics both when used to reinforce loyalty and when made the basis for movements to challenge existing governments. Yet, especially in the examples of Christianity, Islam, and Buddhism, it is not only transnational but also organized precisely to offer a supranational focus of solidarity. This makes it readily available as a source of criticism of the failures of existing states—whether explicitly secular or nominally religious. Such failures are all too apparent in the context of the contemporary crisis. But the same features make it possible for religion to become an important force behind transnational movements for peace and social justice or, as in the case of Pentecostalism, for a combination of spiritual salvation with individual self-discipline and economic advancement. Until recently, social science largely neglected these dimensions of religion, focusing instead on whether or not modernization entailed secularization. As Adrian Pabst discusses in chapter 7, religions' connections to today's basic issues are much broader. In his view, "the task for religions is not to embrace particular modes of political or economic governance but rather to promote models that protect the sacredness of life and uphold hierarchically ordered virtues." Pabst sees religious communities both promoting needed civilizational values and also anchoring dialogue among civilizations. Here, too, the relationship between hope and geopolitics is basic.

It is telling that Vincent Della Sala's chapter 6 account of the contemporary European Union is one of a lost narrative and even doubts about the EU's raison d'être and prospects. European integration has been the greatest project of supranational integration and governance in the modern era. It has achieved peace on the continent—one of its main purposes. Europe has prospered enormously, though how much this is due to the EU is unclear. But whether or, more moderately, how well it holds together in the current context of crisis is in doubt. Della Sala offers a broad view of the EU's response to the economic crisis and relates his discussion to broader considerations about transnational forms of governance. Yet Della Sala is neither skeptical nor overly optimistic regarding the future prospects of the EU. What perhaps matters most for the purposes of this volume is his calm recognition that "European integration as the harbinger of peace and stability no longer captures the imagination of…Europeans." Does this also mean that the EU no longer offers an attractively institutionalized and more secure model for globalization?

In the context of examining contemporary crisis and possible futures, it is important both to recognize the continuing power of nation-states (China for instance, not just the United States) and to recognize the significance of phenomena typically obscured by the unreflective dominance of nation-states over social science knowledge. Take the issue of offshore capitalism, for example, addressed in chapter 9 by Vadim Volkov. The story of financialization (and indeed of globalization) in recent decades is a story not just of flows across national borders but of the establishment of headquarters, sites of legal incorporation, banks, and other key parts of the corporate world in tiny countries like Cyprus or the Cayman Islands. This enables firms to use the capacity for instant financial transfers to evade the taxes, regulations, and laws of the nation-states in which they do business and to further distance financial capitalism from the "real economy." Some previously secret activities can become more open because they can be registered in an offshore haven. Yet much conventional economic data simply ignores the rise of offshore capitalism or tacitly accepts the notion of financial "flags of convenience" (thinking that Cyprus is really a major investor in Russia is like thinking that Liberia really runs major shipping firms). At the same time, the notion of a legitimate, interstate, global economy is rendered more and more an illusion. Pressed by both post-9/11 security concerns and the current financial crisis, a number of tax and police agencies made an effort to stem the growth of offshore capitalism. After several publicized scandals, however, the campaign petered out. The tax havens proved integral to global finance, a perhaps unintended "freedom" offered by neoliberalism.

Environmental issues knit together countries that border bodies of water, are affected by airborne currents of pollution or radioactive fallout, or at the extreme suffer the effects of climate change in common. In a similar sense, religious communities and civilizations crosscut conventional political cartography. Offshore capitalism is also a matter of flows that would never be predicted by conventional political geography. Communication is central to all of these. Increasingly this means communication outside the circuits of traditional media.

Ravi Sundaram shows in chapter 8 that it is important not just to notice the global communication flows made possible by new media but also to recognize that these are increasingly challenging older ideas of property rights. Digital media have challenged near monopolies of certain producers and distributors. Backed by the United States and other states, some firms brand all "unauthorized" copying of "intellectual property" as piracy. At the same time, many corporations are remaking media in order to try to maintain a system based on private property—relying on dedicated applications rather than more open Internet access, for example. And of course, some of the same technologies that shape the circulation of music and videos are also at work remaking the flows of information and money in global capitalism—in both its legal and formal and its illicit, often offshore varieties. Struggles between ownership and access affect a wide range of technologies, forms of cultural production, and products of scientific creativity. Brazil, for example, challenged the international intellectual property rights regime when it copied antiretroviral drugs, treating large numbers of Brazilians with HIV/AIDS and also forcing change globally. Whether the reassertion of private property in cultural goods dominates or the genie of massive unregulated copying and circulation is out of the bottle, the media matter enormously. Moreover, each of these scenarios (and their likely mixture) is unstable. There is no protection of private property interests that doesn't sharply limit access and perhaps more deeply undermine both creativity and circulation. There is no elimination of private property interests that isn't a deep challenge to capitalism.

Religion and the environment are both extraordinarily important themes in the modern world that until recently have not been central themes for social science. Communications has recently grown in prominence as an interdisciplinary field, but this comes after decades of being held as it were at arm's length by the conventional social science disciplines. Offshore capitalism is more and more basic, but it remains at the margin of conventional economics—or for that matter political science.

There are several reasons for this. In the pursuit of mathematically satisfying models, economists have often focused on certain abstractable characteristics of markets and related phenomena rather than questions of what was important in the real world. International relations has long been organized with a focus on relations among states that, drawing on a myth about how Europe resolved its religious wars, treated religion as essentially a domestic matter. Environmental concerns mattered only as they became foci of state power relationships (and thus didn't matter as long as states didn't act on such concerns). In less extreme form, most of the social sciences shared the two biases—even though they prided themselves on being more realistic than economics or international relations. That is, they gave the greatest prestige to work that improved answers to already established disciplinary questions, advancing cumulative knowledge on certain (often narrow) topics rather than asking whether the questions posed were adequate to understanding the contemporary world. And they took for granted that the world was structured into nation-states. Ironically this meant they often failed to study that structure itself—the issue of nationalism was marginalized by the very assumption that nation-states were natural; the analysis of the world system itself was left to a small subfield, while most political scientists, sociologists, and others looked inside nation-states or occasionally compared them. History absorbed the nation-state framework into its very construction of objects of study. Anthropology and geography were partial exceptions and have generated important alternative perspectives as a result (though they have their own disciplinary biases, such as a widespread tilt toward particularism and sometimes relativism in anthropology).

In short, the issues raised in this volume share fitting awkwardly into the conventional disciplinary structure of social science—and yet being manifestly central to issues of governance and global futures.

CHAPTER I

Crises in Parallel Worlds: The Governance of Global Risks in
Finance, Security, and the Environment

David Held and Kevin Young

The world has recently witnessed the largest and most widespread financial crisis in many decades. What is the significance of this event? Most commonly, the calamity is seen through the prism of policy failure, albeit on a massive scale—a failure of corporate governance, a failure of financial risk models, or a failure of monetary policy. Even more widespread is the view that the financial crisis has signified the failure of a particular ideology, neoliberalism, and its emphasis on efficient markets and deregulation. While there are elements of truth to each of these observations, comparatively less attention has been paid to the ways in which the crisis relates to the character of governance arrangements at the global level. Yet it is from the deficiencies of global financial governance that some of the most important lessons can be drawn. In this chapter, we argue that the global financial crisis and its fallout speak to broader problems of contemporary world order. Rather than a calamity specific to the domain of financial affairs, the recent global financial crisis is only a symptom of more general problems of global governance. These deficiencies, we argue, are present not just in the system of global financial governance but also in the domains of security and global environmental governance.

Our argument proceeds as follows. In section 1, we outline some of the basic characteristics of contemporary global governance, briefly describing some central problems therein. We argue that the three policy domains of finance, security, and the environment have remarkable similarities both in the way in which they underscore global interdependence and in the ways in which the governance of these domains remains woefully inadequate to manage contemporary global risks. Each of these policy domains suffers from what can be called a "capacity problem": that is, existing institutions are inadequate to address the global nature of risk and are unfit for that purpose. They also suffer, to varying degrees, from a "responsibility problem": namely, that the spread of risks and the costs borne by their realization are not commensurate with those involved in their governance.

In section 2, we outline the manifestation of the capacity and responsibility problems in the domain of global financial governance, highlighting the interrelated governance weaknesses among existing institutional configurations. In section 3, we outline similar deficiencies in the domains of the environment and security. In section 4, we describe prospects for the future of global governance in light of these weaknesses. We argue that recent attempts to address deficiencies in global financial governance, imperfect as they are, reflect the fact that focused, politicized attention to the global nature of risks can yield progressive reform. A continued trajectory of progressive reform is hindered, we argue, by the dual challenges of institutional inertia on the one hand and vested interests on the other. We conclude by offering some thoughts on the political space for further transformation in the future.

1. Global Governance and the Paradox of Our Times

It is now increasingly acknowledged that complex global processes, from the financial to the ecological, connect the fate of communities to each other across the world. Despite the fractures and conflicts of our age, societies are becoming more interconnected and interdependent. As a result, developments at the local level—whether economic, political, or social—can acquire almost instantaneous global consequences, and vice versa. Thus, global interconnectedness means that emerging risks or policy failures generated in one part of the world can travel quickly across the world to affect people who had no hand in their generation. Yet the problem-solving capacity of the existing system of global institutions is in many areas not effective, accountable, or fast enough to resolve current global dilemmas. What has recently been called the paradox of our times refers to the fact that the collective issues with which we must grapple are of growing extensity and intensity and yet the means for addressing these issues are weak and incomplete.[1]

Contemporary global governance is pervaded by a variety of different international organizations and actors. A thickening web of multilateral agreements, institutions, regimes, and transgovernmental policy networks has evolved over the past six decades, intervening in and regulating many aspects of national and transnational life. This evolving system is far from coherent and complete, lacking ultimate legal authority and a means to uphold international law, but it is much more than a system of limited intergovernmental cooperation. With the United Nations as its institutional core, it comprises a vast range of formal suprastate bodies and regional organizations, as well as regimes and transnational policy networks embracing government officials, technocrats, corporate representatives, pressure groups, and nongovernmental organizations (NGOs).[2] Although these bodies and networks lack the kind of centralized, coordinated political capabilities and enforcement capacities that are associated with national governments, it would be a mistake to overlook their expanding jurisdiction and scope of global public policymaking.[3] International organizations play an increasingly prominent role in the governance of the global economy, by setting standards, facilitating communication, enforcing rules, providing financial assistance, and coordinating policy responses. They are accompanied by an increasingly dense array of nonstate actors organized transnationally with the objective of affecting such global policymaking, and states and regional state groupings of all kinds are themselves embedded in this complex web of interactions, responding and coordinating their policies in accordance with external and supranational prerogatives.

Despite the existence of such a complex system of global governance, global public goods, such as financial stability, seem to be chronically undersupplied, and global bads, such as environmental degradation, build up and continue to threaten livelihoods. Though there are a variety of reasons for the persistence of these problems, at the root the problem is a political-institutional one, a problem of governance. Problem-solving capacities at the global and regional levels are weak because of a number of structural difficulties that compound the problems of generating and implementing urgent policies. These difficulties are rooted in the postwar settlement and the subsequent development of the multilateral order that followed in its wake.[4] The multilateral order founded after World War II was designed for a different era—and thus many of its institutional arrangements were designed for a world that no longer exists. Furthermore, the extensity and intensity of many pressing problems today, from climate change to the regulation of global financial markets, sharply increase the governance capacity required of multilateral institutions—something they have not delivered particularly well.

The difficulties faced by these more contested agencies and organizations stem from many sources, such as geopolitical resistance and the tension between state sovereignty and universal values built into them from their beginning. Many global political and legal developments since 1945 do not just curtail sovereignty but support it in many ways. From the UN Charter to the Rio Declaration on the environment, international agreements often serve to entrench the international power structure, with this institutional inertia acting to undermine effectiveness in addressing global issues. The division of the globe into powerful nation-states, with distinctive sets of geopolitical interests, was embedded in the articles and statutes of leading international governmental organizations (IGOs).[5] Thus, the sovereign rights of states are frequently affirmed alongside more universal principles. Moreover, while the case can be made that universal principles are part of "the working creed" of officials in some UN agencies such as the United Nations Children's Fund (UNICEF), the United Nations Educational, Scientific, and Cultural Organization (UNESCO), and the World Health Organization (WHO) and in NGOs such as Amnesty International, Save the Children, and Oxfam, they can scarcely be said to be constitutive of the conceptual world and working practices of many politicians, democratic or otherwise.[6]

Elements of international law do establish principles for justice beyond borders, but the reach of contemporary regional and international law rarely comes with a commitment to establish institutions with the resources and authority to make declared universal rules, values, and objectives effective. The susceptibility of the United Nations to the agendas of the most powerful states, the partiality of many of its enforcement operations (or lack of them altogether), the underfunding of its organizations, the continued dependency of its programs on financial support from a few major states, and the weaknesses of the policing of many environmental regimes (regional and global) are all indicative of the disjuncture between universal principles (and aspirations) and their partial and one-sided application.

Such problems of governance have a variety of different dimensions;[7] however, it is possible to group these succinctly into two categories, noted in the introduction. The first is called the *capacity* problem. While the globalization of persistent risks means that a growing number of issues span both the domestic and the international domains, the character and scope of institutions are insufficient to deal with the systemic nature of these risks. Institutional fragmentation and competition between states can lead to such policy issues being addressed in an ad hoc, dissonant manner. Even when the global dimension of a problem is acknowledged, there is often no clear division of labor among the myriad international institutions that seek to address it: their functions often overlap, their mandates conflict, and their objectives often become blurred. In this regard, existing multilateral institutions are seldom afforded the institutional resources to tackle what are effectively global-level policy issues. The United Nations, for example, lacks the resources to effectively realize the Millennium Development Goals, the global action plan by the United Nations to achieve eight major antipoverty goals by 2015; international security arrangements lack the orientation and resource capabilities to promote human security; and existing multilateral financial governance institutions lack the capacity to engage in effective financial regulatory reform and control.

The second problem is the *responsibility* problem. Put succinctly, the existing system of global governance suffers from severe deficits of accountability and inclusion. Less economically powerful states—hence, their entire populations—can be either marginalized or excluded from decision making altogether. This is witnessed not only in the structures of formal representation of states in existing international organizations but also in the decision making and agenda setting of global forums more generally. The severity of this problem is exacerbated, and its persistence sustained, by the fact that the relative costs associated with global risks can be larger for people who play little or no role in the generation of the problem in the first place. The recent global financial crisis is a stark example: the negative consequences of the near meltdown of the Anglo-American banking systems have had rapacious consequences for the economic and social well-being of people in sub-Saharan Africa, for example.

In what follows, we highlight the concrete manifestations of the capacity and responsibility problems. In so doing, we argue that strikingly similar deficiencies within global governance can be seen within three of the major policy domains that affect the basis of people's interconnectedness: finance, security, and the environment. Each of these domains constitutes a part of what can be referred to as the global commons: the collectively shared domains that tie diverse populations, interests, and concerns together into a global community of fate. Each of the three policy domains has at its core a central element that has a strong bearing on human welfare regardless of geography and culture. In the case of finance, it is the international organization of the supply and management of credit. In the case of the environment, it is the complex resource systems of the natural world, natural systems that do not acknowledge modern notions of sovereignty. In the case of security, it is the access to basic means of physical well-being, most commonly understood as the protection from arbitrary violence. Despite the importance of each of these core elements to the well-being of every human being on the planet, the governance of each of these policy domains remains plagued by difficulties. Finance, the environment, and security all remain, to different degrees, subject in their governance to both the capacity problem and the responsibility problem.

2. Deficiencies in Global Financial Governance

The recent financial crisis demonstrates an important feature of our contemporary world. The interconnectedness afforded by globalization, for all its benefits, also disperses global risks at a rapid rate. The globalization of financial markets has integrated the global economy in unprecedented ways, and yet the rules and institutions that monitor and regulate financial market activity have not kept pace. The rapidity of financial flows and the evolution of private-sector techniques have outstripped the grasp of any single national regulatory authority to govern them; and at the global level, this problem is even more pronounced. The system of global financial governance was weak and largely unprepared for the events of autumn 2008. To be sure, many of the proximate causes of the financial crisis can be attributed to workings within the US financial regulatory system and are thus national and not global in character. However, the transmission of financial shocks as a result of the subprime crisis and the collapse of the US investment banking industry were unmistakably transnational in character. The seizing up of liquidity was a global phenomenon, as were subsequent shocks to stock market capitalization and the rapid changes in the cost of credit. The financial crisis is but one mechanism through which globalization has unified human experiences: the foreclosed and unemployed US worker and the rural African farmer both experience the negative consequences of the crisis they had no hand in making, even if they remain as distant others to each other.

The capacity problem runs deep in global financial governance. The existing system of global financial governance has been, for most intents and purposes over the past twenty years, weak and highly fragmented. While the International Monetary Fund has played an important role in coordinating emergency financing in exchange for structural and institutional reform of national economies, it has not played a major part in the regulation of financial markets. On the contrary, its institutional focus has been on the regulation of governments and government policies, rather than on financial market activity per se. The World Bank has even less to do with the governance of finance on a global scale—despite its importance in development assistance and the shaping of government policy options. At the center of the global financial regulatory regime has been a complex of institutions that have constructed an elaborate system of standards and codes that have sought to govern the conduct of financial activity and its regulation. Across sectors, there has been considerable institutional fragmentation. There is one institution for international standards in securities markets (the International Organization of Securities Commissions, or IOSCO), one for accounting (the International Accounting Standards Board), one for money laundering and illicit finance (the Financial Action Task Force), one for insurance (the International Association of Insurance Supervisors), and one for banking regulation (the Basel Committee on Banking Supervision).[8]

Some institutions, such as the Bank for International Settlements, the Joint Forum, and the Financial Stability Forum, have existed as overarching institutions that seek to monitor and conduct research on global financial risks and to disseminate ideas. By facilitating communication—formally and informally—between and among national and subnational regulatory regimes, these institutions have performed a valuable function. Such communication has helped stimulate some important advances, such as the limitation of financial regulatory competition among states, the provision of emergency liquidity, the occasional coordination of monetary policies, and the combating of money laundering. Yet the capacity of this system both to detect and to take action on the buildup of global financial risks has not been borne out. The buildup of these risks can be traced back to regulatory deficiencies in the Anglo-American banking systems and to the financialization of capitalism more generally.[9] However, it is notable that the existing institutions of global financial governance did not restrain existing tendencies but rather bolstered the Anglo-American models from these countries and made them models for others across the world. For example, strong confidence in banks' own internal risk assessments was a cornerstone of both the Federal Reserve in the United States and the Financial Services Authority in the United Kingdom, and this confidence was translated into the international regulatory standards for banking in the Basel II Capital Accord. Other regulatory agenda items, such as the regulation of derivatives transactions and hedge funds, seldom even made it onto the agenda of multilateral forums, despite their importance in the financialized economies of New York and London.[10]

This complex system of existing institutions has noticeably lacked any centralized locus of authority. Rather than what most people imagine by regulation, which implies mechanisms of enforcement for rules of conduct, these institutions have governed global finance by facilitating communication among regulators and by aiding the construction of standards agreed to among different national regulatory authorities. The standards generated—such as the Basel Concordat and the Basel Capital Accord of 1988, for example—have played an important role in countervailing international competition among regulators. However, enforcement of such standards has been weak at best, given that there has been no formal mechanism to punish noncompliance. This system has relied on a combination of informal agreement and market-based mechanisms of discipline to ensure that standards are enforced.[11] Governance among institutions has been weak at best. One of the most significant efforts to institutionalize cooperation across sectors of finance has been through the Joint Forum, which has brought together regulators in the insurance, securities, and banking industries across countries to coordinate a common approach to the risks posed by large financial conglomerates. Yet the output of the Joint Forum has generally been limited to making recommendations to other international financial institutions.[12]

Compounding and reinforcing these weaknesses have been the severe deficits of accountability and inclusion within existing institutions. Despite recent changes, the voting rules within both the IMF and the World Bank remain structured in such a way as to encourage the governance of development institutions by states that are themselves highly developed, especially the United States.[13] Other financial governance institutions have until very recently operated under a different decision-making rule but still managed to exclude the vast majority of the world's population from any representative hand in formal decision making. For example, the Basel Committee on Banking Supervision, the global institution that effectively sets the regulatory standards in banking for the entire world, has maintained a highly exclusive approach to its membership, preventing developing countries from formal participation.[14] Until 2008, its membership reflected the configuration of international financial power in the 1970s, even while states such as Japan, France, and Germany experienced a relative decline in the position of their largest banks and countries such as China and Brazil experienced a relative rise.[15] While some institutions have had a less embarrassing record of participation in governance, such as the Bank for International Settlements,[16] the general picture of the responsibility problem has persisted, and this despite UN declarations such as the Monterrey Consensus, which insisted that global financial governance institutions review their membership to include adequate participation from developing countries.[17] As several authors have pointed out, this skewed representation has had clear negative consequences, such as the increased cost of capital to developing countries.[18] The responsibility problem is particularly striking when one considers the global dispersion of costs associated with the recent financial crisis, which have fallen not only on the developed Anglo-American economies but also on many of the most economically vulnerable parts of the world population.[19] As has been pointed out by Supachai Panitchpakdi, secretary-general of the United Nations Conference on Trade and Development (UNCTAD), while few developing countries have been directly exposed to securitized mortgages or failed US financial institutions, the vast majority of them have been significantly affected indirectly through reduced availability of credit, stock market panics, and the slow-down in the real economy.[20]

3. Global Governance of the Environment and Security

Global Governance of the Environment
Until the middle of the last century, most known forms of negative environmental impact were largely localized. Since then, the impact and scale of environmental change have dramatically intensified, with problems such as declining biodiversity, deforestation, and a plethora of water-resource problems becoming effectively globalized.[21] The failure to generate a sound and effective framework for managing global climate change remains one of the most serious indications of the deficiencies of the current system of global governance. There have been important advances in this area, and in this regard not only states through multilateral cooperative efforts but civil society networks have played a prominent role in pushing this issue onto the global agenda.[22] Nonetheless, like other pressing global public-policy challenges, the threats posed by global climate change are vastly greater than even those relatively coordinated efforts currently existing at the global level can handle. In parallel with the domain of finance, global environmental governance suffers from institutional arrangements that are not fit for its purpose; that is, it suffers from capacity and responsibility problems.

The capacity problem in global environmental governance is striking. While a number of individual international environmental agreements exist, and may even possess admirable characteristics, they are often both weakly enforced and poorly coordinated among each other. Furthermore, they are supported by a plethora of different international organizations fulfilling various functions. The current global environmental governance regime features a diverse set of players whose roles are largely uncoordinated: the UN Environment Program (UNEP), the Global Environment Facility, the Environment Management Group, the

Organisation for Economic Co-operation and Development (OECD) Environment Directorate, the Commission for Sustainable Development, the United Nations Economic and Social Council (ECOSOC), and the Environmental Chamber of the International Court of Justice, to name the most prominent.[23] The current constellation of over two hundred international environmental agreements suffers from a problem of what might be called anarchic inefficiency. Firm institutionalized commitment to solve pressing issues has been only slowly, and unevenly, forthcoming. There have been some important advances in the governance of climate change, with the Kyoto Protocol being an important first step, followed by increasing recognition and multilateral commitment at the UN level at the Bali and Poznań conferences. However, the general failure of the Copenhagen Summit in December 2009 to deliver a system of mutually binding commitments demonstrates the limits to this momentum when discussion turns from principles to commitment.

Global climate change has recently been called a threat more serious than that of international terrorism and the greatest market failure the world has ever seen.[24] If this failure is to be addressed, it will require considerable administrative capacity in order to encourage and institutionalize industrial and energy reform and to ensure an ongoing multilateral engagement with the problem. The goal of achieving this capacity, and the means to get there, will be undermined if countries at all stages of development are not directly involved in the shaping of solutions. In this regard, there is a strong parallel with global financial governance: the levels of accountability and inclusion represent serious challenges. Poorer developing countries very often lack the resources and technology to come into compliance because of the relative costs they face.[25] Existing efforts are modest in comparison to the scale of these costs. The United Nations Collaborative Program on Reducing Emissions from Deforestation and Forest Degradation in Developing Countries is one example of early (and modest) multilateral success.[26] However, other sources of global funds for adaptation are insufficient at current levels.

In Copenhagen, the dominant states of the world brought enough bargaining power to the table to ensure that no global deal went through that might damage their perceived short-term competitive interests. The Copenhagen Accord is marked by the absence of long-term emission targets, the omission of watertight pledges on new funding, and no clear indications of how to turn the Accord into a legally binding treaty. The big emitters—the United States, China, India, and the countries of the European Union—will continue to be able to act without a binding framework to enforce emission reductions and to speed up the pace of a transition to a low-carbon economy. Several commentators have recently argued that international climate negotiations could benefit from a more diffuse and incrementalist approach to collective agreements on climate-change policy since a global-level "all or nothing" approach is difficult to achieve and gives powerful states extensive veto power.[27] Such an approach might be viable and would do well to integrate the interests and collective power of the poorest and most vulnerable populations of the world—as it is they who are expected to be most negatively affected by climate change. A plethora of developing countries in Africa and Latin America and South Asia are expected to experience considerable reductions in cereal yields, and populations susceptible to diarrhea, cholera, dengue fever, and malnutrition are expected to be larger in these countries as well.[28] And even while some negative effects from climate, such as extreme weather events, heat stress, growing water scarcity, and the reshaping of coastal geographies, might be mitigated in the future, the ability to do so will clearly be a function of access to resources—leaving the poorest populations in the world subject to what Archbishop Desmond Tutu has recently dubbed the prospect of "adaptation apartheid."[29] The asymmetry of capacities to meet the costs resultant from climate change has a strong bearing on the massive global asymmetries in carbon footprints, making the responsibility problem in global environmental governance all the more striking.[30] Once again, the parallels with global financial governance are striking.

Global Governance of Security

If the global financial system integrates a common infrastructure for the management of credit, the international security system ensures an arrangement for the management of conflict and violence. Although institutional arrangements in the security domain are very different from those in financial governance, the capacity problem persists there as well. While a complex set of rules and institutions frame this domain of governance, much of their structure and content reflect security dilemmas of a world that no longer exists. Indeed, of the sixteen major armed conflicts that were active in fifteen locations around the world in 2008, not one was a major interstate conflict,[31] yet most of the world's armed forces are still based on a model of nation-states at war with one another. Global military spending, fueled by this model, has been on a sustained upward trend. Total global military expenditure for 2009 is estimated to have reached US$1.531 trillion, representing an increase of 49 percent since 2000.[32] To put this in perspective, the total is US$222 for every person on the planet, thirteen times the total spent on all types of development aid, seven hundred times the total amount spent on global health programs, and roughly the same as the combined total GDP of every country in Africa. But, at the present time, this model cannot deliver in many areas where security is most urgent. As in the domain of finance, institutional capacity exists, but it is the wrong kind of capacity, and as such there is a need to create a new type based on cooperation and collaboration of armed forces and on new ways of deploying them.

The dismal record of the wars begun in Afghanistan in 2002 and Iraq in 2003 exemplifies these trends. Both wars gave priority to a narrow security agenda that was at the heart of the Bush administration's security doctrine. This doctrine contradicted many of the core tenets of international politics and international agreements since 1945.[33] It set out a policy that sought order through dominance, that pursued the preemptive and preventive use of force, that relied on a conception of leadership based on a coalition of the willing, and that aimed to make the world safe for freedom and democracy—by globalizing American rules and conceptions of justice. The doctrine was enacted as the War on Terror. The language of interstate warfare was preserved intact and projected onto a new enemy. As a result, the terrorists of 9/11 were dignified as soldiers, and war was prosecuted against them. But this strategy was a distortion and simplification of reality and a predictable failure. In pursuing dominance through force, the War on Terror killed more innocent civilians in Iraq than the terrorists killed on 9/11, humiliated and tortured many Iraqis, created numerous innocent victims, and acted as a spur to terrorist recruitment.[34] It showed little, if any, understanding of the dignity, pride, and fears of others and of the way the fate and fortune of all peoples are increasingly tied together in our global age. Instead of seeking to extend the rule of law, ensuring that no party—terrorist or state—acts as judge, jury, and executioner, seeking dialogue with the Muslim world, strengthening the multilateral order, and developing the means to deal with the criminals of 9/11, the United States and its allies (notably the United Kingdom) pursued old-war techniques and have made nearly everyone less secure.

Contemporary security arrangements exemplify the responsibility problem as well. The most enduring concern in this regard, which came to a head at the 2005 UN World Summit, is the lack of representativeness in the membership and decision-making procedures of the UN Security Council, the preeminent governance body in the field of security. Established by the great power victors at the end of World War II, the Security Council reflects the geopolitical power structure of 1945 rather than 2010, the most obvious manifestation of which is the composition of the five permanent members and the veto power they are accorded. As the Council's powers expanded, beginning in the 1950s with its ability to establish UN peacekeeping forces and accelerating after the Cold War, when the Council began to intervene more readily in civil conflicts than it had in the past, countries became extremely concerned with their lack of control over such interventions. As the number of independent states steadily increased after 1945 due to decolonization and the collapse of the Soviet Union, the new members of the United Nations lobbied intensively for reform of the Security Council in order to enhance their representation and to confine the use of the veto to strictly security-related issues. Broader membership and improved voting procedures were seen to be essential for giving the Council's decisions greater legitimacy. Some have gone so far as to argue that the future of the Council as well as the United Nations itself hinges on an expansion of Council membership. As the Carnegie Commission's *Preventing Deadly Conflict: Final Report* explained, "every year that the Security Council continues with its present structure, the UN suffers because the increasing lack of representativeness of the Council membership diminishes its credibility and weakens its capacity for conflict prevention."[35] Eventually, as James Sutterlin has remarked, "if the interests of the majority of member states are not more adequately represented than is now the case, it is unlikely that they will, over the long run, comply with the Council's decisions."[36]

4. Reform: Inertia and Interests

Thus far, we have argued that the recent financial crisis reflects general deficiencies in the system of global governance, deficiencies reflected not only in finance but also in the policy domains of security and the environment. Inasmuch as these parallels exist, it can be contended that the dilemmas in global financial governance are not particular to this domain but rather extend more broadly to features of global governance itself. Thus, the recent financial crisis is but a costly and powerful example underscoring the profundity of the dilemmas we face in managing some of the most extensive global risks that persistently confront us. In this section, we move the argument forward and ask how very recent governance reforms can be interpreted and what further transformation the future might hold. We argue that some substantive reform has taken place but that the trajectory of reform is unlikely to continue. Detailing recent institutional and policy changes in global financial governance, we note the two problems of institutional inertia and vested interests.

Aside from the significant creation of the IMF and the International Bank for Reconstruction and Development (IBRD), the changes that the Bretton Woods conference of 1944 brought into being concerned institutionalizing a particular exchange-rate regime and doctrine for the mobility of capital across borders. These changes were in response to the perceived threats of international capital mobility and competitive devaluations that had occurred in the interwar period.[37] Today's threats bear some similarities but are also different in significant respects, as they have to do with systemic risks associated with particular financial instruments and practices, rather than the mobility of capital per se. Rather than simply requiring an understanding or set of agreements among states, these risks require effective regulation—a much more technically detailed and invasive form of intervention into the behavior of economic agents.

Since the acute onset of the financial crisis in November 2008, there have been a number of substantive reforms to the system of global financial governance. These have been more than cosmetic and have demonstrated that focused, critical public attention and a renewed commitment to multilateralism in the face of demonstrable failure can lead to progressive reform of global governance institutions. In particular, the São Paulo and Washington, DC, G20 summits in November 2008 saw an unprecedentedly successful attempt by developing countries to extend their participation in key institutions of global financial governance. Countries such as Brazil, China, and India argued for inclusion in the Financial Stability Forum—a substantial reform that soon grew to expand participation to the entire G20 plus Spain and the European Commission.[38] The Financial Stability Forum has now been renamed the Financial Stability Board (FSB), and the new institution has also expanded its institutional capacities through a full-time secretary-general, a steering committee, and three standing committees.[39] In addition to serving as a centralized hub of global financial governance coordination, the FSB will also undertake reviews of the existing international standard-setting bodies, to ensure higher levels of accountability. Furthermore, the G20 has commissioned the FSB to develop "supervisory colleges" to track major international financial institutions and to work with the IMF to assess the systemic risk associated with large financial institutions and potentially risky financial instruments as they emerge. These changes in institutional capacity reflect a proactive function previously weak in the system of global financial governance. How far the new FSB will go to mitigate the new and evolving global financial risks of the future remains to be seen, but these changes are exemplary of an important, albeit partial step toward resolution of both the capacity problem and the responsibility problem that have traditionally marked global financial governance.

Strong reactions to the global financial crisis have enhanced the governance capacities of existing institutions. The IMF, which was seen by many observers as an increasingly redundant international institution, has been given a new lease on life with the tripling of its resources.[40] Recognizing the disastrous effect of the global financial crisis on basic infrastructure in the developing world, the World Bank has also launched a new program to fill the funding gap caused by the crisis, providing at least US$15 billion per year over the next three years.[41] Serious issues of accountability still exist with the governance of the IMF and the World Bank, but in this regard the increasingly well-organized assertions of the G24 group of developing countries to increase the representation, participation, and negotiation capacities of underrepresented countries and regions give ground for optimism about future change.[42]

Massive participatory reform has also taken place. The G20's call for participatory reform of international standard-setting bodies has also meant extensive reform of global financial governance institutions with direct regulatory functions. For example, the membership of the Basel Committee on Banking Supervision has also been expanded, first in March 2009 to include Australia, Brazil, China, India, South Korea, Mexico, and Russia and then a second time in June 2009 to include the entire G20, along with Hong Kong and Singapore. The International Organization of Securities Commissions has also experienced similar reforms on its Technical Committee, with expanded participation from developing countries.[43] Within all these institutions, broader questions of governance remain, such as transparency of decision making and a fuller participation of stakeholders.[44] Nonetheless, despite these ongoing challenges, it is remarkable how such a historically closed policy network can be opened up in the face of major events.

Have these recent transformations in global financial governance amounted to any new policies? Although it is still early to make such judgments systematically, some recent proposals for new global financial standards suggest that the future agenda will reflect more stringent standards than in the past. There is already a noticeable change in discourse—with a major focus of multilateral and technocratic elite forums on macroprudential regulation, as opposed to microinstitutional regulation.[45] A significant change is the reconception of risk as systemic in character—as an emergent property rather than a calculable parameter arising from a predicted distribution. At the request of the G20, the Joint Forum on Financial Conglomerates has engaged in a detailed set of recommendations to address gaps in the scope of financial regulation in the banking, insurance, and securities sectors—with the explicit aim to identify areas of systemic risk not already accounted for in current regulatory frameworks.[46]

Actual policymaking proposals have also followed this change in discourse. One centerpiece of the precrisis regulatory regime, the Basel II Capital Accord (completed in 2004), has witnessed a noticeable overhaul. The Basel Committee on Banking Supervision (BCBS) began by introducing new stringent regulatory standards that involve increasing the size of capital buffers that can be drawn down in periods of financial stress, measures to increase the quality of bank capital, and for the first time, a global leverage ratio (a minimum ratio of debt to equity). Earlier regulatory safeguards due to expire in 2009 have been renewed;[47] complex financial transactions in banks' trading books are now associated with higher capital requirements; and the BCBS has introduced higher risk weights for particular securitization exposures such as collateralized debt obligations (CDOs).[48] Most significant, a new global regulatory capital accord, the Basel III Accord, has been produced and now been endorsed by the recent G20 Leaders Summit in Seoul.[49] In addition to these significant changes, areas of finance that have traditionally been left off the regulatory agenda, such as hedge funds and credit derivatives, are now being seriously considered as arenas for new regulatory reform initiatives in the EU, in the United States, and at the global level.[50] Even the IMF, typically the bastion of neoliberal thinking on financial regulation, has shifted its stance, recently proposing a financial transactions tax in a report to the G20—a remarkable event given that only a few years ago such an idea was largely confined to heterodox economists, activist organizations, and a handful of developing-country leaders.[51]

Each of these changes has its faults, and these changes may not be revolutionary in character; but they do represent an important set of changes in both thinking and policymaking when compared to the years preceding 2008. Given the relative paucity of stringent regulatory reforms before the crisis, there can be little doubt that, if the trajectory of reform continues, the future will feature a much stronger and more comprehensive system of global financial governance. But the important question is, will this trajectory continue? To this, we can answer that it is doubtful. Previous experience with institutional reform in global financial governance suggests that changes take place in the immediate aftermath of crises but then taper off. Following the East Asian financial crises of 1997–98, new institutions such as the Financial Stability Forum, the G20, and the Chang Mai Initiative were formulated as an outgrowth of direct concern about financial stability. As Randall Germain has noted, these changes were not entirely epiphenomenal;[52] indeed, in light of recent changes, we can see the concrete importance of the G20. However, most of these reforms did not alter business as usual in global financial governance, and in some cases they were associated with an acceleration of neoliberal policy programs.[53] In the present context, there are already some signs that multilateral efforts to address global financial governance issues are beginning to wane in their ambitions, as can be observed in the recent communiqués coming from the G20 finance ministers, which have not provided concrete plans for implementing their ambitions announced in 2009.[54] There are similar signs within the IMF at the moment.[55] If we consider the parallels with other domains, we can notice that the ambitions and discourses of global reform proposals tend to outpace the actually agreed-upon covenants for change. The extensive commentary and bold statements on climate change before Copenhagen stand in stark contrast to the outcomes of Copenhagen, for example. Efforts in the early 2000s to address UN Security Council reform were similarly ambitious but led to no concrete change, despite several concrete proposals.[56] These parallels with other areas of global governance suggest that the recognition of a collective threat, the waning legitimacy of existing institutions, and the need for multilateral solutions are clearly insufficient conditions for substantive reform.

The principal challenges for the future can be understood through two phenomena. On the one hand, there is considerable institutional inertia within the existing system of global governance to retain existing structures and arrangements and thus to prevent more substantial change. Proposals for reform within the existing system are likely to be incremental in character, rather than revolutionary, since the latter would upset the existing equilibrium of power and administration within and among existing institutions. Inertia within existing international arrangements can of course be affected through leadership. However, the emerging polycentricity of global finance puts this possibility in doubt for the future. While the US Treasury and Federal Reserve have traditionally exercised a leadership role in global financial affairs, their position is not as strong as it used to be—not only because of waning legitimacy and the more fragile position of the US dollar but also because of other voices on the geopolitical stage. The People's Bank of China has begun to speak with a resonant voice on some critical issues, and its structural power and autonomy in financial affairs is growing.[57]

On the other hand, a continued trajectory of reform in the future will have to contend with the constellation of interests that seek to preserve the status quo at the expense of more robust forms of global financial governance. With the full resurgence of large financial institutions and financial market activity, there will come an even stronger resurgence of private authority alongside them. Any transformation of the economic process produces not only new ways of generating and distributing value but also new coalitions of groups with an active interest in preserving the status quo. Vested interests attempt to block regulatory reform if they can, and they are organized not only within the United States and within other national contexts but also at the EU level and at the global level. As Eleni Tsingou has recently emphasized, private-sector interests have already been proactively responding to reform proposals and attempting to set the agenda at the global level.[58] Already new transnational advocacy associations have been forged in the financial sector, for example, the Association for Financial Markets in Europe (AFME) and the Global Financial Markets Association (GFMA), the latter of which is a transnational forum for the securitization industry, with representatives from Asia, Europe, and North America. Such new institutions join already existing groups, such as the Institute of International Finance (IIF) and the International Swaps and Derivatives Association (ISDA), two transnational associations with considerable reach and technical expertise that are all too happy to try to shape new policy proposals when they can.

While private-sector interests are well represented in transnationally organized forums and often enjoy privileged status with standard-setting bodies such as the Basel Committee, there exists no equivalent force that represents a check on private-sector interests. As Eric Helleiner and Tony Porter have emphasized, there is a distinct lack of a countervailing power to the constellation of highly technocratic financial standard-setting bodies that dominate the system of global financial governance.[59] Constellations of NGOs, think tanks, and academic networks exist, as do reform-oriented groupings of developing countries, such as the G24.[60] However, the comparative advantage of such groups is in their attempts to set the agenda of discussion; they cannot at present begin to match the level of technical expertise on financial regulatory matters that private-sector groups have at their disposal. Without this capacity being matched in some way, it is doubtful that a countervailing power to private-sector mobilization can be generated; and therefore, the future trajectory of reform is likely to be insufficient.

Conclusion

The recent global financial crisis has awoken many people to the adverse consequences of global interconnectedness. The decisions and nondecisions in one part of the world have led to serious consequences not only for remote others but for the entire world. The fact that problems with an obscure set of financial instruments in the US financial heartland could lead to an increase in poverty in some of the poorest and most desperate parts of the world is a reality we are forced to face. In this chapter, we have taken a global governance perspective to argue that the three policy domains of finance, security, and the environment have remarkable similarities both in the way in which they underscore global interdependence and in the ways in which the governance of these domains remains profoundly inadequate to manage contemporary global risks. Following the recent global financial crisis, efforts have been made to address some of these deficiencies. Imperfect as these reforms have been, they offer some evidence that focused, politicized attention to the global nature of risk can yield reform in a progressive direction. As we have argued, many of the changes that have taken place in the past year and a half were unthinkable only a few years ago. However, despite these positive changes, we have also argued that a continued trajectory of progressive reform is hindered by the dual challenges of institutional inertia and vested interests. It remains to be seen how and if the significant reforms begun in global financial governance can be reproduced in resolving the security and environmental challenges ahead. Certainly, the creation of effective institutions to address climate change and the movement to a low-carbon economy, on the one hand, and effective military capacity to resolve new conflict patterns, on the other hand, is a long way off.

Nonetheless, a new space for global politics has emerged as a result of both the failures of old institutional structures and the development of political opportunities created by a widely shared sense of urgency about finding new ways forward. Can the 1945 multilateral order be reforged in the years ahead to reflect the changing balance of power in the world and the voices of nonstate actors that have emerged with such force and impact over the past few decades? The crucial tests going forward concern the creation of new, effective, and just global bargains on financial market regulation, climate change, and the renewal of a nuclear nonproliferation treaty, as well as global investment in a low-carbon future and in the capabilities to cope with crises. If we fail to meet these tests and to build an effective and accountable rule-based multilateral order, then it is highly likely there will be further fragmentation of the global order into competing regional power blocs pursuing their own sectional interests.

The world system we now have is one in which global institutions and rules reflect historical patterns in the distribution of economic, political, and cultural power. It is a system that has not been able to adapt rapidly enough to transformations in the global distribution of economic activity. As Richard Falk has put it, the existing shape of the world order is "dysfunctional so far as serving fundamental human needs are concerned."[61] Established modes of national governance have the power to tax, subsidize, and provide public goods in ways designed to improve the lot of their societies. On the other hand, the escalating demands for global governance raise new challenges. What instruments and targets are the legitimate ones to consider in this new world? What authority and legitimacy can be accorded new governance systems so that they can successfully tackle the problems emerging in the modern global economy and polity?

Reform cannot be achieved without representative and effective global institutions that have the capacity to create credible regulatory frameworks and to invest directly in the provision of global public goods and the mitigation of global public bads. While the administrative incentives within existing multilateral institutions are complex, Weber's quip that institutions are determined by their sources of revenue nevertheless seems prescient for our times. Sustainable, robust, and effective global institutions that evolve alongside new global challenges must be funded by new streams of resources. Momentum already exists not only for new international carbon taxation but also for financial-transaction taxes. Recent developments on the latter front provide grounds for optimism. Only a few years ago, efforts to realize a financial-transaction tax were marginal to global politics; today the idea is seriously discussed by heads of state and international organizations.

A new global deal must be as ambitious as it is practical—the challenge is not to create an entirely new system of global governance from nothing but to break the deadlock of mediocrity and inefficiency within the existing system in order to build on the progressive foundations of the postwar settlement. Engendering a more effective and just system of global governance requires not only political will but mobilization. One is reminded of the fact that the progressive transformation of local and national systems of governance—though still far from perfect—was the product not only of need, not only of demands, but also of social mobilization to advocate and institutionalize change. A coalition of political groupings could emerge to work with such an agenda, comprising European countries with strong liberal and social democratic traditions; liberal groups in the US polity that support multilateralism and the rule of law in international affairs; progressive reformers within existing international institutions; developing countries struggling for access and voice in global governance; nongovernmental organizations campaigning for a more just, democratic, and equitable world order; transnational social movements contesting the nature and form of contemporary globalization; elements of geopolitically resurgent states, such as Brazil, India, China, and Russia; and finally, those diverse economic forces that desire a more stable global economic order.

Although some of the interests that might coalesce around such an effort would inevitably diverge in significant ways, there is nevertheless an important and sizable overlapping sphere of concern among them for the strengthening and protection of the global commons. How far the elements of such a coalition can go to unite around the multiplicity of concrete issues that require urgent attention and to what degree they can overcome fierce opposition from well-entrenched geopolitical and economic interests obviously remains to be seen. The stakes in such a process of struggle are high but are dwarfed by both the tremendous costs of inaction and the potential gains for creating a more inclusive, just, and sustainable world order.

If coalitions are to be built and if a historic bloc is to emerge for meaningful transformation of the multilateral order, such activity will have to have some animating ideology at its core. Most reform efforts in this direction to date have been guided, most often implicitly, by cosmopolitan principles of the equal moral worth of all human beings, regardless of nationality, wealth, or geography. Additionally, the aim of global governance reform itself might be guided by the concept of a global commons—not only a shared set of resources but a shared community of fate, the very basis of contemporary globalization. Such efforts could, at their normative core, enshrine the principle of equivalence—the principle that the reach of a good's benefits and costs should be matched with the span of the jurisdiction in which decisions are made about that good.[62] At its root, this principle suggests that those who are significantly affected by a global public good or bad should have some say in its provision or regulation. Such a principle of equivalence could be circumscribed by a concept of the right to protection from grievous harm. In this way, all-inclusiveness would require deliberation and engagement in policies that seriously affect life expectations and chances.[63] It would also help to underwrite effectiveness, in that in the protection of a global public good such as financial stability and soundness, there are inherent problems when that global public good is protected and managed by a minority of stakeholders since any minority group will necessarily suffer only a portion of the full consequences of its actions when it is ineffective.

CHAPTER 2

Green Social Democracy or Barbarism: Climate Change and the End of High Modernism

William Barnes and Nils Gilman

> Economic growth has become the secular religion of advancing in-
> dustrial societies: the source of individual motivation, the basis of
> political solidarity, the ground for the mobilization of society for a
> common purpose....If there is no commitment to economic growth,
> what can the Soviet Union—or Japan, or the United States—hold
> out as a social goal for its people?
> —Daniel Bell, *The Cultural Contradictions of Capitalism,* 1976

> If one were to choose a single word to characterize [what it means
> to be an American in the twenty-first century], it would have to be
> *more.* For the majority of contemporary Americans, the essence of
> life, liberty, and the pursuit of happiness centers on a relentless per-
> sonal quest to acquire, to consume, to indulge, and to shed whatever
> constraints might interfere with those endeavors.
> —Andrew Bacevich, *The Limits of Power,* 2008

The long-term future of societies all over the planet will be shaped in large part by their experiences of and responses to the ramifications of global warming, especially as those ramifications intersect and interact with other burgeoning environmental and human problems. It is already too late to avoid a cascade of local and regional "natural" disasters in the medium term (i.e., by midcentury). Yet near-term action to drastically reduce greenhouse gas (GHG) emissions is imperative if a long-term civilizational catastrophe is to be avoided.

What is the nature of this looming catastrophe?[1] Briefly: indefinite business-as-usual GHG emissions are likely to increase planetary temperatures by at least several degrees, perhaps even by as much as the planet warmed at the end of the last ice age. Left unabated, GHG emissions and the consequent global warming will engender frequent extreme weather events, produce extensive flooding in some areas and permanent drought in others, dramatically alter hydrologies on every continent, and destroy the agricultural productivity of many of the world's breadbaskets. In the longer term, unabated global warming will raise sea levels by many meters, destroying seaside cities that are home to hundreds of millions of people and great swaths of today's industrial infrastructure. All of this is nearly certain to lead to massive refugee flows, as large areas become incapable of supporting more than sparse human population. Nor are these effects likely to unfurl smoothly or incrementally, allowing societies clear projections and ample time to adapt; instead, they will probably unfold as interlocking acute crises, producing social and political breakdowns in weaker nation-states and possibly interstate conflicts.[2] Ultimately, if the alarms of someone like James Lovelock are to be believed, the human-carrying capacity of the planet may decline by an order of magnitude.[3] Short of thermonuclear war, modern civilization has never faced a more dire existential threat.

And it gets worse—because climate change is intruding into a world fraught with other ecological and political problems. Quite apart from any direct impact of climate change, inequality within and between societies has increased in recent decades; so has material and existential insecurity among the billions of poor people, particularly in the Global South, in the form of rising crime, social violence, and governmental weakness.[4] Additionally, the world is running out of cheap petroleum, accessible and clean fresh water, and many other resources, even as global demand for them continues to rise.[5] Moreover, no matter what we do going forward, increasing extreme-weather-related disasters—especially in coastal Asia, Central Africa, and the Caribbean—are already baked into the future as the result of the GHG already emitted over the past two hundred years. It is this world—not the world of the 1950s or 1960s—into which the effects of accelerating global warming are intruding ever more powerfully. If humanity fails to build up societal capacities for mitigation, emergency response, and remediation in advance of this oncoming cascade of disasters, then as the disasters accumulate toward the middle of this century, all of our attention and resources are likely to get sucked into short-term remediation efforts—with nothing left over to address longer-term solutions.

To moderate these consequences will require nothing less than a profound remaking of contemporary industrial modernity. In brief, the large majority of all industrial and mechanical processes that rely on hydrocarbons for fuel, or that generate substantial greenhouse gases as byproducts, will have to be either converted to clean/green technology or curtailed—on a planetwide basis. Unfortunately, barring a technological deus ex machina, it is highly unlikely that effective clean/green technological substitutes will be developed and deployed to replace current carbon-intensive industrial processes within the time frame required to avoid catastrophe. Absent such new technologies, the only choice for avoiding a climate catastrophe will be to cut back on our aggregate industrial output. This in turn will necessitate far-reaching changes in energy-intensive lifestyles—not just for a decade or two of "emergency" but for all practical purposes permanently. In other words: irrevocably downshifting our production and consumption patterns is the only route open to us if we want to hold open a long-term future for our civilization.

Much has been written about what might be done economically and technologically to combat these looming climate-change issues. What gets less attention, however, is the magnitude of the *political* requirements for addressing climate change.[6] In recent years, a steady accumulation of scientific evidence and opinion has generated a broad consensus among policymakers and informed publics that anthropogenic global warming is both real and a very serious long-term threat to human well-being.[7] That is good. And yet that consensus has not converted to political action; attempts to create GHG-abatement policies and protocols have stalled, and the political will to make necessary changes remains nonexistent. Absent a radical revision to the very conception of modern political legitimacy, such political will is unlikely to emerge. That is not just bad; that is potentially civilization killing.

This chapter attempts to move away from the wishful thinking that so often infuses and clouds climate-change debates and instead move toward realistic (albeit terrifically challenging) action. Rather than join the unrealism of the political and technological hopes of most environmentalists, we instead find promise in a different direction—one based on the possibility of retrieving, reformulating, and reinstating a once-prominent alternative form of "capitalist" political economy—early industrial "producerist republicanism"—as a constituent element of a forward-looking Green Social Democracy.

The Inevitable Failure of the Copenhagen Summit

Most serious climate-change experts, activists, and organizations declared the December 2009 Copenhagen climate-change summit—a forum designed to create a planetwide GHG-policy breakthrough—a failure. Environmentalists generally blamed this failure on the United States and China: specifically, on the blindness, venality, and unfairness of Americans (Republicans in particular) and on the short-sightedness of Chinese rulers. Consider, for example, journalist Gwynne Dyer's advance warning that the Copenhagen summit was not going anywhere:

> Everybody involved knows what the one really fair and effective deal would look like.... The fair and effective deal would take full account of the history, and it would look like this. It would require the rich, industrialized countries to take really deep cuts in their emissions: 40 percent by 2020, say, and another 40 percent by 2035. The developing countries would cap the growth in their emissions at a level not much higher than where they are now—but they must be allowed to go on growing their economies, which means that they will need more energy. All that extra energy has to be clean, or else they will break through the cap. They will therefore have to get their new energy from wind farms or solar arrays or nuclear plants, all of which are more expensive than the cheap coal-fired power plants they rely on now. Who pays the difference in the cost? The rich countries do, by technology transfers and direct subsidies.

Dyer went on to explain that "what makes this lopsided deal fair is the history behind it." Wealthy industrialized countries have burned cheap fossil fuels with abandon for the past two hundred years; in doing so, they saturated the atmosphere with carbon, contributing about four-fifths of the 110 parts per million that humanity added to the preexisting 280 ppm during that time span. Given that most scientists consider 450 ppm the maximum that can be safely allowed into the atmosphere, "all the economic growth of rapidly developing countries like China, India, and Brazil—3–4 billion people—has to fit into that narrow band of 60 ppm that the developed countries left for them. That is why the post-Kyoto deal must be lopsided—but it is still politically impossible to sell that deal to people in the developed countries, most of whom are (willfully) ignorant of that history."[8] Here Dyer was merely expressing the common liberal view that political conflicts are really only tactical or instrumental and that if they look to be fundamental, it is because of ignorance or irrationality on one or both sides. The liberal perspective suggests that the primary obstacle to getting serious about addressing climate change is a lack of education and generosity, and an excess of national chauvinism, on the part of the leaders and citizens of the advanced and wealthy societies—which in turn implies a workable, if arduous, educational and political fix. The underlying assumption is that conflicts over what is to be done need not be fundamental, once we all get our history and science straight.[9]

This chapter asserts, to the contrary, that such arguments misunderstand the deep nature of the political obstacles to implementing a serious GHG-reduction program. The real reason that governments refuse to agree to the necessary reductions in GHG emissions is that such reductions can only happen through massive cuts in production and consumption—cuts that are utterly unacceptable to the publics of virtually all states today, but most especially to the publics of China and the United States, the two biggest GHG emitters. We argue that the world's climate-change dilemma is unresolvable without fundamentally challenging the present constitution of industrial modernity—a challenge that current global elites, as well as the publics that they preach to, are not only unwilling to undertake but incapable of conceiving. We argue that both mainstream contemporary social science, still tacitly in thrall to the normative assumptions of modernization theory, and most domestic and international political cultures, committed to endlessly escalating economic growth, have repressed intellectual and political traditions that might offer grounding for an alternative form of modern civilization.

Unless we can recover those traditions, there is little chance that we will be able to put into place policies to curb the GHG emissions that are leading humanity willy-nilly to ecological and civilizational ruin.

Why a Technological Fix Will Not Work

At this point in the argument, liberals and Green pragmatists usually step forward and say, "But wait, we don't need all this political adjustment; if we can just get the prices right on carbon, this will put in place the right incentives to get people to deploy the technology we need to reduce GHG emissions." The assumption in this sort of claim, often voiced explicitly without much evidence to back it up, is that all the necessary GHG-abatement technology already exists[10] and that only political gridlock, incompetence, or venality is preventing its deployment. Alas, the bitter truth is that replacing today's carbon-intensive energy system with renewable energy sources, on anything approaching the necessary scale and time line, is virtually impossible, and not just for economic reasons.

To realize the futility of the hopes that a technological fix can solve our GHG-emissions problem without requiring a massive reduction in consumption, one must understand the dimensions of the global energy system. The current global economy requires the regular availability of about 16 terawatts of electrical power generating capacity. According to the IPCC's Fourth Assessment Report (2007), reaching a sustainable level of GHG emissions—one that will keep CO_2 under 450 ppm— will require reducing emissions by 80 percent over the next twenty-five years or so.[11] Such a reduction can logically mean only one of two things: either we need to massively cut energy consumption (which necessarily will entail drastic cuts in aggregate economic output), or else we need to generate approximately 13 terawatts of electric power in a renewable manner.[12]

How feasible is the latter? An answer to this question has been sketched by Saul Griffith, inventor, polymath, and recent MacArthur Award winner: "Imagine someone said you need 2 terawatts of wind, 2 terawatts of photovoltaic solar, 2 terawatts of thermal solar, 2 terawatts of geothermal, 2 terawatts of biofuel, and 3 terawatts of nuclear to give you 13 new clean terawatts. You add the existing 1.5 terawatts of biofuels and nuclear that we already use. You can also get 3 terawatts from coal and oil. That would give humanity around 17.5 terawatts"—enough to allow "only" a 10–20 percent decline in energy consumption per capita over the coming generation.[13] "What would it take to do all that in 25 years?" he asks:

> Two terawatts of photovoltaic would require installing 100 square meters of 15 percent efficient solar cells [the best currently available commercially] every second, second after second, for the next 25 years. (That's about 1200 square miles of solar cells a year, times 25 equals 30,000 square miles of photovoltaic cells.) Two terawatts of solar thermal? If it's 30 percent efficient all told [again, the best that is currently commercially available], we'll need 50 square meters of highly reflective mirrors every second. (Some 600 square miles a year, times 25.) The terawatts of biofuels? Something like Olympic swimming pools of genetically engineered algae, installed every second. (About 61,000 square miles a year, times 25.) Two terawatts of wind? That's a 300-foot-diameter wind turbine every five minutes. (Install 105,000 turbines a year in good wind locations, times 25.) Two terawatts of geothermal? Build three 100-megawatt steam turbines every day—1095 a year, times 25. Three terawatts of new nuclear? That's a 3-reactor, 3-gigawatt plant every week—52 a year, times 25.[14]

Griffith also points out that, were this new energy infrastructure built, it would require a space approximately equal to the size of the United States, not even counting transmission lines, energy storage, materials, or support infrastructure—not to mention the costs of decommissioning coal plants, oil refineries, and all the rest of the infrastructure and detritus of two centuries of hydrocarbon indulgence. This, then, is the brutal physics and engineering of what it will take to make a wholesale conversion of the current energy system from hydrocarbons to renewables, without reducing the total energy output.[15]

This physics is also what renders derisory the claims of liberal economists such as Nick Stern, who famously proclaimed that "the costs of action—reducing greenhouse gas emissions to avoid the worst impact of climate change—can be limited to around 1 percent of global GDP each year,"[16] or Paul Krugman, who more recently claimed that a cap-and-trade bill "would reduce the projected average annual rate of growth of GDP between 2010 and 2050 by [only] 0.03 to 0.09 percentage points."[17] A cap-and-trade bill might only cost that much in GDP, but it would fall far short of solving our GHG-emissions problem, which requires putting into place economic incentives that force a sweeping reduction in total energy consumption. Undoubtedly there is some price of energy at which Arizonans will stop cooling their houses in summer and Minnesotans will keep their thermostats at ten degrees Celsius in winter—but that price surely is not 0.09 percent of GDP.

One reason why so many Greens put so much faith in cap-and-trade is their belief that once the price of carbon is set appropriately, this will create incentives that will inevitably push scientists and inventors to come up with solutions to our energy needs. Several things can be said about this dual faith in markets and technology. First, this claim is based on a discredited supply-side-economics view of invention.[18] Just because there is an economic incentive to invent something does not mean that inventing it is technically or physically possible or that, even if it is invented, other social and political barriers to deployment will not arise. For example, vast economic incentives exist to invent pills that would cure alcoholism or drug addiction, and much snake oil gets peddled claiming to provide such benefits. Yet substance abuse has not disappeared from society. Given the addiction of modern civilization to cheap energy, the parallel ought to be unnerving to anyone who believes that technology alone will allow us to pull the climate rabbit out of the fossil-fuel hat. Second, the hopes that many Greens place in a technological fix are an expression of high-modernist faith in the unlimited power of science and technology as profound—and as rational—as Augustine's faith in Christ. It is no coincidence that the phrase "technological fix" was coined in the mid-1960s—the heyday of modernization theory—by Alvin Weinberg, the chief administrator at Oak Ridge National Laboratory during the Manhattan Project.[19] Weinberg claimed that nuclear power would create limitless energy, allowing age-old social problems to be overcome while minimizing political conflict over distributional issues—an argument that should feel uncannily familiar to all those who believe that technological breakthroughs will allow the climate crisis to be overcome without fundamental political conflict.[20]

To review: a drastic reduction (aiming for 80 percent) in global GHG emissions in the midterm (midcentury) is required in order to avoid civilizational-scale climate-change-induced catastrophes in the long term. Such a reduction can only be accomplished by either wholesale conversion of the energy system to renewables or by a massive reduction in total energy consumption.[21] Since wholesale conversion to renewables is a near physical impossibility, however, the only feasible alternative is a drastic reduction in aggregate global production, which will require enormous shifts in the way people in many societies live: less travel, less heating in winter, less cooling in summer, less light at night, less opulent housing, less gadgetry, less elaborate clothing, less meat, ... and the list goes on. *In sum, with regard to all forms of material production and consumption, serious emissions reduction boils down to just one word:* LESS.

The Political Problem of "Less":
Why an Economics of Decline Is So Hard to Imagine

> Anyone who believes that exponential growth can go on forever in a finite world is either a madman or an economist.
> —Kenneth Boulding, "The Economics of the Coming Spaceship Earth," 1966[22]

Just as daunting as the required techno-industrial transformation to an ecologically balanced global economy will be the difficulty of making "less" work politically. Less is something that present-day political classes literally do not know how to think about, much less to sell to mass publics raised on "more." Just look what happened to Jimmy Carter when he made even a modest gesture in that direction—his sensible cardigans are still a political laughingstock, and not just on the right. What would it take for politicians to champion, and publics to accept, levels of consumption well below those to which we have either become accustomed or been taught to long for? Not "less" in the form of a one-time cut to material goods and energy consumption, but a steadily diminishing less, as the necessary changes are phased in over the course of a generation—less, then less, then even less, until, if we are lucky, we reach some kind of a safe plateau as clean/green technology matures and population growth ceases planetwide.

   This political economy of less is not just about *consuming* less; it is also necessarily about *producing* less, which in turn entails a radical restructuring of the industrial base, with literally unthinkable implications for the global economy as it is currently evaluated by mainstream economists and politicians. It will mean a drastically smaller auto industry, no more oil/gas/coal industries, no more industrial farming, vastly less airplane travel, and so on. From an employment perspective, the transformation we are talking about is not just about telecommuting to work on Fridays and otherwise going about your business. What we are talking about, if we are being serious, is a wholesale curtailment of every portion of the economy that involves significant energy consumption. This in turn means massive economic dislocation of all those who have gotten used to working in energy-intensive industries or whose labor in the tertiary ("services") sector of the economy is implicitly piggybacking on energy-intensive practices in the primary ("extractive") and secondary ("industrial") sectors—in other words, virtually everyone. In the long run, it probably means many, many people going back to farming, which will become a much more manual process. In sum, it means an end to industrial growth as we have come to know and worship it.[23]

It is virtually impossible to exaggerate the scale of the revision we are talking about. The problem is profound and its intellectual lineage deep. Begin with the theoretical challenge that an "economics of decline" poses to mainstream social science. To a large degree, the very idea of something called "the economy" is coextensive with the idea of economic growth. When John Maynard Keynes wrote his *General Theory*, there was no reified entity called "the national economy." The first effort to instantiate such an entity analytically and statistically occurred with the 1928–30 Soviet National Accounts, which formed the basis for Stalin's first Five-Year Plan—arguably the first full-spectrum "national economic growth" plan ever put forth by a government. For capitalist economies, the idea of national income accounting was developed in the late 1930s by Simon Kuznets as a way to test the efficacy of Keynesian theories for generating aggregate economic growth.[24] As a body of positive theory, in other words, modern macroeconomics is built around the normative assumption that what economies are supposed to do is grow. And it is not just economics: modernization theory in political science and sociology assumed this from birth.[25] In other words, the political problem we are now facing is underpinned by a fundamental theoretical problem: the very notion of "the economy" takes for granted the idea of an endless "more." Political will aside, officials and policy intellectuals literally do not know how to think about an economy predicated on principles other than expansion and growth. This has been particularly true over the past thirty years, amid the triumphs of the Reagan revolution and neoliberal turbocapitalism.[26]

The problem is equally severe at a political level. From the eighteenth century on, Western visions of progress and national development have treated ever-increasing material abundance as table stakes in any definition of political or social success. Modern and modernizing governments (of whatever ideological stripe, from Teddy Roosevelt and Lenin, through Thatcher and Gorbachev, down to the present American and Chinese leaderships) have staked their claims to legitimacy on the premise and promise of delivering MORE. The ideology of endless growth is the common assumption across all modern political systems; it is the fundament of how modern societies and polities understand what they are all about; it is baked into the core of virtually all contemporary social contracts.[27] With a few frightening exceptions such as Kim's North Korea or Pol Pot's Cambodia, all governments of the postwar period have promised "a rising standard of living" to most if not all of their people. Social compromises and political hegemonies have been brokered on the assumption that continually increasing economic productivity would neutralize distributional conflict. This, pace Dyer, is the real reason why a serious GHG-emissions-reduction program is "politically impossible to sell": not because the masses are "willfully ignorant of history" but because political and economic elites have no idea how to legitimate themselves absent the promise of endless growth.

For rich democracies, the prospect is politically intransigent. What elected politician can hope to sell diminishment to a population that for generations has been taught to consider a rising standard of living a birthright and has internalized the myth that "each generation does better than its parents" (where "better" means more material consumption)? To get a sense for how profoundly politics will have to change in order to fit an age of diminishment, consider how effectively the US Republican Party was able to use the word "rationing" as political kryptonite in the 2009–10 debate over health care. Here was a case in which private insurers are *already* imposing rationing, and the government was *not* planning to impose any additional rationing, and *still* the charge was politically poisonous.[28] Now imagine the government trying to *actually* impose rationing, and of a stringent sort, across every aspect of material production and consumption, in exchange for an uncertain outcome— amounting at best only to a reduction of secular trends from catastrophic to difficult. American conservatives are, in this respect, relatively clear-eyed about the political-economic implications of serious climate-change-mitigation efforts. That they respond by mendaciously denying the climate science itself, and depicting environmentalism as nothing but a Trojan horse for authoritarian statism, should not distract us from the fundamental political truth they are putting their finger on, namely, that any serious effort to restrain greenhouse gases must necessarily mean a full-scale assault on what they (and many others) mean by "the American way of life"—in other words, a dismantling of a way of life defined, to quote modernization theorist Walt Rostow's famous phrase, in terms of "the age of high mass consumption."[29]

As difficult as it may be to imagine American or European or Japanese publics accepting "less" rather than "more" as their national mantra, it is even harder to imagine the emergent middle classes of the Global South willingly leaving the promised land of consumerism just at the moment when they have finally begun to arrive in numbers. Even in authoritarian systems such as China and Russia, elites seek to employ their wider populations in carbon-intensive modernizing national projects, and coercion by itself does not work to keep those populations dutifully on task; some degree of social contract, some substantial payoff, must be offered and at least partially honored. A decline in China's astounding growth rate is often cited as the single factor most likely to destabilize the political system of the world's most populous country.[30]

Ultimately, it is impossible to predict what environmental or political events could sufficiently galvanize political elites and the wider public to break this intellectual and political deadlock. The environmental changes associated with GHG emissions are likely to be nonlinear, and the political reactions to any climate-related disasters are equally unpredictable, thus piling one radical uncertainty on top of another. (If there is anything that the past few years should have taught us, it is that even irrefutable revelations of the rottenness of the contemporary global political-economic order do not necessarily result in commensurate repudiation of the responsible political and economic elites.) Two things, however, are clear: the first is that decisive political leadership, rooted in a fundamentally different conception of the economy, will be absolutely required in order to take the necessary steps; and the second is that denying the magnitude of the necessary change makes the emergence of such political leadership all but impossible. In this latter respect, it must be pointed out that even the most politically hard-headed portions of the contemporary environmental movement are still not admitting the magnitude of the required industrial changes and the consequent political challenges.

Ecological Modernization Theory—Too Little, Too Late

Many avowedly "pragmatic" environmentalists reject the foregoing political analysis as either impossibilist or defeatist, arguing that we must somehow find a way to reconcile decarbonization of the global economy with people's consumerist desires. Recognizing that most people do not want to give up their carbon-intensive habits or aspirations, such self-described "ecological modernization theorists" argue that it is possible to give the modern global political economy an ecofriendly makeover. They promote the idea of making economic growth and affluence "sustainable" while remediating the environmental damage caused by earlier dirty growth and development.[31] The scholars in this tradition, it should be said, are not without their own politically audacious proposals, demanding massive public and private investments in the development and deployment of clean/green technology and substantial institutional reform of capitalist political economy.

What this literature shies away from, however, is the need for any fundamental change in culture or politics beyond that held to be already triumphant in the form of the "post-materialist" culture and politics of the "knowledge workers," the "creative classes," and the modern middle classes generally.[32] As three leaders in the field have recently explained, ecological modernization means

> giving environmental issues and interests a permanent and central position in the decision-making processes of private firms and consumers,…leav[ing] behind prior tendencies within organised environmentalism that favored vitriolic critiques of capitalism and industrialism and focused on making a fundamental break with modernity.

To advance environmental reform efforts, this romantic yearning to revert to an agrarian past premised on "small-is-beautiful" ideals had to be replaced by a more pragmatic posture that created space for dialogue and negotiation between professionalised environmental movements, expanding and diversifying environmental states, and increasingly engaged private sector actors....The incorporation of environmental concerns by mainstream economic actors is possible only when environmental criteria, instruments and concepts are re-formulated to mesh with the logics of modern markets.[33]

To get a richer flavor of this school of thought, consider the work of Ted Nordhaus and Michael Shellenberger, influential popularizers of ecological modernization theory via their bombshell 2004 essay "The Death of Environmentalism" and their much-discussed follow-up book, *Break Through: Why We Can't Leave Saving the Planet to Environmentalists*, which won the 2008 Green Book Award and has been widely acclaimed by centrist reformers, "progressive" business people, and mainstream liberals.[34] Nordhaus and Shellenberger's book is in large part a defense of what they earlier termed the "new values and identities in the post-scarcity consumer societies that emerged after World War II."[35] Rather than criticize the carbon-intensive desires of the contemporary American middle class and its many emulators abroad, Nordhaus and Shellenberger assume that the only viable politics in the face of climate change is one that embraces these historically particular values. Rather than question "the American way of life," they emphasize technological revolution and supportive institutional reform, a political program effectively the same as the Third Way of Anthony Giddens, New Labor, Tony Blair, some of the European Greens, and the Clinton and Obama administrations.[36]

According to Nordhaus and Shellenberger, the main obstacle that ecological modernization faces is the nature worship, antimodernism, and pessimism of tree huggers—all of which represents an insufficient belief in human creativity and human greatness, particularly American creativity and American greatness. To be sure, the version of American greatness put forward during the Reagan and Bush years, most adamantly by the neoconservatives, represented a wrong turn, but that was only a bump in the road. Nordhaus and Shellenberger believe we simply need to get back on the right track. In this view, there is nothing wrong with the general glorification of economic growth, prosperity, and affluence. Indeed, in their reading of the past forty years' history, it is the very completeness of our materialism that made the championing of "post-materialist" values possible. According to Nordhaus and Shellenberger, human beings never rise to ecological consciousness, or other "higher values," unless and until they first achieve material prosperity; and once they achieve such prosperity, they will never agree to give it up. "None of us," they aver, "whether we are wealthy environmental leaders or average Americans, are willing to significantly sacrifice our standard of living."[37] Thus, for Nordhaus and Shellenberger, "prosperity"-like consumption is an entirely unproblematic concept. They assume, like all earlier modernization theorists, that "modernization" and "modernity" naturally and necessarily come as a "package deal" based on a template defined by the carbon-intensive affluence of the contemporary global and especially American upper classes. Like previous modernization theorists, they also assume that the "natural" endpoint of this maturation process is in a convergence on their own preferred values, in this case green and "post-materialist."[38]

This perspective begs a number of crucial questions. First, there is little compelling evidence that people will inevitably transition to "post-materialist" values as they reach the requisite level of material affluence.[39] Why should we believe that the green values and lifestyle of Berkeley intellectuals—rather than, say, the grasping conspicuous consumption of Houston (or Muscovite) cowboy capitalists—represents the true "end of history," the inevitable outcome of providing people with an adequate satisfaction of their material needs? Second, how can we know what constitutes "adequate satisfaction of material needs" as opposed to "overindulgence" that actually stands in the way of, or corrupts the transition toward, recognizing and cultivating "higher" needs and values? And most seriously, there is the question of equity during the transition process: even if everyone were destined to adopt the values of Berkeley liberals once they got wealthy enough, there simply are not enough resources on the planet to deliver nine billion Bobos to paradise.[40]

Of course, Nordhaus and Shellenberger are aware that their vision of expanding today's privileged minority into a much larger number through the application of current (fossil-fuel) technology will have the unfortunate consequence of boiling the planet. Knowing this, Nordhaus and Shellenberger (like other ecological modernization theorists) fall back on the classic high-modernist magic of the "technological fix." They assert, without any real basis, that clean/green technology can allow us to have our high-mass-consumption cake on a global scale and yet eat it in a low-carbon-footprint manner. To be sure, they recognize the huge magnitude of the technological investment and innovation that they are calling for and relying on. But at the end of the day, their way out of the GHG-emissions quandary is to assert that technological breakthroughs can and will lead the way through the coming travails to a new postmodernity that is simultaneously affluent, cosmopolitan, and green. Indeed, they seem to believe that the new technology will not only limit the damage from the climate change that they acknowledge to be already baked in but also make it possible to restart and complete the spread of near affluence throughout the world population without further exacerbating global warming. They can cite no persuasive evidence for either of these positions; indeed, their program is as much a matter of quasi-religious faith as is New Age environmentalism for its acolytes.

Now, it is worth pointing out that the political economy suggested by ecological modernization theory might have been viable, just possibly, if its implementation had begun immediately after World War II—if the New Deal had continued in a green vein, leading to the greening of the Marshall Plan and Truman's Point Four program. This kind of program might still have had a chance of success if launched strongly in the 1960s and continued uninterrupted from there. But the scientific and technical knowledge of the earlier period was insufficient, and Right, Left, and Center all had other priorities and other trajectories throughout those years. Instead we got the glorification of suburban homeownership, the automobile, electric appliances, and consumerism in general as central to the good life.[41] In the late 1950s and early 1960s, a hopeful moment of critique of the affluent society and its culture and politics flowered, only to be overtaken by the conflicts over the Vietnam War, black power, and women's liberation.[42] After some strong environmental beginnings in the 1970s, the subsequent rise of the New Right—carried forward by the Reagan/Thatcher revolution with its glorification of private wealth and denigration of public goods and followed by post–Cold War neoliberal triumphalism—left both ecological modernization and the Third Way largely bottled up in "old" Europe and scattered local refugia (e.g., Portland, Oregon). By now, it is simply too late for the half measures of ecological modernization theory, especially in the wake of the post-2008 crisis of global capitalism.

The preceding paragraph reveals the pivot of our disagreement with ecological modernization theory. Ecological modernization theory remains wedded to the assumption that the post–World War II form of high-consumerist modernization was not a wrong turn but rather a positive developmental stage that generated some unanticipated ecological externalities. By contrast, we assert that we now know enough about the nature and consequences of those externalities, and of planetary sensitivities and limits, to realize that they put the nail in the coffin of modernization theory and its glorification of industrial productivity and high-tech mass consumerism. We must face up to the reality that the past thirty years of "turbocapitalism" have been the culmination of a grand historical wrong turn that began in the last third of the nineteenth century and reached hegemony in the course of the twenty years after World War II.

An Alternative Modernity?

Dealing politically with the problem of "less" requires a profound switching of gears, a radical intellectual and political reorientation that in turn demands a basic retooling of the entire stock of human capital of the social sciences, the professions, organizational management, and public administration. We need to develop an alternative political economy that can survive and cope in the face of the new world that is coming.[43] What would such a political economy look like, and how might we get there from where we are now?

As we have established, it is *not* true that we are close to having—even in the lab—the clean/green technology we need to successfully abate climate change and that all that is lacking is the will to fund full development and deployment. But it *is* true that around the planet there are many people, groups, and communities that know and practice (at least in bits and pieces) something like the techniques, methodologies, and policies needed to step back from high-carbon materialism. The state of Kerala in India, with a population of over thirty million, is perhaps the most striking large-scale example.[44] What we do not have, however, is an example of a national society adopting such practices anywhere near comprehensively—or even moving decisively in that direction. As things stand, the voracious high-carbon-footprint urban sectors of the largest and richest societies are on course to drag the rest of the world down with them, no matter how green the rest of the world becomes.[45]

So is there some way to gather the green lessons, toolkits, and practices that are accumulating around the world and to synthesize them into a set of models that majorities everywhere might be persuaded to choose among, adopt, and enact? Existing environmental movements seem unlikely to get that job done, given the power of the opposition and the recalcitrance of majorities in thrall to the hegemonic culture of carbon-intensive modernity. What we need, then, is a larger narrative with the potential to legitimize radical departure from the status quo to wider audiences, including renunciation of aspirations to affluence and the moral ostracism of those who insist on indulgence in material luxury. Plainly put, centrist ecological modernization policy discourse fails to provide the plausible larger narrative we need to replace the hegemonic orthodoxy of neoliberal modernization theory and "the American way of life." What we need instead is to recover an alternative political tradition that can serve as the historical foundation for a viable contemporary Green Social Democracy.

The twentieth century's leading sources of broad transformative vision, the Marxist and socialist traditions, are largely unhelpful in this respect, given that they always expected to take over and build on the material abundance and technological wizardry of advanced capitalism. In most mainstream versions of socialism, capitalist consumerism was cast not as ecologically unsustainable but rather as the penultimate form of economic modernity, one revolution short of the end game. In the finalized form, the entire population was to enjoy a version of the affluence formerly limited to the wealthy, as well as "higher" values. Even those who saw the early years of the "transition to socialism" as occurring in the context of spartan Third World revolution assumed that the revolution would eventually fulfill itself in a socialism of mass abundance. That a life of higher values might be constructed in the face of not the temporary but the permanent absence of mass affluence was not contemplated in these traditions, at least not in their twentieth-century versions.

We propose looking at a quite different historical tradition, namely, the petty-bourgeois political culture of North Atlantic capitalism's early and middle industrial eras. This tradition did not call for the revolutionary overthrow of capitalism but rather argued for a more modest and cautious (in a sense more "conservative"), more egalitarian and democratic, more decentralized "producerist" capitalism. A twenty-first-century producerist capitalism would seek to recast the socially liberal and politically democratic republican tradition, but in the context of vigorously and comprehensively green economics. Many countries can look back to elements of their own early modern experiences for instances of something analogous to such producerist republicanism. In Russia, they might look back to Bukharin and the New Economic Program years; in China, it would be the World War II cooperatives and the "Yenan Way" born out of that experience; for India, it would involve looking to how the Kerala of the past fifty years has built on Gandhi's movement.[46] But the United States has a particularly instructive history in this regard.

From the American Revolution through the 1930s, the United States had a rich history of democratic populism among skilled craftsmen, artisans, family farmers, and lower-middle-class business people, professionals, and intellectuals, reaching upward into the middle classes and downward into the working classes.[47] What these movements and traditions had in common was the demand that self-managed, self-enhancing work and political citizenship be valorized and protected from the depredations of the federalist aristocracy, slaveholders, Wall Street, and monopolies and other large corporations. Participants in these movements and organizations, including many of the agrarian Populists, were neither wholly modernist nor wholly antimodernist. They were not Luddites or enemies of commerce and industry per se. Many were professionals, teachers, and amateur inventors interested in science; they participated vigorously and rationally in the public spheres and civil societies of their day—indeed, they were among the most important authors of the greatly expanded public spheres of their day. By the later nineteenth century, many participants in these movements were women—pioneers of female civic activism who went on to be key leaders and cadres of the elaborate Progressive civil society of the early twentieth century. The social protections these movements sought included public construction and ownership of major infrastructure and government regulation of corporate capital and the factory system. They wanted to promote and support widespread small production, linked together in a "cooperative commonwealth" through large-scale producer co-ops and vigorous political organization. Political and social identities were rooted in such cooperative and communal arrangements of production, rather than in privatized, individualistic practices of consumption.

Recognizing and revivifying this political tradition provides an Archimedean point from which to critique the pop-modernization-theory view of economic viability and societal success that has become hegemonic over the past seventy-five years. Recapturing the energies and hopes of this lost political assemblage, before it was defeated and co-opted, allows us to more clearly see the assumptions and limitations of the orthodox, growth-centered vision of modernity that has led us to the brink of global ecological catastrophe. From the Civil War to as late as World War II, neither economic theory nor popular political folklore insisted that modernity necessarily came as an integrated package, a package whose central components include the unlimited pursuit of ongoing industrial revolution incarnated in gigantic, ravenous factories; the transformation of the mass of the population into "personnel" within complex, hierarchical organizations; and the elaboration and institutionalization of a culture of material consumerism and high-tech entertainment. Arriving at a hegemonic culture that takes these developments for granted as central to modernity has not been simply the product of the natural progress of efficiency, science, and rationality; rather, a particular pattern of contingent political victories and defeats has played a major role. This pattern need not be accepted as fully irreversible.

We now need to revive aspects of the popular political culture of petty-bourgeois civic republicanism that valued community, solidarity, moral economy, meaningful work, self-management, and democratic citizenship over economistic individualism, material affluence, and private consumerism. Note that we are not saying that any of the earlier incarnations of producerist republicanism could have been fully victorious in its time or that any could be or should be reincarnated whole now. Recovery must include critically minded updating and reformulation in the light of the lessons of the past seventy-five years. In particular, we need to spike that retrieved heritage with a shot of cosmopolitanism regarding race, gender, and sexuality, while giving up the vision of an eventual metamorphosis into a socialism of abundance. Such a project is surely not without intellectual rewards, and, as a leading historian of American Progressivism and petty-bourgeois radicalism has said,

Nor are such utopias unattainable....Charles Sabel, Michael Piore, and Jonathan Zeitlin have created something of a school of political economy that has demonstrated the economic viability of small-scale production within flourishing, democratic economic networks. Historically, Sabel and Zeitlin reconstruct and rehabilitate a craft-based alternative to mass production, an alternative that had impressively strong roots in various cities and regions throughout the nineteenth-century transatlantic world. Flexibility and constant innovation in specialized production formed the foundation for a labor process that revolved around skilled workers,...with owners and workers often attaining a solidarity difficult for us to imagine as part of business relations. And despite the many defeats this small-scale alternative met at the hands of both capitalist and social democratic advocates of a mass-production economy, it did not disappear but merely went underground, showing a remarkable resurgence since the 1970s. Especially strong in western Europe, "flexible specialization," or "small firm networks," provide a contemporary living model of what Michael Albert has aptly characterized as "Capitalism against Capitalism."[48]

The ray of hope that we hold out is that our imagined Green Social Democracy, underpinned by producerist republican values, will ground itself in an acceptance of the limits imposed by the fecundity of the local environment, rather than a Promethean ethos of constant overcoming of those limits. As such, it would encourage localized sourcing, localized production, and localized consumption. It would focus on the conversion of public infrastructure to low-carbon, clean energy as quickly as possible. It would provide universal access to such infrastructure, while making private use of centrally generated power and water quite expensive above a very modest minimum allotment. Tax and regulatory policies would focus on environmental impact and resource management. Governments, educational systems, and civil society would prioritize training, equipping, and enabling the population to become low-carbon "producers" of useful goods and services (especially the "human services") and informed, environmentally conscious, responsible citizens, within local communities, organizations, and enterprises. In other words, it would be something like the comprehensive elaboration of an intensely green version of the "social economy" model that has worked on the local level in Quebec and other places and the "transition town" model that seems to be taking off in England.[49]

There will be so much work to be done in conversion, reclamation, emergency response, human services, community development, and so on that this will be a full-employment economy and for the most part locally focused. Moreover, such a political economy—emphasizing the development of high levels of environmentally conscious human and social capital, largely situated in small, privately or co-op-owned production units and community-based human services, supported and coordinated (but not centrally planned or directed) by environmentally informed larger public institutions—would enable cutting GHG emissions and render societies more resilient and adaptive in the face of climate change. It is reasonable to expect that people whose lives are rich in social capital, educational opportunity, interesting work, and citizenship rights and responsibilities are likely to be more amenable to being weaned off carbon-intensive addictions/enthusiasms or not to develop strong versions in the first place.

This brings us back to the question of whether there is any realistic prospect of overcoming the political obstacles that we have argued are so formidable as to render the programs of mainstream environmentalists unrealistic. Why should our suggested political project fare any better? Is it possible for the global middle classes, with all their long-inculcated yearnings for carbon-intensive lifestyles, to become part of the solution instead of part of the problem? Hope arises from the fact that none of the political economies and political cultures of our world is monolithic or completely controlled by those wedded to the status quo. As climate-change-induced system failures accumulate, along with ever-more-credible warnings of worse to come, the existing high-modernist hegemony will become increasingly hard to sustain.

Recasting doubts about the current hegemony into a green producerist republicanism requires, however, the development of a credible alternative political narrative, one not rooted in an ecologically suicidal ideology of endless growth. This in turn demands the creation of a "usable past" appropriate to that contemporary political narrative. We believe that the constituent elements of such a political narrative are (still) there, deep in the American grain, never having been fully eliminated by the hegemonic carbon-intensive, high-modernist version of the "American way of life." Interestingly, some of the most fervent advocates of producerist republican political culture in current public debate include right-wing constituencies whose knee-jerk opposition to environmentalism may be amenable to neutralization by a green producerist republicanism that invokes new versions of familiar old values.[50] Indeed, one of the main ideological themes of the US Tea Party movement is right-wing, libertarian producerism.

We recognize that realization of this hope on any grand (i.e., sufficient) scale is unlikely, but it is the best strategy we can think of, and in any case, as Mike Davis says, "either we fight for 'impossible' solutions…or become ourselves complicit in a *de facto* triage of humanity" and "'a moral failure on a scale unparalleled in history.'"[51] Unlike much radical green thinking, our analysis is not predicated on semireligious or New Age hopes for a spiritual revolution but, rather, is firmly rooted in class and social analysis. We know that, in order to succeed at a global scale, a broad cross-class transnational coalition must become convinced that commitments to high-modernist affluence are complicit in a civilizational and human catastrophe of unfathomable proportions. Is it possible for the global middle and lower-middle classes, and their existing stocks of human capital and social capital, in the most advanced societies and the largest societies in particular, to metamorphose into being part of the solution instead of part of the problem? It may well be that we cannot retool (technologically, institutionally, culturally, psychologically) fast enough, given the momentum and inertia of the old ways and the power of those who blindly insist on carrying those old ways forward. We cannot know, but what we can say is that it looks like the next couple decades will be our last chance to build the political and human-capital base that might make the required conversion possible.

Even short of this ultimate global political goal, we believe that promoting the sort of producerist republican political economy outlined here is worth pursuing locally. Such a shift will increase local social and political resilience in the face of oncoming climate-change-induced catastrophes. Ultimately, addressing the challenge of climate change requires not just scalable technical solutions but also scalable political and social solutions.

CHAPTER 3

Ecologies of Rule:
African Environments and the Climate of Neoliberalism

Michael J. Watts

I think the multiplication of the enterprise form within the social body is what is at stake in neoliberal policy....The stake of all neoliberal analyses is the replacement every time of *homo economicus* as partner of exchange with a *homo economicus* as entrepreneur of himself, being for himself his own capital, being for himself his own producer....The individual's life itself—with his relationships to his private property, for example, with his family, his household, insurance and retirement—must make him into a sort of permanent and multiple enterprise.
—Michel Foucault, *The Birth of Biopolitics* (2008), 148, 226, 241

Three decades and more after a sequence of droughts and famines swept across the continent, Africa once again—I write in the summer of 2010—confronts a climate-famine-energy crisis of mind-boggling proportions. The *2009 Global Hunger Index* reveals that virtually all countries facing "alarming" and "very alarming" food shortages are African. As if to compound the already bleak prospect of millions of Africans facing starvation and radical food insecurity, the world of high oil prices (and necessarily high fertilizer and pesticide prices too) shows no sign of going away; indeed, the consensus among energy analysts is that we have reached "the end of cheap oil." In short, the current food-energy-climate conundrum appears as a terrifying echo of the 1970s crisis. Africa's development, its security, indeed its very future are again being called into question. The clarion call this time is for a "new" green revolution—delivered by biotechnology and synthetic chemistry—dragging sadly neglected African smallholders into a market place dominated by what the World Bank in its *Development Report* on agriculture sheepishly calls a powerful "multinational agribusiness sector"[1] and for a climate war chest furnished by the North to bankroll the huge costs associated with mitigating and adapting to global climate change, which, in most estimations, will fall with particular ferocity on the African poor.

In the run-up to an oil price of almost US$150 a barrel in 2007–8—a price driven, incidentally, as much by the explosion of commodity-index speculation, especially in oil, as by demand-side growth from East and South Asia—Africa's bottom billion felt a double development squeeze. Not only did prices of fuel and fertilizers spike, but the threat of energy shortages in turn triggered a rapid shift to biofuels production as a low-carbon alternative to petroleum. Rapid expansion in the cultivated area devoted to corn and sugar biomass ran straight into the brick wall of the so-called grain-livestock complex—namely, global increases in the demand for meat, associated with rising living standards in China and elsewhere, absorbed disproportionately large quantities of cereal and grains output for feedstock. Talk of global food shortages in turn spurred a "new scramble" for African land as sovereign wealth funds and other large state and private actors entered into a raft of agreements for large-scale land acquisition—in Madagascar, Sudan, Ethiopia, Ghana, and elsewhere—to provision domestic food markets in Asia and the Middle East.[2] Added into the mix is the recognition—clearly laid out in the 2007 reports of the Intergovernmental Panel on Climate Change (IPCC)—that global climate change, both rising sea level and changes in precipitation and runoff, is likely to have enormous, and disproportionately grave, consequences for semiarid, and especially the Sahelian, regions on the continent, many of which are now densely settled. Climate-induced conflict is seen in the development community as an increasingly likely scenario.[3] In short, Africa faces a veritable perfect storm, whipped up by market, climatic, and Malthusian forces.

Against this foreboding backdrop, the prospect for sustainable African livelihoods is a central plank in what Ananya Roy calls "millennial development," that is to say, the rise of "global poverty as a political issue."[4] The United Nations' annual inventory of poverty in the Global South, measured through the global auditing device known as the Millennium Development Goals (MDG), attests both to the rise of global poverty as an ethical and political arena for the conduct of multilateral humanitarianism and to the centrality of Africa within it. Paul Collier, in his hugely influential book *The Bottom Billion,* gave sub-Saharan Africa pride of place within his pantheon of low-growth, conflict-ridden failing states. Even the most cursory examination of the work of Jeffrey Sachs, William Easterly, or any other development flavor of the moment would reveal how central Africa is to the political machinery of global poverty eradication. As much of the continent celebrates fifty years of political independence, it is already clear that many of the MDG target goals will not be achieved in Africa by 2015 and in some cases may not be achieved, if current trends continue, until the *next* century.[5] The prospects for sustainable development, in this scenario, are bleak, and environmental crises—from tropical deforestation to desertification—are at once a cause and an effect of being poor.[6]

On this wider canvas of contemporary crisis, my brief is to reflect on Africa as a sort of laboratory for the invention and circulation of development ideas and practice and on how the laboratory's scientific contributions have changed over the past half century. Helen Tilley has explored Africa's laboratorial history across the colonial era for a number of arenas—race, medicine, and demography, for example.[7] What concerns me here is Africa as a laboratory for *environmental ideas*—not for ecological science narrowly construed, though it certainly served in this capacity too, but for what now passes as sustainable development, or the intersection of environment and development as a form of political practice or rule (what one might call environmentality or green governmentality).[8] The history of Africa as a laboratory for environmentalism is deep—stretching back four to five centuries. Climate, forests, rivers, and rangelands all became parts of a very considerable transdisciplinary enterprise that began even before the partition. Richard Grove's pathbreaking work shows, for example, how some African islands that suffered the ravages of large-scale production systems from the sixteenth century—and by virtue of their island biogeography were ecologically sensitive in any case—were the earliest markers of conservation thinking around issues such as deforestation, soil erosion, and water use.[9] I shall focus on the shifts in thinking since the 1960s—and the rise of green governance in various forms—and argue that the move toward market-driven forms of green governance was not simply reflective of a shift to neoliberalism within the worlds of development theory and practice as such but in fact was deeply *constitutive* of it.

Nature has always provided the ground and substance for economics and political economy. Michel Foucault provides a way of assessing these relations through the apparatuses and rationalities of modern government.[10] In the same way that he sees a link between governmentality and the medicalization of social structure—social and disciplinary interventions to administer populations in the name of security and life—so one might explore the relations between governmentality and the environmentalization (or the "greening") of the social. Green governmentality as a form of biopower is not simply about the deployment of particular knowledges—the statistical and quantitative machinery to establish "norms of nature" as a problem of government—and calculative rationalities derived from the ecological sciences but potentially is an entire political machinery.[11] These technologies and rationalities of normalization are rooted in evolutionary and biological thinking that encompasses, as Goodie shows,[12] "everything in the physical and biological environment" necessary to life and survival in the broadest sense:

> We can expand Foucault's analysis of governmentality to investigate how the ordering of "things" progressively included variables such as "life," "health," "sustainability" and the "environment" to generate new rationalities of government aimed at making visible the relations between "things" via the production of ecological rationalities of government....We can enlarge the problematization of modern governmentality by suggesting that the problems of "life," "environment" and "government" have now coincided with the emergence of "ecopolitics," crystallizing a new nexus of power/knowledge which deeply reorganizes in a relational way the three movements constitutive of modern governmentality, namely: government, population and political economy.[13]

The ecological rationalities of government were European and extra-European in genesis, emerging from the ecological impact of an expansionary European mercantile and capitalist economy. It was in the colonies that scientists first came to fully grasp the transformative power of humans on the biophysical landscape, and it was from—to use

Jason Moore's language—"capitalism as a world-ecology"[14] that biopolitics, understood and enlarged to include the conduct of all that is necessary to support life through the management of populations, was to emerge. Africa continues to be a forcing house for the development of these green forms of governmentality, now shaped by the demands of adapting to global climate change on the one hand and neoliberalism on the other. If as Foucault suggests, neoliberalism is "a whole way of being and thinking," a "grid of economic and sociological analysis," then to the same extent the current concern with building adaptive capacity through resilient community and other institutions in Africa is entirely consistent with the neoliberal tenet of life as entrepreneurship. In this world of development as adaptation, civil society becomes part of the ensemble of the technology of liberal governmentality: it provides the ground on which populations, subject to economic laws and principles of right, can be managed.

Colonial Green

The colonies were always much more than a canvas on which Europe painted a modern picture of itself. Enrique Dussel says Europe was a center within an interdependent system, even if the notion of modernity's self-construction rested on Europe's being hermetically sealed off from its empire.[15] Provincializing Europe entails not only recognizing that European imperial projects were compromised in what they could achieve in political and economic terms but also acknowledging that the colonies were centers of experimentation and agency; they actually became the laboratories of modernity.[16] As Helen Tilley notes in her important book *Africa as a Living Laboratory*, the colonies provided the bricks and mortar of disciplines, theories, and institutions.[17] Ecological rationalities of government in fact emerged not just within the context of deforestation and pollution in Europe but also within the crucible of colonial rule conceived as a solution to such problems:

> Thus the mergence of these [ecological] rationalities appears intimately related to the expansion of Venetian, French, Dutch and English maritime powers, all competing for commercial activities

on strategic locations which include oceanic island colonies and various plantations particularly sensitive to deforestation and erosion.... [This] led to new environmental awareness of land,...botany, meteorology and map-making.[18]

Nowhere was this more the case than in Africa in the wake of the partition of the continent in the last quarter of the nineteenth century, when three-quarters of the globe came under European domination. The political emancipation of the bourgeoisie, as Hannah Arendt described this period,[19] also launched the process of scientific development, which began with the exploration and trade expansion between the sixteenth and eighteenth centuries across the Atlantic, Indian, and Pacific Oceans, on its path to "a world wide preeminence."[20] The transnationalization of science promoted by the professionalization and growing standardization across the biophysical sciences (geography, anthropology, botany, evolution, and so on) had the effect of converting Africa—by 1900 the largest imperial landmass—into a sort of gigantic scientific workshop. The geographical displacement of European costs of industrialization onto the colonies makes the point that "much of the ideology of modern conservation thinking actually emerged out of the colonial rather than metropolitan conditions."[21] Formal colonial rule brought forth armies of scientists, research centers, commissions, and field expeditions and at the same time had the effect of Africanizing science—that is to say, converted Africa, in key domains, into an object of scientific scrutiny, on the one hand, and drew Africans and African knowledge into a constitutive process of what Tilley calls "vernacular science," on the other.[22]

Africa's laboratories were many and multifaceted (see Rabinow on urban sanitation and Grove on islands and conservation)[23] and were achieved through institutions, networks, and the circulation of ideas—and importantly an interplay between field and laboratory sciences—that were often at the heart of imperial government broadly construed. The disciplines of ecology, geography, and anthropology were central to the vernacularization of scientific knowledge. In other words, the localization of scientific knowledge (that is to say, a clear distinction between what was universal and what was site specific) had a way of entering into the archive of global science even if "Africans themselves were rarely at the helm of decision-making."[24]

Paradoxically, some of this knowledge even entered subsequently into the debates over the future of Africa itself and its colonial status. The market, new crops and new farming practices, the role of colonial scientific practitioners, and an array of African actors collectively constituted the mix within which both ecological and conservation ideas and practices were debated as part of the wider challenges of colonial rule. A number of historical moments and substantive issues were central to the genesis of a vernacular science of African ecology. First was the late-nineteenth-century sleeping-sickness debate and the relations more generally between livestock, human populations, and the local environment. Another was the nature of climatic and rainfall variation and the ability of peasants to adapt to such perturbations. Thirdly, the Great Depression of the 1930s became an incubator for what the colonial office in western and southern Africa saw as a debilitating intersection of overpopulation (by humans and animals), soil erosion ("desertification"), and deforestation.[25] The big push toward colonial conservation—and various patterns of resistance to conservation measures—became part of a wide-ranging discussion, with connections to the Dust Bowl debates in the United States, that animated scientific and colonial-administrator constituencies across the French and British colonial empires in the 1930s. And finally, there was the process by which nineteenth-century imperial hunting (both colonial and precolonial) grew into a scientific concern with biodiversity, charismatic megafauna, and the push toward conservation areas and national parks,[26] a process that from the vantage point of communities that depended on local animal populations appeared as a process of enclosure and criminalization of customary rights of use and as an authoritarian land grab by colonial states.

African agency was obviously constitutive of this vernacular ecology and incipient environmental conservation. On one side stood African knowledge of the environment. A growing cadre of anthropologists, often working in conjunction with district and agricultural officers sensitive to the flexibility and adaptability of African peasants and pastoralists, often promoted the utility of indigenous knowledge (and practice) over what was seen as a hasty and inappropriate application of European farming methods.[27] By the 1890s, the World's Exposition in Chicago was promoting the science of "ethno-botany";[28] early in the twentieth century, agricultural officers in northern Nigeria could be heard singing the praises of peasant farmers and their local knowledge.[29] And on the other side stood a number of Africans (typically not scientifically trained) who worked closely with the colonial research apparatus and in this sense approximated what in a different setting Steven Shapin has called invisible technicians.[30] By the 1950s, a body of scientific data and a network of research institutions had come into being in which it was possible, says Helen Tilley, to "make one's career out of African [scientific] materials and to never once step foot on the…continent."[31] The green current running across colonial rule in Africa was deeply dialectical, emerging from the local and the global, the universal and the vernacular, the cosmopolitan and the parochial.

Postcolonial Green: From the Sahel to Stockholm via Rome

The period between the late 1960s through the early 1980s was an extended decade of economic and political turbulence driven by the oil boom and bust, by financial liberalization and the launching of structural adjustment programs, and by the massive human ecological crisis triggered by the drought-famines that extended across the West African Sahel to the Horn and to eastern and southern regions of the continent. At base, this was a crisis of the agrarian and pastoral economies—peasants and herders for the most part, who occupied the great swaths of the semiarid savannas, which is to say the ecological heart of the continent. The great drought-famines of the 1970s were framed by two important events: the first was the UN Conference on the Human Environment held in Stockholm in 1972, and the second was the release of the Club of Rome's report *Limits to Growth* in the same year. Both were foundational to the rise of a sort of "international environmentalism" addressing what were later to be understood as the challenges of "sustainable development." Both were fundamentally shaped by a robust Malthusianism. For the Club of Rome, founded as a global think tank in 1968 by an Italian industrialist and a Scottish international scientific civil servant (respectively, Aurelio Peccei and Alexander King), the oil crisis was a harbinger of a larger structural problem of resource scarcity, population pressure, and ecological degradation. Methodologically, the Club outsourced its study to the MIT (Massachusetts Institute of Technology) Systems Dynamics Group, which assigned a team made up of seventeen researchers from a wide range of disciplines and countries, led by Dennis Meadows.[32] They assembled vast quantities of data from around the world to feed into the Club of Rome model, focusing on five main variables: investment, population, pollution, natural resources, and food. Calibrated to examine the interactions among these variables and the trends in the system as a whole over the next ten, twenty, and fifty years assuming extant growth rates, its scenarios predicted various sorts of system collapse or system unsustainability. In all, twelve million copies of the book have been sold, and it has been translated into thirty-seven languages.

Limits to Growth became a touchstone for the global modeling of human ecological problems (in a sense a forerunner of the IPCC) and also provided a compelling narrative of global catastrophism, which came to stimulate a debate over what King, then at the OECD, called "the temple of growth," but it linked the "predicament of mankind" to questions of global inequality and calls for a New International Economic Order. All of this, it should be said, was in parallel with two other important events. One was the UN Stockholm Conference, which laid the foundation stones for the genesis and proliferation of international treaties and multilateral regulatory frameworks around global environmental issues. The other was the arrival at the World Bank of Robert McNamara, whose presidency between 1968 and 1981 was to emphasize making the institution a development bank focused on the productivity crisis of the rural poor, the land-poor smallholders of the Third World.

These events helped shape how a run of African droughts, and the massive famines and food crises that attended them, was framed and understood as a particular sort of environmental crisis and as a development conundrum (see figure 3.1). Peter Taylor has referred to the prevailing discourse as "neo-Malthusian environmentalism" and interestingly made use of, as a historian of science and an ecologist, influential studies conducted by the Systems Dynamics Group at MIT that analyzed agropastoral systems in the West African Sahel in the wake of the 1970s crisis.[33] By 1973, the semiarid Sahel region had experienced five years of drought and developing crisis. Many pastoralists (livestock herders) and farmers were in refugee camps, their herds decimated and their crops having failed again. Prevailing analysis at the time focused not only on famine relief but on the causes of the crisis and on prospects for the region's future, a view that heralded drought and famine as a forerunner

Figure 3.1: The model of Neo-Malthusian environmentalism

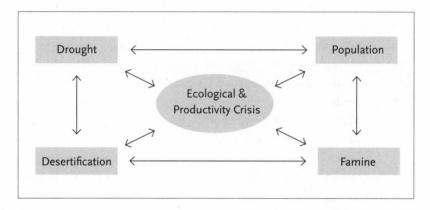

of future demographically driven scarcity and shortage (through human increases and related settlement into increasingly marginal and overexploited environments and animal overstocking on open ranges): in short, a Malthusian dystopia. The consensus was that the ecological resource base of the Sahel region had been seriously damaged. Once emergency relief was under way, discussion turned to longer-term measures needed for recovery and for prevention of future disasters. The US Agency for International Development (USAID) funded a one-year, US$1 million project at MIT to evaluate long-term development strategies for the Sahel and the bordering "Sudan" region. The computer model (in a sense, a regional variant of the Club of Rome's global models) included a capacious menu of factors and mathematical relationships, all converted into a systems analysis anchored in (and confirmatory of) the "tragedy of the commons."[34] As calibrated, the model determined that overstocking and overgrazing were inevitable. Soil degradation and eventual desertification could be avoided only if all the pastoralists replaced their individual self-interest (and outdated forms of communal property) with "long-term preservation of the resource base as their first priority," perhaps requiring them to enter ranching schemes that privatized or strictly supervised access to pasture.[35]

The environmental and related agrarian crisis of the 1970s proved to be a veritable laboratory for economic ideas. Ecology, food, and climate fed into arguably one of *the* founding documents in the rise and consolidation of neoliberal development and the rise of the "Washington

Consensus," namely, the Berg report (named after Michigan economist Elliot Berg), released as *Accelerated Development in Sub-Saharan Africa* by the World Bank in 1981. At the core of Africa's crisis was "domestic policy" and a poor export performance in basic commodities in which the continent had a comparative advantage. Distorted markets and state marketing boards became the conceptual front lines in a ferocious assault on the African state, a critique backed up with the prescriptive heavy artillery of structural adjustment and stabilization. The solutions to the environment-development crisis resided in a technical fix (bringing the green revolution and irrigation, and improved transportation, to the continent) and in exploiting export markets by unleashing the peasant innovativeness from the yoke of the state. The African peasant emerged, in this account at least, as one part indigenous ecologist and one part diminutive capitalist (and rational economic agent).

What sort of ecological assemblage—what sort of ecological rationalities—lay behind the African food-climate-ecology crisis of the late 1960s and 1970s? It is worth recalling that a European version of the politics of food was central to Foucault's account of the rise of biopower, in which the "old power of death" was not abandoned but justified through the "calculated management of life" and appeals to the improvement of and the control over populations.[36] Central to this shift was the rise of apparatuses of security—what Foucault called the spaces of security, the management of uncertainty, mechanisms of normalization, and the population as a realm of conduct—around the problem of scarcity (*la disette*) as a crisis of government. Food (and the securing of the city) and famine now, as a matter of government, turned on questions of subsistence rights, the trade in grains, the management of droughts, and the control of food riots. The "antiscarcity" system of the ancien régime—the customary entitlements of the Elizabethan period in England, for example, famously described by Karl Polanyi[37]—was gradually displaced by the logic of the market and by concerns with agro-ecology, transportation, and farming practice. Famine was no longer a natural act or bad luck: subsistence became a realm of governmentality. There was not, as Foucault noted, "scarcity in general," but rather,

> We allow the phenomenon of dearness-scarcity to be produced and
> develop on ... a whole series of markets, and this phenomenon ... will

itself entail precisely its own self-curbing and self-regulation. So there will no longer be any scarcity in general, on condition that for a whole series of people, in a whole series of markets, there was some scarcity,...and it may well be that some people die of hunger after all. But by letting these people die of hunger one will be able to make scarcity a chimera and prevent it occurring in this massive form of the scourge typical of previous systems.[38]

Those who did perish were not the object of management (populations) but, to use the figure of nineteenth-century England, delinquents and "paupers," not the hardworking and upstanding "laboring poor" who simply required discipline and guidance to normalize their behavior congruent with the freedoms of the market.[39]

There was an African colonial version of this story that preceded the crisis of the 1970s. The colonial state was engaged in a biopolitical balancing act. On the one hand, the old indigenous antiscarcity system—the moral economy of subsistence[40]—was eroding, often quickly and under force, while on the other hand, the effects of commercialization and states' exactions vastly expanded the likelihood of famine, which raised the possibility of millions perishing in what Mike Davis calls "late Victorian holocausts."[41] British imperialists reluctantly and ineffectively institutionalized a minimalist antifamine policy (colonial welfare) for the indigent and invoked, with varying degrees of commitment, the "will to improve" colonial subjects who suffered from various indigenous deficits (recalcitrance, foot dragging, economic irrationality) and incompetencies. The food and ecological crisis of the 1970s represented a formalization of this emerging food-environment-security nexus. Not unlike David Nally's stimulating account of "colonial biopolitics" in the Irish famine,[42] development practice focused on agricultural (and pastoral) rationalization, population control or resettlement, and state discipline.

While African starvation—whether in Ethiopia or Burkina Faso— loomed large in the media and in the expansion of a century-long process of the international humanitarianization of hunger,[43] at base the emaciated famine victim was always draped in the sackcloth of Malthusian overpopulation and demographic urges. Garrett Hardin after all raised the specter of the "lifeboat ethic"—letting die, in Foucault's terms—as the cost associated with the implacable logic of overpopulation, overgrazing, resource scarcity, and inadequate property rights displayed in the Club of Rome report. The commons stood in as a metaphor for the old antiscarcity system, which, as Malthus and others predicted in the early nineteenth century, would compound the problem of food security, improvement, and growth. Climate, environment, and populations needed to be managed: improvement, market forces, and property rights were its modalities. It was the vision of John Stuart Mill and Adam Smith, confirmed by the raft of market studies conducted in the wake of the famine by, perhaps appropriately, Elliot Berg and his associates at the University of Michigan, who confirmed that markets were efficient and "non-monopolistic" but required investments in transportation and credit to realize their potential.[44] Africa, wracked by food insufficiency, political corruption, and poor weather, at least was populated by some form of *homo economicus*.

From the very outset, however, these emergent forms of green rule—largely state centered and rooted in a variety of national and multilateral development institutions without a substantial nongovernmental institutional presence—were unstable and in a sense were gradually imploding from within and without. The counterrevolution in development theory that the Berg report represented transformed the economic and political landscape of the state from the late 1970s onward. Structural adjustment unleashed a process of the fragmentation of public authority and contributed to the emergence of multiple forms of indirect private government, as Achille Mbembe called into question what sort of tentative green governance could be thought and brought forth.[45] As some African states imploded and fell into civil war (Sierra Leone, the Democratic Republic of the Congo, Somalia), others were institutionally and financially eviscerated in a way that simultaneously limited the capacity of the state to govern at all and made the boundaries between public and private ever more porous.[46] But perhaps more crucially, the neo-Malthusian model and its technicist beliefs and assumptions were increasingly questioned by a new wave of social science research rooted in careful ethnographic and local studies of human ecological dynamics and the intersection of social and ecological relations of production among rural producers (which in a statistical sense represented the majority of Africans).[47]

The challenges to Malthusianism and its various appendages came from along several fronts. First, Amartya Sen's pivotal book *Poverty and*

Famines decisively broke the purportedly causal connection between drought and famine.[48] Food crises and starvation bore no necessary relation to absolute food decline, and the effects of drought were typically mediated by farming practice and the market (in the latter case compounded by the deleterious effects of price increases and entitlement declines). Second, a body of work operating under the sign of peasant studies saw African communities as less composed of self-interested individuals (*contra* Hardin) than enmeshed in processes of commodification and social relations of production that rendered significant proportions of the rural populace vulnerable to all manner of ecological events even in "normal" times. The effects of climate and of ecological conditions were, in other words, experienced differentially in relation to class, asset holding, and the operations of the market. This realization had direct implications for who was vulnerable, how ecological processes were experienced, and in turn, how people and land might recover (in short, their resiliency). Third, there was a proliferation of work on common property resources—in which Nobel laureate Elinor Ostrom was a central player—that retained the significance of common property in Africa but, contra Hardin, emphasized how customary institutions and rules, rather than open access, were their defining qualities; and indeed, within them lay a capacity for environmental governance. Fourth, the sense in which indigenous knowledge and vernacular peasant practice could be captured and deployed was sharply constrained by studies of the social relations of production in farming communities, which revealed that the adaptive capacity much praised by geographers, anthropologists, and rural sociologists could be, and often was, undercut, eroded, or lost by the operations of the market. This was the heart of James Scott's influential book on the moral economy of the peasantry after all.[49]

Finally, there was a turn toward discursive analysis, led by the likes of Melissa Leach, Jeremy Swift, and others, to point to what they called dominant models or narratives of environmental crisis that reflected particular readings or constructions of local African conditions.[50] In part, the framing of particular environmental problems—for example, desertification and the deterioration of rangelands—was also questioned by the rise of a "new ecology" that focused on disequilibrium and a rethinking of the old static systems models of tropical ecology.[51] As a consequence, critical approaches to both ecology and conventional policy questioned the neo-Malthusian, technicist, and Hardinian models of the African ecological crisis. This was then an epistemological challenge. Outside experts drew on a long line of orthodoxies in which Africans were depicted, to quote Richard Grove, as botanical "levelers."[52] Science was in this account politically and culturally embedded.

By the 1980s and into the 1990s, these intellectual developments— partly rooted in the field of political ecology, partly in ecological science and science studies, and partly in anthropological critiques of development[53]—represented a fundamental challenge to the legitimacy and standing of the conventional narratives of Africa's environmental conditions, its actors, and its agents.

Rule by Carbon: Climate, Development, and Poverty Redux

It is a striking image: a global capitalist whose personal wealth is rooted in an industry, air transportation, distinguished by its massive carbon footprint and a Nobel Prize–winning US politician and former vice president honored for his contributions in placing global climate change, and the scientific work of the Intergovernmental Panel on Climate Change (IPCC) in particular, on the global political agenda (see figure 3.2). Tossing the globe into the air, British tycoon Sir Richard Branson announced to the world in 2007 that he was offering a US$25 million prize for the scientist who discovers a way of extracting greenhouse gases from the atmosphere—a challenge to find the world's first viable design to capture and remove carbon dioxide from the air. Big Science meets Big Business meets Big Politics. It is above all a *planetary image,* in its own way a bookend to NASA's famous planet Earth photograph AS17-22727, taken during the final Apollo mission in 1972. It is a picturing, or rendering, of a certain sort of global nature, global politics, and global science all at once. If the NASA image came to be the lodestar for the United Nations Convention on the Human Environment held in Stockholm in 1972, perhaps the Branson-Gore photograph captured the sentiments not just of the December 2009 UN Climate Conference in Copenhagen (COP 15) but of the biopolitics of global warming generally. Copenhagen in some respects gestured back to Earth Day 1972, to the *Limits to Growth* report and its World3 computer model.

Figure 3.2: Vice-President Al Gore and Sir Richard Branson announcing a scientific prize for carbon capture in 2007. AP Photo/Kristy Wigglesworth

The United Nations Framework Convention on Climate Change (UNFCC), which the United Nations adopted at the Rio Earth Summit, aimed to achieve the stabilization of greenhouse gas concentrations in the atmosphere at a level that would prevent dangerous anthropogenic interference with the climate system.[54] The Kyoto Protocol, which was signed in 1997 and came into force in 2005, was established to realize these goals. CO_2 emissions are now 30 percent higher than when the UNFCC was signed; atmospheric concentrations of CO_2 equivalents are currently 430 parts per million.[55] At the current rate, they could more than triple by the end of the century. In effect, this would mean a 50 percent risk of global temperature increases of five degrees Celsius (the average global temperature now, for example, is only five degrees Celsius warmer than the last ice age).[56]

Over the past two decades, global climate change has become the vehicle for two new, powerful discourses, both of which represent important departures from the sort of theory and policy debate I outlined earlier. The first is referred to as "global environmental governance," and the second, as "global environmental sustainability" (in contradistinction to the earlier language of "environmentalism" during the 1970s). The proliferation of institutions and organizations and of principles, norms, and decision-making procedures—what are conventionally seen as an "international environmental regime"—is reflected in the explosive growth of interstate treaties, on average, sixteen a year since the 1972 Stockholm Conference on the Human Environment and nineteen a year since Rio. The treaties that developed in the wake of Stockholm focused on limiting specific sorts of pollutants (SO_2, NO_2), banning ozone-depleting gases, protecting key species (regulating commercial whaling), and preserving endangered ecosystems (wetlands). As Mathew Paterson points out, this form of global governance "corresponds to an era where capitalism was itself organised and governed through extensive planning, from tripartite corporatist management in many Western countries, to the nationalisation of many industries, and extensive multilateral management through the Bretton Woods system."[57] But this model was to shift. By the 1980s, the Brundtland report (*Our Common Future*) enshrined sustainability as a political discourse that sought to address both the growing North-South conflicts (the relations between poverty and global sustainability) and the growing counterrevolution by firms and states to the idea of regulation, that is to say, to attempt to install an environmental governance "compatible" with no limits to growth (the precondition of neoliberal capitalism).

Remnants of "managed capitalism"—that is to say, remnants of a Keynesian project—did endure, but by the 1990s, on the back of a major neoliberal push in the United States, the United Kingdom, and Germany and through the multilateral development institutions such as the IBRD and the IMF, these relics rapidly disappeared. Deregulated markets, privatization of state-owned industries, the deregulation of exchange rates and financial flows, and assaults on corporate taxes and the welfare state were all buttressed by the power of global regulatory institutions and international agreements praying at the altar of free trade and robust property rights (for example, the WTO, TRIPS, GATS). In a radically new ideological environment, environmental problems were now subject to the implacable logic of the markets, prices, and capital flows. As Paterson put it, "global environmental governance . . . . [became]

increasingly guided by an imperative less to *organise* and directly *manage* capitalist growth to pursue sustainability, than to enable private actors to pursue their economic interests in ways which simultaneously promote sustainability."[58] What began with state-directed command and control ended with governments creating markets for environmental goods and services and subsidizing (that is to say, providing) new incentives for green industries. Much of this new model of green governance was constituted by voluntary agreements for new practices and standards set by industry for itself (for example, the ISO 14000 series on environmental management standards) and by rafts of international environmental NGOs, think tanks, and foundations following the money into new forms of market-based green governance.

Global climate change became, hot on the heels of structural adjustment, a theater for "governance through markets": government provides incentives and subsidies, and corporations establish their own (voluntary) standards. Global climate-change policy and struggles over its shape and form emerged from the very specific set of political economic changes over the past four decades, and in specific capitalist order.[59] In this regard, 2010 looks very different from 1970. The likes of Naomi Klein and George Monbiot make the point that in this ascendant neoliberal order even environmental calamity and reconstruction is a source of corporate profit and capitalist consolidation (so-called disaster capitalism).[60] In the current neoliberal order, the short-term future depends on a precise costing of climatic impacts and on getting the prices right.[61]

Implicit in the science behind the global climate change debate is a worldview somewhat at odds with the Darwinian orthodoxy of evolutionary gradualism.[62] Climate could and did of course change historically, but for human occupation and livelihood, this represented a deep historical time—the very *longue durée*. What is on offer now is something unimaginable until recently, namely, abrupt and radical shifts. It is a science of planetary disaster demanding a response—political, policy, civic, and business—of an equal and opposite magnitude and gravity. Here is Al Gore on the matter: "What we are facing is a planetary emergency. So some things you would never consider otherwise, it makes sense to consider."[63] It is a language of survival, security, radical uncertainty, and necessary infringements on freedom and choice, on liberty itself. What might this planetary ecological crisis entail?

For some, therefore, it means that a war on global warming must be declared, quite as draconian as the global war on terror. Are we not faced with inhabiting—once again—the rubble of a ruined world? For others, typically of a social democratic cast of mind, it means pinning hopes on human adaptability and resilience in the face of melting glaciers, the end of irrigated agriculture and a return to dry farming. For the governments, green NGOs, and those others with seats at the table hoping for a leaner, low-fat capitalism, it means negotiating some version of the neo-liberal deal. That is, haggling over the further commodification of the earth and its productions— vegetable, mineral and animal—and legislating limits and rights to pollute, to trade toxins, to crank up derivatives markets recently vilified as a sure sign of the excesses of casino capitalism.[64]

In a discursive sense, then, climate change as a planetary emergency mobilizes powerful actors around the threat of massive risks and uncertainties.[65] It resembles the War on Terror, the Ebola outbreaks, or the threats of nuclear weaponry and points toward what might be distinctive about contemporary ecological futures: namely, that they are "attuned to uncertain and multiple potential futures that do not operate according to statistical, probabilistic or epidemiological rules."[66] But as I hope to show, it also returns us to the expanded sense of security implied by Foucault in his lectures on security and territory. As he put it, "new elements are constantly being integrated: production, psychology, behavior, the ways of doing things of producers, buyers, consumers, importers, and exporters, and the world market. Security therefore involves organizing, or anyway allowing the development of ever-wider circuits."[67] In this rendering, security is "centripetal" and sees variations as inescapable in natural phenomena (rather than operating according to the binary of permitted and forbidden). Security of the environment, when the horizon is global climate and human survival, "tries to grasp the reality of the 'natural' phenomena that it addresses, to understand the way in which various components function together, to manage or regulate that complex reality towards desired ends."[68] Nowhere is this clearer than in the ways in which climate change and environmental security are now conceived of as a way of climate-proofing Africa by building adaptive capacity and resiliency.

Environmental Security and Risk Futures:
African Development as Self-Organizing Resiliency

> [The] logic of resilience, then, is not merely an attitude of prepared-
> ness; to be resilient is not quite to be under protection nor merely to
> have systems in place to deal with contingencies. Resilience implies
> a systematic, widespread, organizational, structural and personal
> strengthening of subjective and material arrangements so as to be
> better able to anticipate and tolerate disturbances in complex worlds
> without collapse, to withstand shocks, and to rebuild as necessary.[69]

The demands of responding to the uncertain but profound effects of
global warming are reshaping the contemporary landscape of African
sustainable development. In place of the managed environmentalism of
the 1970s, and the neo-Malthusian models, is a new language turning
on socioecological resiliency and adaptive community institutions linked
through market governance.[70] Gone is the language of overpopulation,
incomplete markets, poor transportation, and local management deficits;
gone too is any lingering sense of state welfare. There is now an assemblage of ecological rationalities, not all of which have the state as their
guarantor and the nation as their locus of operation, that collectively
expand the sense of security and securitization.[71] The very uncertainty
of the effects of global climate change (global climate-change models are
robust on system dynamics but weak on regional and local predictions) is
antithetical to the sort of predictive modeling exercises practiced by the
Club of Rome. The securitization of the environment—which not only
embraces the threats to food and water systems but now encompasses the
likelihood of conflict and violence around access to scarce resources[72]—
requires not so much a strong or disciplinary state operating within closed
spaces of institutions but something consistent with the global and multiple planes of movements of persons, information, and commodities and
with an environment construed as a supplier of "ecosystem services."[73]

The old modes of calculation—the insurance-based logic of calculable risks assessed through probabilities—are replaced with modalities that
can still render the uncertain future thinkable and something that can be
prepared for and remediated. It is at this point that culture—especially
institutions, many of which are indigenous or hybrids of local custom and

the modern—meets up with the so-called resiliency school and theories of "complex adaptive systems."[74] Its function is to incorporate social and economic systems in an overarching complex science of "socioecological resilience" rooted in civil society (the community looms very large here). The scope and scale (and institutionalization) of resiliency thinking are now vast, encompassing most fields of expertise that address security in the broadest sense (from the IMF to homeland security). It is a vast industry that encompasses vast swaths of the social, economic, and political landscape; its origins, however—and its great strength—remain in the area of green governance and the linking of social and environmental systems. Local knowledge and practice, notions of vulnerability and exposure—in other words the critical responses to the neo-Malthusian approach—have been grafted onto a new turbo-charged systems theory, derived in particular from the work of ecologist C. S. Holling and his associates, and have been brought together in a highly influential think tank called the Stockholm Resilience Center. African communities can now be fine-tuned—paradoxically building on their traditional strengths (for example, the social capital of village communities or city slums) yet supplemented by the expertise of development and state practitioners. The echo of Foucault's account of civil society in a neoliberal order is loud and clear:

> Civil society, therefore, is an element of transactional reality in the history of governmental technologies, a transactional reality which seems to me to be absolutely correlative to the form of governmental technology we call liberalism, that is to say, a technology of government whose objective is its own self-limitation insofar as it is pegged to the specificity of economic processes.[75]

The new ecology of rule, if we can return to the Sahel, is the language of adaptation to climate change and the resiliency of socioecological systems, what Rose in another setting has called "government through community."[76] Geographers, ecologists, and political scientists have been its central theoreticians, addressing the question of how the possible burdens of climatic change, sea-level rise, and possible catastrophic events are to be distributed geographically and in social and class terms.[77] Africa once again becomes a major knowledge laboratory, because it is already clear that the burden of climate change will fall heavily in Africa.[78] The research on adaptation to climate change on its face seems to build on the insights drawn from the political ecological critiques of neo-Mathusianism—in particular, that one must start from patterns of social, economic, and political vulnerability of the poor and the sorts of entitlements they command.[79] The marriage is, however, forced and unstable. Poverty and vulnerability appear in the paradigm of socioecological systems—adaptive capacity, resiliency, and flexibility in local social systems—with no serious account of political economy and the operations of power. It is a managerial view of security rooted in a particular synthesis of the market and nature.

The origins of the resiliency work lay in the 1970s with the work of Holling, which attempted to locate the equilibrium-centered work of systems ecology on the larger landscape of the biosphere as a self-organizing and nonlinear complex system.[80] Complexity science—the hallmark of contemporary systems ecology—represents a meeting point of several multidisciplinary strands of science, including computational theory, non-equilibrium thermodynamics, evolutionary theory, and earth systems science. At the heart of Holling's early work was how systems retain cohesiveness under stress or radical perturbations (such as climate variation). Resilience determined the persistence of relations in a system. In his later work, he explored the implications for management of ecosystems by emphasizing less stability than the unpredictable and unknowable nature of complex system interdependencies, which implied (in policy terms) a need to "keep options open, the need to view events in a regional rather than a local context, and the need to emphasize heterogeneity."[81] Through his Resilience Alliance and later the Resilience Center, resilience and adaptive systems thinking was pushed far beyond ecology to encompass a coevolutionary theory of societies and ecosystems as a single science ("panarchy").[82] Holling extended his view of resiliency by suggesting that all living systems evolved through disequilibrium, that instability was the source of creativity: crisis tendencies were constitutive of complex adaptive systems. What linked the social, economic, and ecological was the idea of capital as the inherent potential of a system available for change.[83] What began as a study of the local ended as an abstract theory of "capital accumulation" marked by episodic change, turbulence, and a lack of predictability. What is striking in such an integrated field theory is that there is no point of intersection between system resiliency and virtually any contemporary account of social power or for that matter of the contradictory dynamics of capitalist accumulation.

At the time that Holling was laying out his first ideas (and in the midst of the Sahelian famine in Africa), Friedrich Hayek delivered his Nobel Prize speech, which, as M. Cooper and J. Walker brilliantly show, has an elective affinity with Holling's ideas.[84] Hayek was moving toward his mature theorization of capitalism as an exemplar of the biological sciences: the extended market order is "perfectly natural...like biological phenomena, evolved in the course of natural selection."[85] In his Nobel lecture, he returned to the epistemology of limited knowledge and uncertain future,[86] a position that led him to explicitly reject and denounce the Club of Rome *Limits to Growth* report. It was to biological systems and complex, adaptive, and nonlinear dynamics that he turned to provide the guide for his "spontaneous market order" of capitalism. Both endorse the view of limited knowledge, unpredictable environments, and order through survival.[87]

The Stockholm Resilience Center in particular has acted as a major purveyor of Holling's and related ideas to the global development community. Indeed, resiliency is now so central to the notion of environmentally sustainable development—the cornerstone of the major multilateral development and international environmental NGOs—that the complex adaptive systems framework (including the sorts of measures of standardization and accounting for assessing ecosystem resilience) has been taken up by the likes of the World Bank and UN HABITAT in such diverse arenas as sustainable urbanism, ecosystem services, and climate adaptation and mitigation. A key policy document, *Roots of Resilience*—bearing the imprimatur of UNEP, the World Bank, and the World Resources Institute—reads,

> Resilience is the capacity to adapt and to thrive in the face of challenge. This report contends that when the poor successfully (and sustainably) scale-up ecosystem-based enterprises, their resilience can increase in three dimensions. They can become more economically resilient—better able to face economic risks. They—and their communities—can become more socially resilient—better able to work together for mutual benefit. And the ecosystems they live in can become more biologically resilient—more productive and stable.[88]

As Cooper and Walker note, resiliency is the form of governmentality appropriate to *any* form of perturbation and uncertainty: "dealing with extreme weather events is not merely analogous to coping with recurrent financial shocks, it is also the means through which economics and social resilience is to be achieved."[89]

The notion of adaptive capacity and government through communities does of course rest on a substantial body of research that demonstrates how rural communities in Africa (and elsewhere) adapt to climate change through mobility, storage, diversification, communal pooling, and exchange by drawing on social networks and their access to resources.[90] Yet what is on offer instead is a bland and bloodless shopping list of "conditions" for adaptive governance, including "policy will," "coordination of stakeholders," "science," "common goals," and "creativity." *Roots of Resilience* offers a full-blown theory of development ("growing the wealth of the poor") in the same way that socioecological governance and adaptive, flexible climate risk management offer a form of neoliberal governmentality for climate change in Africa. The new post-Washington Consensus looks like it is even more consistent with Hayek's mature vision of the market order than its earlier raw and crude neoliberal version. *Roots of Resilience* proposes to scale up "nature based income and culturing resilience," which require ownership, capacity, and connection. Ecosystem-based enterprises, rooted in community resource management, will entail local-state and private-civic partnerships and enterprise networking. Markets in ecosystem services, and delegation of responsibility to communities and households as self-organizing productive units, will constitute the basis for survival in biophysical, political, economic, and financial worlds defined by turbulence, risk, and unpredictability. Some will be resilient, but others will be too resilient or not resilient enough.

We are in the world of tipping points, thresholds, and maladaptation. Ecological resiliency is the calculative metric for a brave new world of turbulent capitalism and the global economic order and a new ecology of rule. Africa, home to the bottom billion, provides a laboratory in which the "poor will be tested as the impacts of change manifest."[91] Resiliency has become, say Cooper and Walker, "the test of one's right to survive in the global order of things."[92] To return to Foucault and his notion of an expanded sense of ecosecurity, resiliency is an apparatus of security that will determine the process of "letting die." Africa, once again, is the testing ground for a vision of security and care in which life is nothing more than permanent readiness and flexible adaptiveness. As Lentzos and Rose note in their discussion of the world of financial turbulence and personal risk management, resilience refers to "a systematic, widespread, organizational, structural and personal strengthening of subjective and material arrangements."[93] It is a deeply Hayekian project—an expression of the neoliberal-thought collective—in which the idea of a spontaneous market order has become, ironically, a form of sustainable development. The challenges of adapting to the radical uncertainties and perturbations of global climate change produce a new sense of *homo economicus;* the African peasant, as Foucault says, becomes "an entrepreneur of himself,"[94] a hedge-fund manager for his own impoverished life.

CHAPTER 4

Economic Crisis, Nationalism, and Politicized Ethnicity

Rogers Brubaker

Economic crises have often been associated with economic nationalism or protectionism on the one hand and with violence or hostility toward ethnic minorities on the other. The Great Depression exacerbated—and was in turn exacerbated by—economic nationalism. In much of central and eastern Europe—and not only in Nazi Germany—the Depression was also associated with a murderous mixture of ethnic nationalism and anti-Semitism, while in the United States and France it prompted efforts to repatriate immigrants. More recently, the Asian financial crisis of 1997–98 triggered a massive wave of violent attacks on the Chinese minority in Indonesia. It is therefore not surprising that the current crisis has raised fears of protectionist nationalism, ethnic scapegoating, and xenophobic populism. A February 2009 cover story of the *Economist* opined that "economic nationalism ... is ... turning the economic crisis into a political one and threatening the world with depression."[1] And United Nations Secretary-General Ban Ki-moon warned in April 2009 of "social unrest, weakened governments and angry publics ... [with frightening] consequences for communities already victimized by prejudice or exclusion."[2]

Yet nationalist and ethnopolitical responses to the crisis have so far been surprisingly muted. The depth and duration of the crisis, to be sure, remain uncertain at this writing, especially in Europe. With the stability and even the continued existence of the Eurozone in question, and with unemployment having reached 20 percent in Spain, the potential for intensified nationalism is clear. And on the level of rhetoric, the European debt crisis has already generated a good deal of nationalism. The debt crisis is easily cast as a morality tale in which personified nations are the protagonists. German politicians, outraged that responsible Germans should have to bail out spendthrift Greeks (and conveniently forgetting that the rescue package would bail out German banks), suggested that Greece sell a few islands or perhaps the Acropolis; Greek politicians responded by claiming that Germany had failed to pay adequate reparations for wartime thefts of Greek gold. Nationalist rhetoric has been visual as well as verbal. The cover of the weekly German magazine *Focus* referred to Greeks as "Swindlers in the European Family" and showed a statue of Aphrodite with a raised middle finger; the Athens daily *Eleftheros Typos* responded with an image of goddess Victoria atop the Berlin Siegessäule holding a swastika.[3]

These and other rhetorical flourishes notwithstanding, the crisis has not to date generated the surge in protectionist nationalism or ethnic exclusion that might have been expected. This chapter seeks to specify the reasons for this initially muted response. More generally, it seeks to explain why economic crises can and sometimes do provoke nationalism and ethnopolitical conflict, but also why they do not automatically or uniformly do so.

When thinking of nationalism in connection with economic crisis, most people are likely to think first and foremost of protectionism, and to understand protectionism narrowly as a set of policies (such as tariffs, quotas, or currency devaluations) through which states seek to protect domestic producers from foreign competition.[4] While such policies are of course important, I am interested here in a broader set of phenomena. There is no single name for these phenomena, which include various forms of nationalism and politicized ethnicity. But they all involve claims to privilege or protect national or ethnic *insiders* in the face of putative economic threats from *outsiders*.

Such claims take two differing forms that I call *nation-statist* and *ethnopolitical,* though they often overlap in practice. In the first configuration, the boundary between insiders and outsiders is defined by citizenship or state frontiers. Nation-statist boundaries divide citizens from foreigners, national territory from foreign territory, and (more ambiguously) national products from foreign products. Claims are made to protect the labor markets, industries, natural resources, financial assets, or welfare benefits of the nation-state and its citizens vis-à-vis some foreign threat or competitor. The threat may be seen as coming from foreign workers, who take "our" jobs at a moment of high unemployment; from foreign goods, which are seen as competing unfairly with domestic goods; from foreign capital, which destabilizes the domestic economy or undermines the domestic currency; or from the IMF or World Bank (or now also the European Union or European Central Bank), which can be seen as imposing an unjust and punitive regime of austerity on the national economy.

In the second configuration, insiders and outsiders are defined by ethnicity, race, or religion (which I subsume under the umbrella term *ethnicity*), rather than by citizenship or territory. Ethnic outsiders—who may be immigrants or a longstanding but marginalized, vulnerable, or stigmatized segment of the citizenry—may be members of the *state* (with respect to their formal legal citizenship), but they are not socially accepted as full members of the *nation*. They are therefore vulnerable to being blamed for, or seen as profiting from, economic distress. Or they can be seen as enjoying illegitimate access to or control of jobs, wealth, welfare, credit, business opportunities, land, or other resources. Claims are made to exclude, restrict, expropriate, or expel such ethnic outsiders or to privilege ethnic insiders (those considered full members of the nation or, in some cases, those claiming priority as indigenous "sons of the soil") in such matters as employment, university admission, or business opportunities.

Before considering nation-statist and ethnopolitical responses to economic crisis in more detail, I want to make three more general observations about nationalism, politicized ethnicity, and economic crisis. First, it is important to emphasize that distinctions between national and ethnic insiders and outsiders, representations of outsiders as a threat, and claims to privilege or protect insiders are by no means restricted to times of economic crisis. As basic forms of social organization, cultural understanding, and political claims-making, nationalism and politicized ethnicity are endemic to the modern world. A world of nation-states is a world in which citizens are routinely, chronically, and pervasively privileged vis-à-vis foreigners and in which ethnocultural insiders are routinely, chronically, and pervasively privileged vis-à-vis others (even in ostensibly civic nation-states such as France and the United States).[5] The privileges enjoyed by insiders are no less important for being largely invisible and taken for granted. The privilege of birthright citizenship, for example, and the taken-for-granted legitimacy of excluding noncitizens from the territory and labor markets of prosperous states contribute massively to sustaining patterns of global inequality.[6] It is therefore not helpful to think of economic crises as *causing* nationalism or politicized ethnicity. Rather, crises may be conducive to redefining understandings of insiders and outsiders (by favoring more restrictive understandings of membership); to reformulating accounts of the threat posed by outsiders (by highlighting economic concerns); and to generating claims to protect or privilege insiders that go beyond the routine privileging of insiders that is inscribed into the basic organization of nation-states.

Second, while crises are socially understood as exceptional, economic crises are endemic and recurrent phenomena in modern capitalist economies. Moreover, crises shade over into chronic and routine forms of economic disruption, trouble, and insecurity. Crisis is in this sense a *gradational* concept, designating phenomena that differ in intensity or degree, but not in kind, from everyday economic phenomena. It is impossible to draw a precise line between "ordinary" economic troubles—such as surges in unemployment, declines in output, spikes in inflation or interest rates, massive indebtedness, plummeting currencies, or the bursting of speculative bubbles—and "crises." For this reason, I do not limit my analysis to economic crises but seek to specify in more general terms the ways in which economic troubles are intertwined with nationalism and politicized ethnicity.

Third, and most important, economic crisis or distress does not uniformly or automatically foster or intensify nation-statist or ethnopolitical responses. One key reason for this is that economic distress is not self-interpreting. Political responses to economic distress depend on how economic troubles are framed and interpreted. And the prevailing idioms used to interpret economic troubles differ sharply across time and place. Anti-Semitism, for example, was a much more pervasive and legitimate public idiom in the interwar period than it is today.[7] The same holds for autarkic nationalism: despite intensifying criticism of globalization *à l'américaine*, few narratives of the current crisis are informed by a vision of an autarkic national economy.

A further reason for the variable and contingent relation between economic crisis and nationalist or ethnopolitical response is that differing forms and degrees of economic dependence and interdependence impose differing constraints on efforts to protect national economies. The intricate network of indebtedness linking EU countries, for example, as well as the profound dependence of many countries, especially Germany, on intra-EU export markets, blurs the line between inside and outside, national and foreign; this makes it more difficult—nationalist rhetoric notwithstanding—for prosperous countries such as Germany to protect their own economies by refusing aid to Greece and other heavily indebted countries.[8] Nationalist responses have also been limited in some hard-hit countries by the urgent need for IMF assistance, while low commodity prices have made "resource nationalism" a less viable strategy than it has been in the past.[9] A final reason is that institutional environments and constraints differ markedly. EU member states, for example, cannot protect their labor markets from citizens of other EU states. And trade regimes (even outside the EU) are much more institutionalized and "legalized" today than they were in the 1930s.

Nation-Statist Responses to Economic Distress

Most discussions of "nationalism" in connection with economic crisis have focused on measures undertaken by the state to protect the domestic economy. These include tariffs, quotas, currency devaluations, and other measures intended to restrict imports and protect domestic producers. It is understandable that such measures have been the center of attention. Since measures such as these are apt to provoke countermeasures from other states, they risk setting in motion a protectionist spiral. Given the importance of interstate trade to the world economy, such a spiral would sharply reinforce the economic downturn. This is what happened in the Great Depression, and that precedent understandably weighs heavily on current discussions, all the more so as the current crisis occasioned a "sudden, severe and globally synchronized collapse" in world trade.[10]

Governments have indeed responded to the present crisis with a certain amount of protectionist rhetoric and a variety of protectionist initiatives, including not only tariffs but a range of nontariff measures. Yet both rhetoric and policies have been relatively limited in scale and scope; they have not unleashed anything like a tariff war or a series of competitive devaluations. In the United States, for example, despite intensifying jawboning about China's enormous and chronic trade surpluses and undervalued currency, and despite the "buy American" provisions of the stimulus package, it does not appear as of this writing that much more attention than usual has been paid to competition from foreign goods.

The absence to date of signs of a dramatic protectionist spiral in response to the current crisis has led some observers to conclude that fears of protectionism are overblown. The institutional environment is very different today than in the 1930s: most international trade today occurs within customs unions or free-trade zones, and World Trade Organization (WTO) rules and procedures have "legalized" the international trade regime. The ideological climate also differs sharply from that of the 1930s: the disenchantment with neoliberalism has not entailed a reenchantment with autarchy.[11] In less conspicuous ways, moreover, states routinely and chronically seek to protect domestic producers; this continued to be the case even at the apogee of neoliberalism.[12] In this view, protectionism was "the dog that didn't bark" during the current crisis; the response to the crisis represented a move "from a situation with a good deal of protectionism to a situation with a little bit more protectionism." Dani Rodrik concludes that "the international trade regime has passed its greatest test since the Great Depression with flying colours."[13]

Others—notably Simon Evenett and the Global Trade Alert monitoring group he directs—warn against complacency. The institutional and ideological landscapes are indeed different, they concede, and protectionism today does not look like protectionism in the 1930s. But they see continued dangers in reciprocal, mutually reinforcing forms of "murky protectionism," involving such initiatives as antidumping measures, discriminatory provisions in stimulus packages, credit guarantees, subsidies to and bailouts of domestic firms, licensing requirements, and even "green" policies that favor domestic firms. And the pressures for further and stronger measures may increase as unemployment continues to increase or stays high for a prolonged period.[14]

Nation-statist forms of closure include not only measures seeking to protect domestic producers but also measures seeking to protect domestic workers or taxpayers. Historically, economic distress has often occasioned an intensification in antiforeigner rhetoric (though it is not, of course, the only source of such rhetoric). Narratives of crisis have blamed immigrants for causing or aggravating economic distress by taking jobs from citizens, claiming welfare benefits, and burdening public services. And such rhetoric has often been accompanied by a tightening of restrictions on the entry, residence, employment, or socioeconomic rights of foreigners. In France, the major European country of immigration during the 1920s, both public opinion and legislation turned sharply restrictive after the economic crisis deepened in 1931.[15] In the United States, where restrictive legislation had curtailed mass overseas immigration earlier, Mexican immigrants—whose numbers had continued to increase during the 1920s—became targets of federal deportation drives and local repatriation programs.[16]

More recently, the institutionalization of regimes of rights for foreign workers has constrained the policies of liberal states. In response to the oil crisis and rising unemployment of the 1970s, for example, northern and western European countries ceased recruiting new workers, but they could not simply send workers home on any large scale, and indeed foreign populations continued to grow as a result of family-reunification policies. Where such rights regimes have not been institutionalized, states have faced no such constraints. Economic distress, for example, prompted (or at least was used to justify) mass expulsion of foreign workers from Ghana in 1969 and from Nigeria in 1983 and 1985.[17]

There is widespread concern among migrants in many labor-importing countries (and in remittance-dependent source countries) that migrant workers will be disproportionately affected—through lay-offs, scapegoating, or administrative measures—by the current crisis. Undocumented workers in particular, often tolerated in boom times, are everywhere more vulnerable during periods of sharp economic contraction. Foreign workers in some regions seem particularly vulnerable. The major labor-importing countries of Southeast Asia, hard hit by precipitous drops in exports, have stopped issuing or renewing work permits, stepped up efforts to deport undocumented foreigners, and provided incentives or directives to replace foreign with national workers or to lay off foreign workers first.[18] And in the Persian Gulf states, which employ armies of foreign labor on a strictly temporary basis, foreign workers have no right to long-term residence if they lose their jobs.

Yet the connection between economic crisis and restrictive measures toward foreign or undocumented workers is not as close as might be expected. In the first place, like the protection of domestic producers, the protection of domestic workers is a chronic and routine form of nationalist rhetoric, policy, and practice; it is by no means limited to periods of economic crisis. The labor markets of all prosperous nation-states privilege their own citizens (or European Union citizens in the special case of the EU). All insiders have unconditional access to the labor market, while only certain categories of outsiders (such as permanent residents, persons with work visas, or other categories privileged by a country's immigration law) enjoy legal access. Others may work or reside without permission; but the risks, costs, and insecurities they bear in taking what are often dirty, dangerous, or demeaning jobs without the most basic legal protections are evidence of the chronic and routine *closure* of labor markets, not evidence of their *openness*.

This routine privileging of insiders means that even when restrictive measures toward foreign or undocumented workers *coincide* with economic distress, they are not necessarily *caused* by that distress. The much-discussed restrictive legislation enacted by Arizona in April 2010, for example, was not a response to the economic crisis. Undocumented workers had been the focus of rhetorical concern and of federal and state-level enforcement initiatives in workplaces and along the border long before the crisis. The Arizona measure, along with a series of earlier measures in that state, was a response to a major shift in the geography of undocumented border crossing since the mid-1990s, as fences and stepped-up border enforcement in California and Texas diverted cross-border flows to Arizona.[19] The focus of concern in Arizona has been crime tied to drug trafficking and human smuggling, not competition for jobs.

Several constraints may limit efforts to protect domestic workers at the expense of foreign workers in times of economic distress. First, labor markets are often segmented, with foreign workers concentrated in jobs citizens do not want; this limits competition for jobs and blunts pressures for protection. Second, competition is further limited by the sensitivity of migrant labor, both legal and undocumented, to labor-market conditions. In the United States, for example, both flows and stocks of undocumented workers have declined substantially since 2007.[20] Third, powerful and organized business interests in access to cheap labor have often trumped a diffuse public preference for a more restrictive immigration policy.[21] A further constraint on certain kinds of programs targeting undocumented workers in the United States is the concern of both political parties to avoid alienating the rapidly growing Latino electorate.[22] Finally, legal and institutional constraints may limit the privileging of domestic labor. Wildcat strikers at British refineries and power plants in January 2009, for example, protested the subcontracting of construction work to Italian and Polish workers and called for "British jobs for British workers"; but the strikes attracted little political support (no doubt in part because the subcontracting was perfectly legal under European Union rules), and they soon petered out.

Yet although restrictive measures against foreign or undocumented workers are not a direct, automatic, or uniform response to economic distress, crises do provide powerful and resonant rhetorical resources for proponents of such forms of closure. Other things being equal, closure against foreign workers becomes a more attractive nation-statist strategy as the magnitude and duration of unemployment increases. Limiting foreigners' (or certain categories of foreigners') eligibility for welfare benefits becomes a similarly attractive strategy in response to prolonged or severe budget crises.[23] With the current crisis still unfolding, especially in Europe, it is certainly possible that closure against foreigners will intensify.

Questions about the nation-statist response to the current crisis concern not only the short- and medium-term efforts to protect domestic producers or workers from "outside" competition or to protect domestic wealth by managing trade imbalances, currency reserves, and exchange rates. They also concern longer-term changes in the architecture of global political economy. Some observers have suggested that the current crisis will mark the end of neoliberalism.[24] This large and important issue is beyond the scope of this chapter; I limit myself here to two observations. On the one hand, neoliberalism was already in retreat in the Global South before the crisis;[25] the crisis may well further diminish the prestige of the neoliberal model. On the other hand, it is by no means clear that the crisis will substantially weaken neoliberalism in the United States itself. Political struggles over regulatory reforms are still under way at this writing, but the proposals on the table are relatively modest; and even these have encountered strong opposition and aggressive lobbying from financial institutions. If by neoliberalism we mean a project aimed at the "restoration and consolidation of class power," as David Harvey has observed, then it may well emerge from the crisis relatively unscathed.[26]

Ethnopolitical Responses to Economic Distress

Nation-statist responses to economic crisis can shade over into ethnopolitical responses. Efforts to protect labor markets from outsiders, for example, may define outsiders in nation-statist terms by their legal status as foreign or undocumented workers; yet such workers are often implicitly identified in cultural, religious, or racial terms. While official rhetoric is often nation-statist, referring to "immigrants" or "foreigners," informal popular discourse tends to be more ethnic, referring for example to Turks, Muslims, or Africans.

Ethnopolitical responses to economic crisis can emerge when groups marked as ethnic outsiders (regardless of their citizenship status) are represented or understood as responsible for, or as illegitimately benefiting from, economic distress or when such outsiders are represented or understood as having illegitimate access to or control of jobs, wealth, credit, business opportunities, welfare benefits, land, or other resources to which, it is argued or implied, ethnocultural insiders should enjoy privileged access. This is most likely to happen in settings characterized by a pronounced ethnic or cultural division of labor or, more generally, when economic categories coincide more or less closely with ethnic categories. When this is the case, economic and ethnocultural cleavages are superimposed, and economic oppositions of interest—between creditors and debtors, owners and workers, landlords and tenants, workers and strikebreakers, or shop owners and customers—can be interpreted in ethnic terms.

Such redoubling of economic and ethnic categories and cleavages has been most pronounced in colonial and postcolonial societies. In colonial Burma, for example, tensions between Telugu dockworkers and Burman strikebreakers led to riots in 1930 that sparked Burmese nationalist agitation, while Chettiar moneylenders from south India— as they foreclosed on loans and emerged as large landowners during the Depression years—became the central targets of the nationalist movement.[27] But economic and ethnic categories and cleavages are super-imposed in other settings as well. Throughout much of eastern Europe, sharp differences of language and religion historically distinguished town dwellers from surrounding peasants until well into the twentieth century, and in many parts of the region, landlords, too, were ethnically distinct from peasants.[28] As a result, economic conflicts and agendas were readily ethnicized.[29] The interwar Romanian state, for example, found it politi-cally irresistible to undertake a far-reaching land reform in newly acquired Transylvania, where large landowners were almost exclusively Hungarian, and peasants largely Romanian. And Romanian nationalists were quite open about their desire to "conquer" or "colonize" the ethnically "alien" cities and towns of Transylvania, which were dominated economically, demographically, and culturally by Hungarians, Germans, and Jews.[30]

In settings such as these, crisis does not *create* ethnoculturally defined oppositions of economic interest, but it can *highlight and drama-tize* such oppositions; and in this way, it can help political entrepreneurs mobilize people around them. A striking example is furnished by the economic crisis of 1997–98 in Indonesia. Chinese in Indonesia had long occupied a distinctive economic niche, controlling a substantial fraction of private economic wealth and dominating retail and wholesale trade. They had also long been defined as outsiders (regardless of their for-mal citizenship status), in opposition to the "indigenous" majority. The combination of conspicuous wealth and political outsiderhood rendered them vulnerable to periodic waves of discriminatory measures and vio-lent attacks. The 1997–98 economic crisis, occurring in the context of a preexisting political crisis as the Suharto regime was verging on col-lapse, provided a catalyst for a new wave of violent attacks, as ethnopoliti-cal entrepreneurs, with the tacit support of government spokespersons, blamed economic distress on the speculation, hoarding, and price gouging of Chinese shopkeepers and traders, while some Islamist activists called for a national jihad against currency speculators and hoarders.[31]

Chinese in Indonesia (and throughout Southeast Asia) belong to a broader category of politically vulnerable but economically powerful (or economically visible) minorities, discussed in the literature as "middle-man minorities,"[32] "trading diasporas," or "market-dominant minori-ties."[33] Such minorities—which have included Jews in many settings, Lebanese in West Africa, Indians in East Africa, Fiji, and Burma, and (with a certain amount of conceptual stretching) immigrant entrepreneurs such as Korean shopkeepers in south Los Angeles—may control (or be perceived to control) a disproportionate amount of wealth or a disproportionate share of key economic positions.[34] This in itself makes them vulnerable to political challenges.[35] But politically vulnerable minorities may be especially vulnerable in a context of economic crisis when they occupy an identifiable economic niche (in production, trade, or finance) that enables political entrepreneurs to represent them as contributing to or benefiting from the crisis. Jews, for example, have often occupied, or have been represented as occupying, key positions in finance; this has facilitated their being implicated in narratives of blame for financial crises.[36]

Certain specific aspects of economic crises may be more easily ethnicized than others. A sudden rise in prices for basic commodities, for example, may focus attention on those who can be blamed (in vernacular understandings) for the rise in prices or can be seen as profiting from it (as was the case for Chinese in Indonesia). A sudden change in the value of a currency may focus attention on those who can be identified as currency speculators. Agrarian distress can focus attention on ethnoculturally "alien" landlords (or intermediaries such as leasing agents or estate farmers).[37]

Not all politically vulnerable minorities can be identified as contributing to or profiting from economic distress. As outsiders to ethnoculturally defined national communities, for example, Muslim immigrants in northern and western Europe and Roma or Gypsies in eastern Europe are certainly politically vulnerable minorities, but their position in the economy scarcely allows them to be seen as contributing to or benefiting from the current crisis (though they can be represented as illegitimate claimants on public services). The vulnerability of such minorities in times of economic crisis stems not from narratives that identify their putative role in the crisis but rather from diversionary scapegoating strategies of incumbents—for which the crisis may provide a greater incentive than usual—and heightened popular receptivity to scapegoating efforts.

Just as economic crisis does not directly or automatically engender nation-statist measures against foreign producers or workers, nor does it directly or automatically engender an ethnopolitical reaction against ethnic outsiders. Even in the Indonesian case mentioned earlier, violence against Chinese cannot be explained primarily by the economic crisis but rather is explained by the preceding and concomitant *political* crisis of the Suharto regime, as well as the longstanding political construction of Chinese as outsiders. A similar point holds for the recent sharp right turn in Hungarian politics. The economic crisis no doubt contributed to the spectacular breakthrough of the extreme-right party Jobbik, which won 17 percent of the first-round votes in the parliamentary elections of April 2010. But the radicalization of street protest, coarsening of political rhetoric, and striking intensification of anti-Gypsy rhetoric, mobilization, and violence in Hungary all predated the economic crisis and emerged from a preexisting political crisis.

Like nationalism, politicized ethnicity is endemic to modern polities: it is a chronically available form of discourse, policy, and practice. And ethnic exclusion can be promoted as a response to any kind of economic differentials or economic change that can be interpreted in ethnic terms, even in periods of prosperity. Economic crisis can provide an additional rhetorical resource for political entrepreneurs who seek to interpret economic circumstances in ethnic terms; but crisis is neither necessary nor sufficient for ethnic exclusion to occur. Moreover, the intertwining of economic distress and struggles for political power does not always intensify nation-statist or ethnic exclusion. It may foster discourse centered on class and other specifically economic categories.[38] In Latvia, one of the countries hardest hit by the crisis, where the economy shrank by nearly 20 percent between March 2008 and March 2009, nationalists were resoundingly defeated in local elections of June 2009, while substantial gains were recorded by a left-leaning party associated primarily with the large Russian-speaking population.[39]

As of this writing, ethnic exclusion has not been a pronounced response to the current crisis. Racialized conservative narratives that blamed the US credit crisis on government efforts to increase homeownership among minorities did not get much traction, nor, at the other end of the political spectrum, did Brazilian President Lula Da Silva's remarks blaming the crisis on "white people with blue eyes."[40] While surveys have suggested that substantial minorities in both the United States and Europe blamed Jews at least to some extent for the financial crisis, political anti-Semitism has been marginal.[41] Populist-nationalist and radical-right parties have scored recent electoral successes in France, the Netherlands, and Italy, as well as in Hungary. But such parties—which have advocated both nation-statist forms of "national preference" and ethnic forms of exclusion against Muslims, non-Europeans, and (in east-central Europe) Gypsies or Roma—have been a familiar presence in the European political landscape for decades; their electoral fortunes have waxed and waned in rhythms that do not appear to closely match economic rhythms.[42] On balance, there is no clear evidence that the current crisis has generated substantial and sustained forms of ethnic exclusion.

Conclusion

Given the chronic availability of nationalist and ethnic idioms in modern polities, one might expect economic crises to foster heightened nation-statist or ethnic exclusion. One might expect intensified efforts to blame national and ethnic outsiders for economic distress, to protect domestic producers and workers against foreign (or ethnically "alien") competition, or to treat politically vulnerable minorities as scapegoats. And earlier crises furnish ample precedent for such efforts. This review has suggested, however, that economic crises do not automatically or uniformly generate such responses and that nationalist and ethnopolitical responses to the present crisis have so far been relatively muted.

Some reasons for the muted responses are specific to the present conjuncture. The globally synchronized and patently systemic acute phase of the credit crisis in the fall of 2008 was difficult to interpret in ethnic terms; the economic categories highlighted by the credit crisis did not map easily onto ethnic categories. The credit crisis was more easily interpreted in nation-statist terms. It could be blamed (outside the United States) on outside forces: American profligacy, American-style casino capitalism, the global financial system, or an externally imposed neoliberalism.[43] Yet nationalist narratives of the crisis—or narratives with a more or less pronounced nationalist inflection—have not gone hand in hand with dramatic shifts toward nationalist protection. Legal and institutional constraints, complex forms of economic interdependence, and prevailing cultural idioms have all worked to inhibit radical measures designed to protect domestic producers or labor markets (although more limited forms of protection remain chronic and routine). In the current economic and ideological conjuncture, strong programs of autarchy have little allure, despite the disenchantment with neoliberalism.

I have also suggested a more general analytical reason for the lack of a consistent ethnopolitical or nation-statist response to economic crises. Economic crises—like economic conditions more generally—are not self-interpreting. Diagnoses of and political responses to economic crisis are always mediated in a variety of ways: by preexisting idioms, policies, and practices; by discursive struggles to explain the nature and causes of the crisis; by political conjunctures, opportunity structures, and institutions; and by broader institutional environments. Specifically political factors— institutions, idioms, opportunities, and struggles—are more important than economic factors in explaining variations in nationalist and eth-nopolitical response.

Yet one should not complacently assume that nation-statist and ethnopolitical responses will remain muted. The current crisis has been unfolding in multiple temporalities. The credit crisis that paralyzed mar-kets worldwide in fall 2008 was difficult to diagnose in ethnic terms; but in the longer run, the crisis may well serve to bolster nationalist (and other) critiques of neoliberalism and globalization à l'américaine. And although the global credit crisis subsequently eased, the Greek debt crisis, at this writing, is threatening to spread to Spain and Portugal, raising serious questions about the stability and even continued existence of the Eurozone as a whole.

Developments in the "real economy," meanwhile, have followed rhythms of their own. Unemployment remains high and in some coun-tries continues to increase at this writing (notably in Spain, where it just passed the 20 percent mark), even as other indicators have improved. Should unemployment increase further or remain high for a long time; should heavily indebted countries such as Greece, Portugal, or Ireland face drastic, prolonged, externally dictated regimes of austerity; or should the crisis of the Eurozone deepen—in these and other possible futures, one might expect protests against unemployment, austerity programs, bailouts, or other forms of economic distress to take nation-statist or ethnopolitical forms. Scattered recent reports have already linked anti-immigrant rhetoric and incidents in Greece and Spain to the crisis.[44] Since such rhetoric and incidents have long been familiar elsewhere in Europe, the crisis cannot be seen as their root cause. Yet the crisis certainly does provide important rhetorical resources for those who seek to advance nationalist or ethnopolitical agendas. It is therefore too soon to assess with any confidence the overall scope and form of nationalist and ethnopolitical responses to the present crisis.

CHAPTER 5

War and Economic Crisis

Mary Kaldor

It was during the Vietnam War nearly forty years ago that the first post–World War II financial crisis took place; in 1971, the United States experienced its first external trade deficit, and the system of fixed exchange rates tied to gold was abandoned. And it was against the backdrop of the wars in Iraq and Afghanistan that the financial crisis of 2008 took place.

Was this coincidental? Or is there an underlying connection between economic crises and security crises (war)? This is the question posed in this chapter. I put forward an argument to show that there is indeed a link between the two sets of events. The argument is based on the proposition that the war sector and the economy are two separate but interconnected systems. One is a system primarily designed for destruction. The other is designed for production. Both are composed of a particular organization of people, equipment, and infrastructure, which can be dubbed a technological style or paradigm. This style evolves at a different pace in each system according to the different logics of destruction and production. The economy develops more or less continuously according to the logic of the market. The war sector can change dramatically in major wars but otherwise tends to remain rather static. How each system influences the other varies in different periods according to the different stages of the technological style in each system. In other words, the relationship between the two systems helps to explain both crises and "golden ages."

The present period, I argue, is a period of transition from one technological style to another: from a twentieth-century style based on mass production and the intensive use of oil to a twenty-first-century style based on information and communications technologies. The dominance of the twentieth-century style in the war sector, I argue, is holding back the economic transition and is an important part of the explanation for the economic crisis, which in turn contributes to a growing security crisis. Moreover, the application of the twentieth-century military paradigm in insecure places such as Iraq and Afghanistan worsens the security crisis. A security transition, I argue, is a necessary condition for a new golden age of sustainable growth.

In developing the argument, I draw on theories of long cycles (fifty to sixty years) in economic history. In particular, I draw on technological explanations of long cycles known as neo-Schumpeterian theories. I use these theories as a heuristic device; I do not have specialist knowledge to be able to assess the historical record. But the theories suggest recurring patterns of crises and golden ages related to technological transitions that may help to explain the present crisis. I should emphasize that this is not a technologically determinist explanation. I understand any given technology as a particular combination of knowledge embedded in a specific set of social relations.

The chapter is divided into five sections. In the first section, I outline the neo-Schumpeterian theory of long waves or great surges of development in economic history. In the second section, I outline theories that deal with the role of war in long cycles, and I develop my own argument. In the third section, I discuss how these theories help to explain the current economic crisis. And in the fourth section, I describe the current security crisis. In the final section, I speculate about what this might mean for the future.

The Neo-Schumpeterian Theory of Long Waves

Neo-Schumpeterians, such as Chris Freeman or Carlota Perez, espouse a theory of long cycles or great surges of development in the history of modern capitalism, lasting approximately half a century. The cycles are shaped by the bunching together and diffusion of a set of technological innovations that changes the direction of innovation in the whole economy; they call this a "techno-economic paradigm" or a "technological style." Each surge is characterized by some critical invention that leads to a new set of technologies and infrastructures that all are interlinked and to a new type of "best practice," as shown in table 5.1.

Table 5.1: Five Successive Technological Revolutions, 1770s to 2000s

Technological revolution	Popular name for the period	Core country or countries	Big-bang initiating the revolution	Year
FIRST	The "Industrial Revolution"	Britain	Arkwright's mill opens in Cromford	1771
SECOND	Age of Steam and Railways	Britain (spreading to Continent and USA)	Test of the "Rocket" steam engine for the Liverpool-Manchester railway	1829
THIRD	Age of Steel, Electricity, and Heavy Engineering	USA and Germany forging ahead and overtaking Britain	Carnegie Bessemer steel plant opens in Pittsburgh, Pennsylvania	1875
FOURTH	Age of Oil, the Automobile, and Mass Production	USA (with Germany at first vying for world leadership), later spreading to Europe	First Model-T comes out of the Ford plant in Detroit, Michigan	1908
FIFTH	Age of Information and Telecommunications	USA (spreading to Europe and Asia)	The Intel micro-processor is announced in Santa Clara, California	1971

Source: Carlota Perez, *Technological Revolutions and Financial Capital: The Dynamics of Bubbles and Golden Ages* (Cheltenham, UK: Elgar, 2002), 11.

Since 1771, when Arkwright's Mill was opened in Cromford, England, there have been five long cycles: the industrial revolution characterized by the mechanized cotton industry, factory labor, and the spread of canals; the age of iron, steam, and railways; the age of electricity, steel, and heavy engineering (the first globalization); the age of oil, the car, and mass production (often known as Fordism); and our own era, the age of information and telecommunications technologies. Each era is initiated by some defining moment, such as the first mass production of Ford's Model T in 1908 or the launch of the microprocessor in 1971, by the availability of a cheap factor of production, such as oil (the age of the automobile) or the chip (the age of information technology), and by a core economy from which it propagates—Britain in the first three waves, with the United States and Germany catching up in the third wave, and the United States leading in the two most recent waves, spreading to Europe and Asia. Each cycle goes through four phases: irruption when the new technology begins to be applied; frenzy when such rapid investment in the new technologies and infrastructure takes place that a major bubble forms and collapses; synergy when the techno-economic paradigm diffuses throughout the economy and society in what could be termed a "golden age"; and maturity when technological progress slows down, the core factor of production is no longer plentiful, markets are increasingly saturated, and protest about established ways of doing things develops.[1]

According to Carlota Perez, one of the foremost neo-Schumpeterian theorists, these different phases are to be explained by the different rates at which social and political institutions adapt to the techno-economic paradigm. Economic crises and depressions are to be explained in terms of a mismatch between social and political institutions and the techno-economic paradigm, while "golden ages" represent periods of harmony. It is the mismatch between social and political institutions and the emerging techno-economic paradigm known as Fordism that explains, for example, the depression of the 1920s and 1930s. The United States, at the beginning of the twentieth century, pioneered a new techno-economic paradigm involving the introduction of mass-production techniques, using semiskilled operatives; the spread of manufactured consumer durables, especially automobiles; and the intensive use of energy, especially oil. This marriage of oil and mass production achieved spectacular rates of growth in the United States in the early decades of the twentieth century. But the crash of 1929 revealed the limits to the diffusion of the new paradigm as a result of insufficient market growth both domestically and internationally. Or to put it another way, the spread of Fordism was held back by a set of institutions and social structures constructed in a previous era.

Domestically, the problem was that the distribution of income meant that many of the new goods were only available to higher income groups—something that was masked by a personal credit boom in the 1920s. Credit collapsed in 1929 at a time when demand from farmers fell because of the collapse in the prices of food and raw materials. Internationally, the problem was the dominance of the pound sterling and the way that Britain used its dominant position to protect the British and imperial economy.

Despite Roosevelt's "New Deal," unemployment persisted in the United States until World War II, which led to a massive redistribution of income in the United States as well as a huge increase in American exports financed through lend-lease—the assistance that the United States provided to allies. After the war, a new financial architecture was established, known as Bretton Woods, through which sterling was supplanted by the dollar. Although lend-lease was halted, the United States continued to provide massive economic and military assistance to allies during the early years of the Cold War. This assistance contributed to the financial and physical infrastructure that enabled the rise and spread of mass consumption in the West and that together with suburbanization and welfare led to a new golden age in the 1950s and 1960s. Dollars spent on economic and military assistance returned to the United States in the form of purchases of American goods. As Fordism spread through European economies, ever-increasing levels of productivity were achieved. In the Soviet bloc, the same techniques of mass production married to oil were widely applied, although the growth of demand was largely achieved through military spending by the state rather than private consumption.

But the golden age was followed by the recession of the 1970s and 1980s. This was a period of maturity of the dominant technological paradigm —a period when it becomes harder and harder to innovate within the existing paradigm, when markets become increasingly saturated, when the key factor of production can become scarcer and more expensive, and when other countries catch up with the core country. Already in the 1960s, workers and students began to rebel against the boredom of the mass-production era. Because Europe and Japan were achieving faster rates of growth, the United States experienced its first trade deficit in 1971. Oil was becoming much more expensive, and prices jumped dramatically when oil producers created the organization OPEC and imposed an embargo in the aftermath of the Arab-Israeli war of 1973.

The new techno-economic paradigm is based on information and communications technologies, which allow potentially for huge efficiencies in the use of both labor and raw materials, especially energy. Investment in information technologies began in the 1970s, intensified in the 1980s, and reached a frenzied peak in the Internet boom of the late 1990s. The spread of mass production to new areas such as Asia brought about a renewal of economic growth, but nevertheless, the innovation and wealth-creating potential of the new technologies across all sectors is far from being fully deployed and still remains only a small proportion of the overall economy. For neo-Schumpeterians, our present economic difficulties have to do with the way the institutions and social structures established during the automobile age are blocking the further spread of the information age, much like in the depression of the 1930s. There has been a rapid growth of information and telecommunications technologies and their application to a range of industries in the past two decades but largely within the pattern of demand established during the Fordist era. This pattern of demand was based on mass consumption and, to a lesser degree, military spending, shaped by an infrastructure of roads and airfields and by a global distribution of income that massively favors the West and particularly the United States because of the dominant role of the dollar. Cars and consumer durables have greatly improved. New consumer goods such as iPods and video games have been invented. New, more precise aircraft, missiles, and tanks have been developed in the military sector. Above all, similar patterns of consumption have reached millions of people in places such as China and India. But all the same, the new paradigm is coming against limits. Some of these limits have to do with growing global inequality—billions of people are unable to afford the new products, while consumer markets in the West are increasingly saturated. Other limits are environmental—the need to deal with the polluting and resource-depleting consequences of Fordism and the difficulty of doing so within the existing physical infrastructure. Some have to do with the rising price of oil. And yet others have to do with the difficulty of adjusting patterns of demand in a context in which the dollar remains the dominant currency despite the catching up of Europe, Japan, and above all, China.

So according to the neo-Schumpeterian theory, this is a moment when the economic transition has begun but the institutions and social structures are still frozen in an earlier era and are holding back the next phase of economic growth. As in previous eras, investment in the new technologies was made possible by the role of finance, as I elaborate in the following pages. But because of the obstacles to further diffusion, this has led to a bubble of asset inflation and credit creation. This is what Perez calls a turning point, as shown in figure 5.1. So how do institutions and social structures change? And, in particular, what role does war play in the turning point?

Figure 5.1: The historical record: Bubbles, recessions, and golden ages

great surge	INSTALLATION PERIOD "Gilded Age" Bubbles	turning point Recessions	DEPLOYMENT PERIOD "Golden Ages"	
1st	1771 The Industrial Revolution Britain	Canal mania	1793–97	Great British leap	
2nd	1829 Age of Steam and Railways Britain	Railway mania	1848–50	The Victorian Boom	
3rd	1875 Age of Steel and heavy Engineering Britain/USA Germany	London funded global market infrastructure build-up (Argentina, Australia, USA)	1890–95	Belle Epoque "Progressive Era" (USA)	
4th	1908 Age of Oil, Autos and Mass Production USA	The roaring twenties Autos, housing, radio, aviation, electricity	Europe 1929–33 USA 1929–43	Post-war Golden Age	
5th	1971 The ICT Revolution USA	Emerging markets dotcom and Internet mania financial casino	2007–??	Sustainable global knowledge-society "golden age"?	

⇧

We are here

Source: Carlota Perez, Milliband Lecture at the London School of Economics, May 18, 2010.

War and Long Cycles

Alongside the literature on long cycles in capitalist history is a literature on long cycles in war, which does not necessarily intersect with the literature on long cycles in capitalism. In particular, it is often argued that in the modern period, it is possible to identify a roughly one-hundred-year cycle of what are known as hegemonic wars, with smaller wars bunched together midcentury. Thus, Quincy Wright identified the Wars of the Spanish Succession (1701 to 1714), the Napoleonic Wars (1795 to 1815), and the two world wars (1914 to 1945) as hegemonic wars. Lesser wars bunched together in between include the Seven Years' War (1756 to 1763) and the concentration of wars in the mid-nineteenth century, including the American Civil War, the Crimean War, the Franco-Prussian War, and the Austro-Prussian War.[2]

Those who write about long cycles in capitalism have tended to argue for a link between these two sets of cycles, although the direction of causation is hotly disputed. Some argue that war is a consequence of an upswing in capitalism both because economic growth allows for the buildup of military capacities and because of increased competition among emerging powers. This was the view of Nikolai Kondratieff, the Russian economist whose name is most associated with long cycles. He thought that the long cycle was to be explained by infrastructural investment and that during an upswing war is more likely. "The upward movement in business conditions, and the growth of productive forces, cause a sharpening of the struggle for new markets—in particular, raw material markets. On the one hand, this makes for an expansion of the orbit of the world market and the involvement of new countries and regions in the trade network. On the other hand, it makes for an aggravation of international political relations, an increase in the occasions for military conflicts and military conflicts themselves."[3] In a correspondence with Kondratieff, Trotsky disagreed with this interpretation. He argued that wars were exogenous shocks that pulled capitalism out of its inherent tendencies to stagnation.

The consequences of war for the cycle are also disputed. Some theorists, such as Trotsky, argue that war can have a reordering effect—the "midwife" of a new society, as Marx put it—allowing hegemony to pass from one power to another and mobilizing resources for future expansion.

Others argue that war and military spending are immensely destructive and divert resources from productive use.

Joshua Goldstein and Paul Kennedy have both attempted to combine different explanations. Although the mechanisms for change are different, both suggest that war is more likely during an upswing for the reasons given by Kondratieff and that war has a reordering function at key moments in the cycle.[4] At the same time, they argue that high levels of military spending lead to the relative decline of the hegemonic power, thus setting the scene for challengers during a subsequent upswing.

I agree that different explanations need to be combined. But key to explaining the direction of causality is what I call the techno-military paradigm. A techno-military paradigm comprises a bunching together of technological innovations, a particular combination of men and machines, a "best practice" for fighting wars. The techno-military paradigm evolves according to the logic of war rather than the logic of the market but nevertheless intersects with the logic of capitalist cycles. War needs to be thought of as a social system for destruction, and whether it has positive or negative effects on capitalism (the social system for production) depends on how it is organized and how it intersects with capitalism. If we think of the techno-economic paradigm as an expression of the social system of capitalism in a particular cycle, then we might also use the term *techno-military paradigm* to describe the organization for war in a particular period. In other words, we could think of these paradigms as useful labels or simplifications to describe complex specific patterns of production and consumption that roughly summarize a particular epoch. A key difference between a techno-economic paradigm and a techno-military paradigm is the mechanism for change. The first depends on the market and the second on war. Clausewitz often compared war to business activity, likening battle to the act of cash payment in the marketplace. Failure to adapt to military advances can lead to defeat in battle, while failure to adapt in the marketplace can lead to economic loss. The difference is that whereas the market operates more or less continuously except in war, war, at least in the modern period, has been contained to discrete episodes. In other words, the techno-military paradigm can change dramatically in war and remain rather static in peacetime. Indeed, the techno-military paradigm tends to change only in very major wars—those wars that seem to have been bunched at roughly fifty-year intervals.

Thus, for example, the Napoleonic Wars brought about a profound change in the techno-military paradigm that was to hugely influence Clausewitz. Instead of the relatively gentlemanly wars of the eighteenth century, Napoleon's contribution was the use of massed armies, based on conscription, and the introduction of uniforms. The critical technological innovations of the wars in the middle of the nineteenth century were the introduction of the railway and the telegraph and, in the United States, the mass production of small arms. And it was the mass production of automobiles and aircraft that laid the basis for Allied victory in World War II. In the aftermath of that war, the United States and the Soviet Union both maintained high levels of military spending and continued to develop new military technologies within the techno-military paradigm established in World War II—the use of energy-intensive weapons plat-forms (aircraft, tanks, ships, and missiles). In particular, the quest for oil was an essential component of this national security paradigm.

The debate about whether military spending is a stimulus to or a drag on economic growth thus depends on how the techno-military paradigm relates to the techno-economic paradigm. In the immediate aftermath of a dramatic change in how war is conducted, the techno-mil-itary paradigm can provide a stimulus to the techno-economic paradigm, contributing to political, technical, and social institutions. It is thus a key explanation for the turning point. The geopolitical outcome of major wars is what helps to establish the dominance of a core country, based not only on economic power but also on the way it adapts the techno-military paradigm. Indeed, military power based on a specific paradigm helps to underpin the economic role of the core country, reminding others of past victories. In the aftermath of a major war, the techno-military paradigm can also contribute to the technical infrastructure—building roads, for example—and to new social norms. This is shown in table 5.2.

Thus, the Napoleonic Wars helped to establish both the political and infrastructural conditions for the first techno-economic paradigm. British hegemony and the role of sterling were firmly established, and the Concert of Europe laid the basis for peaceful development in the European continent. The spread of democratic practices on the French model—a necessary condition for countering French offensives—helped to lay the basis for the spread of factory labor. The introduction of uni-forms was a stimulus to the manufacture of textiles; Napoleon's army

Table 5.2: War and Turning Points

Major war	Geopolitical outcome	Techno-military paradigm
Napoleonic Wars 1795–1815	British hegemony Concert of Europe Spread of democratic practices	Mass armies, uniforms, conscription
Midcentury wars: Crimean War, 1853–56 American Civil War, 1861–65 Austro-Prussian War, 1866 Franco-Prussian War, 1870–71	Rise of Germany and United States Bismarckian Concert of Europe	Use of railways and telegraph Mass production of small arms
Two world wars 1914–1945	US hegemony Welfare state	Weapons platforms (tanks, aircraft, ships, and missiles) Intensive use of oil

marched to Moscow in British boots! The wars of the mid-nineteenth century laid the political basis for economic development of the United States and Germany and the spread of a techno-economic paradigm based on railways, coal, and steel. There was no major war at the end of the nineteenth century, which may explain why Perez describes the last decades of the nineteenth century as a "gilded age" rather than a golden age. It took two world wars to decisively establish American hegemony and lay the basis for the spread of the new techno-military paradigm. The establishment of NATO and other forms of military assistance could be said to have provided a stimulus to the spread of the techno-economic paradigm, through the construction of infrastructure—roads and airfields, for example—or new innovations that were applicable for civilian use ("spin-off").

In other periods, however, the techno-military paradigm may rigidify political and economic structures and divert economic and technological resources, inhibiting the development of a new techno-economic paradigm and thereby contributing to economic crisis and the social and political tensions that may lead to war. This, it can be argued, was the case for late-nineteenth-century Britain, where the production of warships and other tools of empire was more profitable than investing in the new mass-production techniques.[5] And the continued political dominance of Britain constrained the development of competitors. During this period, militant nationalism masked growing political and social tensions.

Likewise, by the late 1960s, high levels of military spending, it can be argued, became a drag on innovation in both the United States and the Soviet Union. (Indeed, this helps to explain the later collapse of the Soviet Union.) In the United States, military spending stimulated the economy, but it also crowded out investment in civilian infrastructure, diverting and distorting scientific and technological resources. Thus, the military sector absorbed the bulk of research and development expenditure, and technological skills developed for the design of weapons, which put the premium on performance, were often unsuited to civilian applications, for which cost and simplicity were more valued.[6] Or to put it another way, the inflationary impact of high military spending was not compensated by growth in productivity. At the same time, the continued political dominance of the United States has skewed the global financial system.

It was the high level of military spending that contributed to the first US trade deficit in 1971. The techno-military paradigm did not change during the Vietnam War. The generals applied their notions of best practice derived from the two world wars, even though this was quite unsuitable for a war of counterinsurgency. Of course, there were many articles and books that were written during and after Vietnam, criticizing the way the war was fought. But the defense establishment chose to learn a different lesson, arguing that insufficient resources on the World War II model had been applied.

In the period after Vietnam, there were efforts to adapt the American model of warfare to new technologies, particularly information and communications technologies. Terms such as AirLand Battle and, later, the Revolution in Military Affairs were supposed to herald far-reaching technology-induced changes in the US military. But actually, the technologies were integrated into existing doctrines and institutions. In effect, the emphasis on more and more expensive weapons platforms incorporating new technologies represented an attempt to preserve the twentieth-century techno-military paradigm. Because of the privileged role of the dollar, the United States could maintain very high levels of military spending financed through increasing external deficits and indebtedness. Although of course the United States was at the forefront of the diffusion of the new paradigm with newly emerging giants like Google, Amazon, Microsoft, and Apple, to which military "spin-offs" had contributed, it can be argued that transformation did not translate into improved international competitiveness because of the dominance of the institutions and patterns of demand of the automobile age, of which the unreformed Cold War military was a crucial part. As long as the rest of the world believed that high levels of military spending equal military power and economic preeminence, it was ready to lend to the United States. Huge economic external surpluses were built up by oil producers or by competitors such as China and Germany, and these were used to finance the American deficit.

The wars in Iraq and Afghanistan have magnified this syndrome but, at the same time, called into question both the role of the United States as a core country and the effectiveness of the twentieth-century techno-military paradigm. The cost of the wars, according to official estimates, is of the order of a trillion dollars. This is over and above regular military spending that has continued to increase, totaling perhaps as much as five trillion dollars since 2001. This huge military spending has not been financed by taxes. On the contrary, under the Bush administration, taxes were cut. The wars have merely contributed to the mounting debt. At the same time, the attempt to fight the wars on the basis of an earlier techno-military paradigm seems to be failing. Thus, they are contributing to a crisis that is both economic and military.

The Economic Crisis

The financial crisis of 2008 has been widely interpreted as a failure of regulation and the consequence of excessive faith in markets. And, of course, it is true that a weak regulatory framework allowed the banks to take excessive risks. But it cannot be the whole explanation. As Joseph Stiglitz puts it in his recent book, understanding the crisis is like peeling the layers of an onion.[7] Each explanation raises new questions. Why did the neoliberal ideology become the dominant ideology in the 1980s and 1990s? Why did it sweep the corridors of power both nationally and internationally? Were there alternatives?

For neo-Schumpeterians, the financial crisis of 2008 was an expression of the deeper underlying crisis that has to do with the way the institutions and social structures of the automobile age are blocking the further spread of the information age. The argument is that the first two or three decades of the diffusion of a technological revolution lead to major financial bubbles. As the old paradigm reaches maturity, financiers look around for new profitable opportunities. They invest in the new technological innovations, and this leads in the beginning to extraordinary profits. The resulting enthusiasm brings in huge amounts of money, which allows massive experimentation and even overinvestment, especially in infrastructure. But because the new techno-economic paradigm comes up against social and institutional barriers, these new opportunities cannot be fully exploited. This is the frenzy phase, when the "new economy" is not yet large enough for sustained investment but when finance capital has got used to making big profits. "In order to achieve the same high yield from all investments as from the successful new sectors," says Perez, "finance capital becomes highly 'innovative.' Imagination moves from real estate to paintings, from loans in faraway countries, to pyramid schemes, from hostile takeovers to derivatives or whatever."[8] This is the moment when greater risk is licensed and when a mountain of paper wealth is created, masking the mismatch between the new economy and the social and political institutions. This is a period of unfettered free markets and extreme social polarization when the gains from economic growth are not redistributed. It is a period that celebrates making money and in which selfishness is considered "good." And it is in this context that financial schemes become increasingly wild. Most people have heard of the canal mania or the railway mania or the dot-com bubble.

In this interpretation, neoliberalism and Keynesianism can be understood as responses to different phases of the cycle. Neoliberalism often becomes fashionable during the phase of maturity, when state institutions and excessive regulation appear to be a brake on the economy. Neoliberalism frees up finance capital to invest in the new techno-economic paradigm, but it cannot construct the institutions needed to promote the spread of the paradigm. In the 1970s, both Left and Right reacted against the dominance of the state.

The Right argued that the market was intrinsically creative and that the dismantling of regulations would result in increases in productivity.

The Left were more interested in releasing democratic potential. Hence, both Right and Left called for an alternative to the dirigisme of the postwar period.

It was neoliberalism that won the argument and dismantled many of the institutions of the postwar period, thus freeing up capital investment for the new innovations. But a neoliberal ideology was incapable of providing the framework needed to establish the institutions that could diffuse those innovations throughout the economy. After the bursting of the dot-com bubble in 2000, investors sought ever more imaginative ways of taking risk and making profits. A pyramid of growth was built on asset inflation, especially housing. Between 1980 and 2007, the ratio of the stock of assets to world output jumped from 1.4 to 4.4, and in the United States, the ratio of debt to GDP jumped from 168 percent to 380 percent.[9] Perhaps the only question is not why it happened but how these huge global imbalances were masked for so long.[10]

Thus, it can be argued that neoliberal prescriptions are important for breaking down the institutions of an earlier era and for financing the new techno-economic paradigm; this is why a neoliberal ideology tends to be characteristic of the irruption and frenzy phases of a cycle. But while neoliberalism may be effective at creative destruction, it is incapable of institution building. State-led policies are critical to set in motion the diffusion and full deployment of the techno-economic paradigm—the golden age.

An intriguing aspect of the contemporary story is the way in which neoliberalism was associated with a commitment to military Keynesianism. The same Right that argued for a minimal state in the 1970s also argued for increases in military spending. Under President Reagan, a new formula was adopted—a new Cold War and neoliberalism at the same time. The combination of a tight monetary policy and increased military spending greatly increased levels of borrowing. In other words, the US economy was stimulated while the rest of the world followed neoliberal prescriptions with names such as "structural adjustment," "convergence criteria," or "transition strategies." Military and economic assistance to the rest of the world was also cut, and developing countries were forced to borrow instead, contributing to the loss of hope and the rise of resentment and desperation that are part and parcel of the security crisis I describe in the next section. In the Bush era, this syndrome was magnified further. Huge increases in US military spending not only to finance the Afghan and Iraq wars but also to preserve the twentieth-century techno-military paradigm were actually accompanied by tax cuts. It was anachronistic projects such as the F-22 fighter jet or missile defense that were taking up much of the military budget.

In many of the commentaries on the crisis, there are calls for a new Keynesian program. The implication of the neo-Schumpeterian argument is that the new Keynesianism has to be concerned with more than just boosting demand. It must also address the content of demand. Keynes thought it was enough to dig holes if that would stimulate the economy. In a way that was true for the previous cycle, both consumption and military spending provided an outlet for the new paradigm. But actually it matters what is demanded and who does the demanding. Today's crisis is global and environmental. If increased demand consists of increased consumer and military spending in the United States and the United Kingdom, none of the underlying structural problems will be addressed and we can expect even worse crises in the future, arising from public rather than private indebtedness. In other words, it is not a choice between growth as usual or sustainable growth. If we continue to stimulate economic growth within the Fordist paradigm, the world will come up against economic as well as environmental limits. For economic growth to be economically sustainable, it has to be socially and environmentally sustainable as well. Thus, any stimulus has to be directed toward overcoming global social polarization (and that requires a new form of global money) and toward environmental protection if it is to provide an outlet for the new techno-economic paradigm. But how is this to be achieved? How do social and political institutions adapt?

In the past, the answer was a major war, in which political conditions were transformed and a new techno-military paradigm was established to stimulate the spread of a techno-economic paradigm. At present, high levels of military spending within a twentieth-century techno-military paradigm sustains the imbalances in the world economy and represents a drag on institutional restructuring. Under what circumstances might this change?

The Security Crisis

The big difference between this crisis and earlier moments of transition is the unlikelihood of hegemonic or Great Power war. Indeed, this is perhaps the biggest break with modernity (the period between the late eighteenth and mid-twentieth century associated with the rise of the state). The two world wars were mind-bogglingly destructive—perhaps as many as seventy million people died. In the aftermath of that experience, war of this type became unacceptable. The United Nations Charter prohibited the use of force internationally except in self-defense or if approved by the Security Council. The Cold War kept alive the idea of a Great Power clash, but it ended peacefully. Of course, there have been interstate wars—the war between Iraq and Iran or the wars between India and Pakistan—but they have become increasingly rare, and in any case, they are not the same as hegemonic wars. The prohibition of war was underpinned by a growing awareness of humanity as a single community, linked with the increased importance of human rights and facilitated by the information and communications technologies of the fifth Kondratieff cycle. Kant's famous phrase that a right violated in one part of the world is felt everywhere has become closer to reality.

War, of course, was never the only mechanism through which social and political institutions adapted. Another very important mechanism was politics—debate, struggle, elections, influence, and so on. Although politics is often slow and unwieldy, the experience of the smaller European states—Scandinavia or the Benelux countries—does testify to the possibilities for institutional flexibility in response to domestic and international politics. As the importance of war and threats of war have lessened, so, it can be argued, something called global politics is beginning to supplement and even supplant international relations based on diplomacy and war. There are more and more international or even supranational institutions responsible for regulation in a wide array of fields. And although treaty making remains the stuff of interstate relations, it increasingly involves public debates, advocacy campaigns, lobby groups, and the like.

But of course, global politics is still dominated by Great Power interests, and the display of the instruments through which past victories were achieved is considered an important way to pursue those interests. The United States continues to emphasize the importance of military power largely based on a techno-military paradigm drawn from the wars of the mid-twentieth century, and to a lesser extent, this is also true of Russia and China. In other words, hegemonic war or Great Power war, thank goodness, is increasingly unlikely as a mechanism for change. On the other hand, the attachment to the techno-military paradigm of the twentieth century, the idea of a grand conflict, represents a huge obstacle to global political and economic change.

Of course, the decline of major wars does not necessarily mean the decline of war in general. Today's bouts of political violence are, however, very different from the wars of modernity. They are very similar to the wars that have always happened in the periphery—insurrections, revolutions, civil wars—the wars that were considered sideshows. It can be argued that this type of war is not new but merely more visible; it was formerly obscured by our preoccupation with Great Power clashes. Indeed, I use the term "new wars" not necessarily to show they are new but to show they are different from the wars of modernity, even though they may have some new features that have to do with globalization.

Major wars were turning points that contributed to the reordering of political institutions and social structures. Contemporary wars, as was often the case with earlier bouts of violence that took place between major wars, are disintegrative. Like neoliberalism in the economic sphere, they unravel institutions but cannot create new ones. They are disordering rather than reordering.

Indeed, the word *war* may be a misnomer. What we are facing is the spread of insecure spaces where people fear being killed, kidnapped, robbed, tortured, raped, or expelled from their homes; these are spaces where people may lack access to water, food, electricity, or health care or where they are increasingly vulnerable to natural or manmade disasters. Such spaces range from parts of global cities to whole regions. Cité Soleil in Port au Prince in Haiti is one such example, characterized by a toxic mixture of crime and poverty, where police and UN peacekeepers dared not enter even before the earthquake. But so is the Horn of Africa, Central Asia, especially Afghanistan and its neighbors, and the Caucasus. Into these spaces rush private actors such as warlords, criminal gangs, militias, jihadists, pirates, adventurers, and mercenaries, creating a market in violence that transcends borders and reaches into the heart of the developed world through terror, drugs, human trafficking, and the like.

Insecure spaces are also described as ungoverned spaces. They are characterized by what are variously described as fragile, weak, failing, failed, collapsed, shadow, or quasi states. This phenomenon is often attributed to backwardness, the incomplete character of the state-building process. But actually it may well be something to do with our contemporary times. It may represent the unraveling of the state-building process under the impact of globalization. Typically, these spaces exist in areas that were formerly governed by authoritarian or totalitarian states. The rise of neo-liberalism in the West in the 1980s and 1990s was paralleled by a wave of political and economic liberalization in the rest of the world. The spread of democratization in large parts of the world—Latin America, Africa, Asia, and eastern Europe—was accompanied by the imposition of neo-liberal recipes. This gave rise to a process characterized by declining government revenues, declining legitimacy, growing informalization (i.e., the emergence of a shadow economy) and criminalization, and a weakened rule of law. It also facilitated the reemergence of privatized forms of violence—organized crime and the substitution of "protection" for taxation; vigilantes; private security guards protecting economic facilities, especially international companies; and paramilitary groups associated with particular political factions. In particular, reductions in security expenditure, often encouraged by external donors for the best of motives, have often led to breakaway groups of redundant soldiers and policemen seeking alternative employment. In many of these regions, political violence based on ethnic or religious identities, for example, can be viewed as a legitimation, a cover for a more pervasive political economy of insecurity, in which the classic distinctions of the modern period, between public and private or between political and economic, are broken down.

These are the circumstances that underlie contemporary insecurity. It is the lack of state authority, the weakness of representation, the loss of confidence that the state is able or willing to respond to public concerns, and the inability and/or unwillingness to regulate the processes of privatization and informalization that give rise to a combination of political and criminal violence. Moreover, this unraveling process tends to be reinforced by the dynamics of the violence, which has the effect of further disordering political, economic, and social relationships in a negative spiral of insecurity—an ongoing crisis of fear that is no longer bounded in either time or space. Massive migration, transnational terrorism, the search for messianic leaders, "persistent conflict" and ever-present emergencies are all symptoms of this form of aggravated insecurity—the outcome of the combination of an authoritarian past and a neoliberal present.

Yet as long as our security capabilities are still framed in classic Great Power terms and based on the twentieth-century techno-military paradigm, we cannot address this type of insecurity. The wars in Iraq and Afghanistan can best be understood as wars of this new type. The application of modern war techniques merely made them worse, as I have extensively argued elsewhere. It has exacerbated the typical conditions of insecurity. And this has also happened in other places where twentieth-century military techniques have been applied—Israel/Palestine, Chechnya, Kashmir. In other words, continued military spending at high levels based on the twentieth-century model is not only an obstacle to economic transition; it is a security obstacle as well. It prevents us from establishing the kind of security conditions necessary to overcome global social polarization, in turn necessary for renewed capitalist development based on the full diffusion of a new techno-economic paradigm.

Possible Futures

My basic argument is that security transitions are critical for economic transitions. The neo-Schumpeterian interpretation of the economic crisis implies that what is needed to bring about a new phase of economic growth is not just a Keynesian stimulus and a rejection of neoliberalism but a far-reaching institutional adaptation to the new techno-economic paradigm based on information and communications technologies. Such an institutional adaptation would include reform of global institutions, including issuing global money, a focus on environmental sustainability and combating climate change, and a fundamental redistribution of income and wealth on a global scale.

A security transition is an essential part of this institutional adaptation. Indeed, a focus on security is a way of illustrating the neo-Schumpeterian argument—one way of thinking about institutional adaptation. In the past, security transitions have occurred as a result of major wars. Thus, the Napoleonic Wars opened the way politically, socially, and technically for capitalist growth in Europe in the nineteenth century.

The wars of the mid-nineteenth century laid the basis for the rise of the United States and Germany and the spread of railways. And the two world wars ended European hegemony and established the framework for the postwar golden age of consumerism and competitive armament. By the same token, failure to adapt has contributed to crisis. Up to 1914, Britain continued to produce ever more elaborate warships so as to remind competitors of the Battle of Trafalgar; yet it can be argued that this contributed to Britain's economic decline. And in this chapter, I have argued that the persistence of what I have called the twentieth-century techno-military paradigm, which is intrinsically linked to the political narrative of US hegemony, is a huge obstacle to the kind of institutional changes needed to overcome economic and financial crisis (not to mention social and environmental crisis). Indeed, the application of the twentieth-century techno-military paradigm in Iraq and Afghanistan can be said to have precipitated (along with the subprime mortgages) the financial crisis of 2008, both because of the cost and because of the way the wars undermine the political narrative of American power. Like Vietnam, these wars have not produced a transformation in the techno-military paradigm; like earlier minor wars, they have a disordering rather than a reordering effect.

The big difference between today's crisis and past crises is that major war, which leads to a change in the techno-military paradigm, is unthinkable. What is needed instead is a transition to a new set of institutions for global security that is no longer based on war. Of course, the wars in Iraq and Afghanistan have led to some "new thinking" within the American military. There is a widespread sense that the United States cannot afford to fail the way it failed in Vietnam. In the army and the marines, there is a new emphasis on population security and civil-military cooperation, which is at the heart of General David Petraeus's strategy for Iraq and General Stanley McChrystal's strategy (now taken over by Petraeus) for Afghanistan, even though the wars are still framed politically in more traditional terms. Something similar has been taking place among other militaries, especially in Europe, that have taken part in UN missions in "new war" situations. Indeed, in many defense ministries, a struggle is going on between those who see the future as dealing with "nontraditional threats" and those who insist that the main task is still to prepare for a future global war against a "peer competitor."

The argument suggests a framework for sketching out four different idealized scenarios for the future, based on different economic and security combinations. This is outlined in table 5.3 with two axes, economic and security, each one divided into business as usual or fundamental change. Thus, neoliberalism means business as usual in the economic sphere, and Keynesian stimulus betokens change; the Fordist paradigm means business as usual in the security sphere, and I have used the term *human security* to indicate change. Of course, reality will not fit neatly into any of these boxes and is likely to involve a bit of each, depending on political choices that are currently being made.

Table 5.3: Possible Futures

	Neoliberalism	Keynesian stimulus
Fordist military paradigm	A return to premodernity; spread of "new wars"; permanent crisis	A return to modernity; sluggish growth; more and more corruption and rent-seeking; growing geopolitical competition for resources, especially oil; possible return of "old war" in a few decades
Human security	More security; faltering growth	Move toward global rule of law and global sustainable economy

The first scenario, in the top-left box, is the continued combination of neoliberalism and the twentieth-century techno-military paradigm—business as usual in both economic and security terms. According to the logic of the argument, this would mean a return to the conditions of premodernity—growing insecure spaces in Central and South Asia, the Horn of Africa, East and Central Africa, and the cities of Latin America, from which the rich West cannot insulate itself. In these spaces, violence, once again, becomes integral to everyday economic processes, and the distinctions between public and private and between political and economic break down. These are spaces where the environment is sacrificed for everyday survival and where continued social and political polarization are a local expression of global disequilibrium. Such spaces are likely to spread to parts of Europe; the neoliberal response to the Greek crisis may be followed by similar crises among the PIGS (Portugal, Italy or Ireland, Greece, and Spain) and in central Europe. The economic tensions can easily be manipulated by unscrupulous politicians along ethnic, religious, or xenophobic lines. The continued use of conventional military force in the quest to defeat the troublemakers—terrorists or Al Qaeda—makes things worse, although levels of military spending are constrained by overall limits of public spending. Moreover, the failure to restore global equilibrium would mean periodic financial crises, and the failure to address climate issues is likely to mean more natural disasters. The Icelandic volcano, which has little to do with climate change, is nevertheless a foretaste of the possible ripple effects of such disasters.

The second scenario assumes a global economic stimulus but no change in the techno-military paradigm. What this means is that more money flows into different parts of the world, but it is still skewed in favor of the United States and the United Kingdom and toward consumer and military spending. Some of the surplus will reach other regions, but in insecure areas, it is likely to be captured by rent seekers, vigilantes, pirates, and speculators, as happens with aid now flowing into Afghanistan. Like the first scenario, the failure to address global imbalances means that there continue to be financial crises and that whatever growth is achieved is limited.

In some places, as the Russians have done in Chechnya, stability is reimposed by a massive and destructive use of force, and new authoritarian regimes are established, making extensive use of improved surveillance capacity. Even so, the equalizing potential of the new technologies means that it is much more difficult to impose authoritarian regimes on a classic twentieth-century model, and so this leads to continuing asymmetric violence (suicide bombers, improvised explosive devices, and the like, coordinated through mobile phones and the Internet), which legitimizes further uses of conventional military force. In this scenario, growth is still biased toward the use of carbons, and competition for scarce resources, especially oil, is expressed in geopolitical terms. This scenario is characterized by arms races and the proliferation of weapons of mass destruction, cyber warfare, and perhaps a return to an "old war" in a few decades, when China, Russia, and India have built up their military capacities and the memory of the twentieth century has faded. In this scenario, who knows which will kill the planet first—climate change or "old war."

The third scenario is the transformation of national militaries into what I have called elsewhere human security forces, but without any global economic stimulus. What I mean by human security is that, in a world where war is no longer an option to settle interstate differences, we move toward a global rule of law and global politics. In this situation, most states are responsible for upholding the rule of law domestically, and the security apparatus available for external use is directed toward the enforcement of international law. In other words, this involves a shift from a war paradigm to a law paradigm, and the forces required to uphold a law paradigm are more like police than militaries. It is a phasing out of techno-military paradigms. Of course, it requires technology, and much of the technology of the fifth Kondratieff cycle is highly relevant— improved communication, the use of mobile phones and the Internet, for example. Although it sounds utopian, this transformation is beginning to happen in growing numbers of international missions deployed to uphold cease-fires in Africa or the Balkans, even though there is a very long way to go.

But human security is also intrinsically linked to economic, environmental, and social development. Some funds might be released through a massive restructuring of military budgets (currently, the United Nations peacekeeping budget is 0.56 percent of total global military expenditures), and the new secure conditions would allow a more effective use of aid budgets and a limited degree of growth. But without a broader economic stimulus, these new human security forces would find it increasingly difficult to cope with the growing political tensions associated with high levels of unemployment, poverty, and disease or with the vulnerability to natural disasters and struggles over resources.

The final scenario is, of course, the ideal scenario. It is the combination of global stimulus and a shift toward human security, which betokens broader institutional change, including policies that provide a socially desirable direction for profitable innovation. This is the scenario that leads to a new golden age of sustainable economic growth based on the diffusion of information and communications technologies and the development of new patterns of demand based on protection of the environment, education, and poverty eradication.

But what happens after that? In this chapter, I have hardly addressed the ways in which politics can bring about institutional change. Each of the scenarios I have proposed depends on different political constellations. The last scenario does imply more flexible and accountable institutions that might allow for more continuous institutional adaptation to supplant the discontinuous adaptation that is characteristic of the war model. In that case, it might be possible to anticipate cycles that are less disruptive and more evolutionary than in the past.

CHAPTER 6

A Less Close Union?
The European Union's Search for Unity amid Crisis

Vincent Della Sala

The recent global economic turmoil has raised questions about the nature of economic governance and the future of capitalism throughout the industrial world. The debate has not spared the European Union, where competing models of capitalism have tried to coexist in an economic and monetary union for at least two decades. Whereas the discussion else-where has focused primarily on what forms of regulation are necessary to govern financial markets, the recent crisis has exposed deep fault lines within the EU and thrown into question some established principles, such as the single market and a commitment to price stability and disciplined fiscal policy. For the first time in its history, there is serious speculation that some member states might withdraw or even be "expelled" from central European institutions such as the single currency. While talk of the demise of the euro and the EU is surely exaggerated, it is an indication that the global economic crisis has raised serious challenges and questions about the nature of European integration and its future.

It seemed all so different when the first signs of the crisis appeared in late 2007 and early 2008. Confident that a new constitutional treaty would streamline decision making and would enhance the EU's role in foreign policy, many observers and European officials looked to the financial crisis as providing an opportunity for the EU to consolidate internally and assume a global leadership role. Europe's remarkable degree of interdependence in the postwar period stood out as an antidote to economic nationalism and unregulated capitalism. It provided a model and possible leadership for transnational governance of the global economy and managing policy issues such as climate change. Yet, two years later, the optimism was gone, and talk of global leadership was replaced with reflection on the effects of the crisis not just on European economies but on the political project of European integration. The history of European integration has been one of "muddling through," bringing together partners who shared little of a common vision of the project beyond the notion that greater interdependence was the pathway to peace, stability, and prosperity in Europe. This broad umbrella provided space for those who saw the EU simply as enhanced cooperation to run a single market and for those who looked to economic integration as the pathway to a full-fledged political union. The broad objective of creating an "ever closer union" was enshrined in the founding Treaty of Rome in 1957 and has served to provide an unnamed and unknown final destination for the integration project ever since.

There are many ways to tell the story of European integration: as the result of bargaining between states that looked to closer economic interdependence as a way of promoting national interests;[1] as the evolution of functional interests;[2] as determined by the creation of an institutional architecture that gradually shaped a European polity.[3] In each of these accounts, ambiguity about the nature of the EU and its final objectives has not been an obstacle to telling the story of a process that has both widened its geographic scope and deepened integration across a wider range of policy areas. Indeed, ambiguity was a strength, as it provided a means to bring together different political systems and forms of economic governance in an effort to create an "ever closer union."

A polity born in the ruins of war and as a response to the ravages of nationalism in the first half of the last century, the EU is no stranger to crisis. Indeed, "crisis" has been as much a motor propelling the European project forward as it has been a threat.[4] At repeated points in time, political actors have been able to make the most of pivotal moments to push forward the process of creating an "ever closer union." The question, then, is what, if anything, is so different in the economic turmoil of 2008–10; and why might it herald a period not of opportunity for the European project but of a very uncertain future? The aim of this chapter is twofold. First, it tries to present a panoramic view of the EU's response to the economic crisis. It shows that there were two closely related phases to the crisis in Europe: the first concerned with systemic risk in the banking sector and the second with the sovereign debt problems of some member states. Second, it tries to draw some lessons from the EU's response for broader considerations about transnational forms of governance. The chapter argues that the recent economic crisis has raised a new set of challenges for the EU and European integration, challenges that highlight fault lines that exist between the creation of an economic union and the lack of a consensus for the creation of the political instruments to govern it.

The Calm before the Storm?

The period between the end of the Cold War and the dawn of the economic crisis in 2007 was one of rising expectations for the European Union. Two major achievements stand out: the creation of the single currency, known as the euro, and the enlargement of membership to include former Communist states in eastern and central Europe. The Treaty of Maastricht (known officially as the Treaty on European Union, or TEU), signed in 1992, came on the heels of the dismantling of internal economic borders (creating what is known as the internal or single market) and the reunification of Germany. In addition to setting out an ambitious plan to create a single currency by the end of the decade, the TEU contained a number of important provisions, raising expectations for some people that the "ever closer union" would lead to a political union.[5] It called for the creation of a Common Foreign and Security Policy (CFSP), an explicit reference to European "citizenship," a role for the EU in justice and internal affairs, and a greater role for the directly elected European Parliament.

The TEU was a singular moment in the history of the European Union, crystallizing the hopes of those who wanted the ever closer union to develop into a political union. Yet the treaty also introduced the notion that integration could be differentiated, with some member states going ahead with more accelerated and intense forms of integration.[6] This was especially the case with the single currency, which many observers felt would create the conditions for a full-fledged political union.

Membership in the single currency was open to those states that wanted to take part (some such as Britain and Denmark refused) and that met certain macroeconomic conditions, known as the convergence criteria. Largely the result of German pressure, the convergence criteria set out that member states had to rein in public finances (with debt-to-GDP ratios at 60 percent and deficit-to-GDP ratios at 3 percent) and to maintain price and exchange-rate stability before gaining entry into the single currency. The aim was to ensure that the national economies governed by the single currency would begin to share similar macroeconomic conditions so as to avoid asymmetric shocks that would cause internal tensions. An important part of the single currency was the creation of the independent European Central Bank (ECB), with a mandate to ensure price stability and without the power to bail out any member state that ran into sovereign debt problems.

The implementation of the single currency was a crowning achievement of the integration process. By 1999, eleven of the twelve member states that had wanted to join had been admitted (Sweden also refused to join, and Greece met the convergence criteria and joined in 2001), and coins and notes were introduced in 2002. The single currency did create a monetary union, but it was an asymmetrical one, as the instruments to maintain price stability were largely in the hands of the ECB, while member states retained almost exclusive control of the instruments of fiscal policy.[7] Member states were willing to give up the power to set monetary policy, but they jealously guarded their fiscal powers and refused to set up an EU fiscal policy that would raise revenue and distribute resources. Concerns that this might lead to large discrepancies between fiscally conservative and more spendthrift member states were assuaged by the Stability and Growth Pact (SGP), which essentially committed member states in the euro zone to maintaining the same fiscal discipline that had been in the Maastricht treaty once the euro was implemented. It also introduced mechanisms that could lead to sanctions for member states that did not keep public finances under control. The paradox of the creation of the single currency was that while it was seen by some people as essentially a political project to create pressure for a strengthening of European institutions, it was part of an economic union that had few political instruments. In the glow of its successful introduction, this was not perceived as an immediate problem, but the single currency masked deep fissures within the EU. More ominously, as events later confirmed, the SGP had limited policing powers and could not offset possible imbalances in the asymmetrical monetary union.[8]

Although the single currency may not have delivered the political gains that some people would have liked, the second major achievement of the past decade clearly demonstrated the attraction of the EU as a model for integration and ensuring political stability. The EU nearly doubled its membership from fifteen to twenty-seven members with the entry of ten new states in 2004 and of Romania and Bulgaria in 2007. With the exception of Cyprus and Malta, the new members were all former Communist states and, as in the case of the three Baltic states, part of the Soviet Union. For those new members, entry meant more than just being part of the largest economy in the world; it signaled a definite, if not definitive, step in the consolidation of the fledgling democracies.

The widening of membership raised worries that the institutional machinery designed for the original six members of the European Economic Community might not function with twenty-seven members. Reaching agreement among the member states, even on issues decided by a qualified majority, presented significant challenges, as did ensuring representativeness and accountability in decision making. Finding an architecture was seen as even more imperative, as enlargement had made evident some of the major policy differences among the member states. This was apparent in a range of issues, from foreign policy (with the war in Iraq a prime example) to climate change. Moreover, the single currency and the expectations raised in the 1990s were accompanied by concerns that important policy decisions were now being made by supranational institutions that were not directly accountable to voters. The need to adapt the EU's institutions to wider membership and to respond to calls for greater accountability and transparency led to a movement to provide Europe with a formal constitution.

A constitutional convention was launched with great fanfare in December 2001, and it produced an ambitious document in 2003. It was then the subject of extensive bargaining between the twenty-five governments (Romania and Bulgaria were only observers, as they were not scheduled to join until 2007), resulting in a tome of close to five hundred pages. Meant to bring Europeans closer to the EU's institutions, the draft "Constitution for Europe" only highlighted what a complex and undecipherable beast the EU had become. Its main institutional innovations were an enhancement of the European Parliament's role in some areas of decision making, the introduction of a figure responsible for foreign policy, and the creation of a presidency to chair meetings between the member states.

All seemed to be proceeding according to plan in 2005 until French voters rejected the constitution in a referendum in May, followed by the Dutch a week later. What is important for our discussion here is not so much the specifics of the draft constitution or of the reasons for the referenda defeat. More significant were some of the fissures that emerged in the referenda campaigns, especially in France. Opponents of the text ranged from those who felt it propelled integration too far and too quickly to those who saw it as arresting the movement toward the creation of a supranational polity. Important opposition came from those who saw the draft constitution as the entrenchment of "Anglo-American" capitalism and neoliberalism. For instance, the highly visible "NO" campaign in France used a picture of a supposed Polish person working in France. It sought to highlight not only that French jobs were being exported abroad but that service jobs at home would also be lost to migrant workers from member states in eastern and central Europe. The campaign was a prescient sign that appeals to economic nationalism had some resonance.

A compromise document was agreed on after the French and Dutch referenda defeat. Known as the Lisbon Treaty, it was signed in October 2007 and finally enacted in December 2009, after yet another referendum defeat in Ireland in 2008. It contained essentially the same institutional changes found in the defeated draft constitution, but gone were the references to a "constitution." What had started as a triumphant process to create a sense of constitutional patriotism in a polity that eschewed the more traditional forms of belonging was now simply a debate about changes to the treaties on which the EU rested. The high expectations in the wake of the end of the Cold War had given way to an institutional and political vacuum in the EU, along with growing unease over economic liberalization, precisely at the same time as the global economic storm hit land in Europe.

A Crisis within a Crisis

When the first signs of turmoil in financial markets began to appear in the United States, it was widely assumed that it was not going to spread to Europe. While housing and asset bubbles burst in Britain, Spain, and other parts of the EU, it was generally assumed that European banks had not engaged in the sorts of high-risk activities that had swept through American financial markets. Indeed, there was an immediate sense that the crisis would set in motion a number of processes that would propel the European Union to challenge America's economic supremacy. What had seemed a distant possibility only a few years before now seemed in reach, and many people began to speak of the euro as the new reserve currency of choice to reflect Europe's emerging dominant position in the global economy.

There was reason to be optimistic that the financial storm would not reach Europe's shores. A combination of closer regulation, stricter capital requirements, and a greater aversion to risk seemed to promise that banks in continental Europe would not face the same kinds of liquidity problems that would plague American financial institutions. The housing bubbles in Spain, Britain, and Ireland were worrying, but it was generally felt that these would not lead to any systemic risks. There was more than a little finger-wagging at reckless "American" capitalism. And for those sectors of European society that had always remained suspicious of, if not hostile to, forms of economic liberalization, the crisis in the United States was vindication of the European model of the social market economy. Additionally, it was widely assumed that any response to the crisis would require greater cooperation and coordination among states across the Atlantic and Asia as well. There was the sense that a new age of multilateralism was at hand and that no one would be better placed to set the pace than the European Union, which could serve as a model for supranational governance.

It was reasonable for Europeans to remain relatively optimistic about their prospects, but already in August 2007, signs of a shutting off of the financial taps began to appear in Europe. In August, BNP Paribas told its investors that it could not value the assets in two of its investment funds. The European Central Bank, worried about the drying up of funds for interbank loans, pumped liquidity into the markets almost immediately. A few weeks later, in scenes reminiscent of another era, depositors of the British bank Northern Rock were lining up outside its branches to pull out their savings in the wake of reports that it had asked the Bank of England for emergency loans because it could not raise funds in financial markets. British savers and Europeans became aware of what modern banking had become, even in Europe. European banks, like those elsewhere, were not just deposit-taking institutions but active players in complex financial markets. By October, the Swiss bank UBS was announcing losses of over US$3 billion as a result of exposure to sub-prime debt instruments. The news did not get any better in the new year, so that by the time the storm hit in September 2008, with the collapse of Lehman Brothers and the rescue of AIG, it was becoming apparent that Europe would not be spared. What followed over the next two years were two closely related dimensions of an economic crisis that revealed deep political differences within the EU. The first concern was with the imme-diate consequences of the broader crisis in global finances and the fears that it might lead to systemic risk for European banking and finance; the second and later development was a fear that sovereign debt crises among member states could undermine the euro.

Member states intervened in the final months of 2008 to ensure that important banks stayed afloat and that systemic risk would be avoided: Belgium and the Netherlands partially nationalized Fortis; there were repeated attempts by the German government to save Hypo Realty Estate; the Belgium and Luxembourg governments bailed out Dexia; the British government nationalized the mortgage lender Bradford and Bingley and announced plans to spend £50 billion to buy preferred shares of major banks; and so on. Added to this, the ECB and practically every member state in the European Union pumped money into the bank-ing system, either through eased credit facilities, nationalization, or some other form of recapitalization. It became apparent that member states of the European Union, while stressing that a coordinated response was necessary, were taking steps to ensure that their banks and depositors were protected at all costs. The Irish government, worried about a run on the banks by depositors, guaranteed all bank deposits and some debt instruments; Germany, Sweden, Italy, and others followed suit, partly out of fear of capital flight to insured havens. EU competition authorities struggled to keep up with the wave of measures designed to save national banking systems. Meanwhile, attempts to create a European rescue fund that would lessen the possibility of discriminatory state aid fizzled out relatively quickly. The French government was the strongest proponent of the plan, while the strongest opposition came from Germany, whose finance minister was quoted as saying that German money would never be used to save banks in Italy or Greece.

Even those countries that had a history and reputation of having fairly conservative banking systems, such as Austria and Italy, were suddenly put on heightened alert because of their exposure to loans in the former Communist states of eastern and central Europe. Encouraged to take out loans in foreign currencies, borrowers in these countries suddenly faced unsustainable charges as local currencies dropped and banks tightened the supply of credit. Austrian banks had exposures in eastern and central Europe totaling 70 percent of the country's GDP. Stoking fears that developments in the new entrants could cripple banks in western Europe was news that the slowdown in the global economy and the liquidity crisis had led EU member states, such as Hungary and Romania, to seek out IMF loans to avoid defaulting on sovereign debt.

The exposure of banks in western Europe to troubled loans in eastern and central Europe brought into relief a structural problem in European banking and financial markets. The creation of a single market and currency have gone a long way toward creating integrated capital flows and allowing financial operators to think across national boundaries. However, the regulation of those markets remains a national concern, as do the mechanisms to deal with liquidity and solvency issues. To whom should Austrian and Italian banks turn when their exposure in Hungary or Poland causes problems for their balance sheets and operations at home? A special committee was set up, chaired by Jacques de Larosière, whose mandate was to come up with a series of recommendations for regulatory structures to govern transnational financial markets. The group found that "as the crisis developed, in too many instances supervisors in Member States were not prepared to discuss with appropriate frankness and at an early stage the vulnerabilities of financial institutions which they supervised."[9] Time and time again, the work of the committee found that national supervision and regulation had failed, partly because national regulators were concerned with domestic banks and not the consequences for the broader European market. This only compounded the structural problem that there was no effective European regulatory system. The future financial regulatory system will be based on enhanced cooperation between national authorities and on mechanisms to guard against systemic risk, but there will not be a Europe-wide body to govern banks.

The de Larosière report was only one indication that there was a tension between the creation of Europe-wide capital markets and the lack of corresponding governance instruments. The case of the proposal for European-issued debt instruments (referred to here as joint European bonds) helps illustrate some of the challenges that the creation of a single currency and market have raised. The liquidity problems in world markets led to a growth in the spread in European bond prices. There was a flight to safety, and not surprisingly, borrowing became more expensive for governments facing budget problems and/or already carrying heavy debt loads, such as Portugal, Ireland, Italy, Greece, and Spain (mercilessly called the PIGS in financial circles). There was a widespread discussion that ensued as to whether it would be feasible to have joint European bonds as a way to ensure that some members of the eurozone would not be paying a premium to service their debts. The European bonds, it was also argued, could challenge US Treasury bills as a safe haven at a time when markets were drying up. Presumably, this would have also been part of a longer-term process (accelerated by the financial crisis) to have the euro replace the dollar as the global reserve currency. A number of economic commentators supported the idea, along with the governments that had the most to gain from a single European bond that would presumably be set at rates lower than what they were facing as yields began to widen. The political hurdles to the plan were, and remain, significant, as it forces member states that see themselves as having been "virtuous" in their fiscal policies to assume greater responsibility for those that have not undertaken structural economic reforms. Rather than create solidarity among the richer and poorer members, the bonds could create further tensions.[10] Opponents of the Eurobonds, especially in Germany, saw them as the thin edge of a wedge for creating mechanisms for fiscal transfers within the EU.

Although the dimensions of the financial crisis were not to be underestimated, it was in the real economy that the EU faced its greatest challenges. GDP fell by 4 percent across the EU in 2009, and double-digit unemployment in the eurozone returned after an absence of almost a decade. In response, individual member states and the European Union (to the tune of €200 billion) introduced various forms of stimulus packages. The constraints imposed by the Stability and Growth Pact were largely ignored in the face of an immediate crisis, and the average public-sector deficit for the sixteen members of the eurozone went from 2.0 percent in 2008 to 6.8 percent in 2009. More significantly, some member states, such as Ireland, Spain, and Greece, had deficit levels over 10 percent, while others, such as Denmark, Finland, Austria, Sweden, and Germany, had levels below or just above the 3 percent threshold of the SGP. The haphazard approach to using public spending carried two risks for the EU. The fear was that without coordination and without structures to impose a solution, short-term breaches of commitments to fiscal restraint would become medium-term practices. Any relaxing of the commitment to fiscal restraint central to the single currency would make the objective of greater convergence of macroeconomic fundamentals more elusive. The second fear was that the imbalances that existed between the member states would only get worse, leading to possible problems for the single currency.

What became clear as the debate progressed in Europe was that there were fundamental differences between the member states about how to use the state to govern the economy in the wake of the crisis. Britain, which had been the bastion of the Anglo-American model and liberal market capitalism, was essential to any solution but seemed, as is often the case, more on the sidelines in European debates. This was probably due to the fact that Britain is not part of the single currency, and its being home to one of the most important financial centers in the global economy meant that its interests were different from others'. The Labour government's massive intervention that led to the effective nationalization of major banks and an initial bout of spending seemed to suggest that even the normally austere Gordon Brown was willing to jettison nearly three decades of liberal policies. However, the Conservative-Liberal coalition that came to power in 2010 introduced drastic cuts to public spending in an attempt to rein in public finances.

The more potentially harmful divisions in the European Union over managing the economy were those between France and Germany.[11] Even before the rescue packages of 2008–9, the French government of Nicolas Sarkozy had indicated in July 2007 that it would not meet the target of balanced budgets by 2010 that had been agreed on only a few months earlier. Although the SGP rules do allow for member states to overshoot targets provided they meet certain conditions, the important point here is that Sarkozy's commitment to core principles of EU macroeconomic governance was lukewarm even before serious troubles began. He pushed to remove from the founding principle of the EU in the Lisbon Treaty reference to "free and undistorted competition." He was quoted as saying, "Competition as an ideology, as a dogma, what has it done for Europe? It has only brought fewer and fewer people who vote in European elections and fewer and fewer people who believe in Europe."[12] The French government's position throughout the 2008–10 turmoil was to call for stricter regulatory controls of financial markets, pushing for greater oversight of hedge funds and limits to executive salaries. But it also introduced in December 2008 a stimulus package of €26 billion in public spending, along with over €11 billion in tax breaks for investment. The measures were in line with stimulus packages in other eurozone countries. What did raise some concern was the very explicit statement that aid to the automobile sector would be contingent on the money going to plants in France and not elsewhere in the European Union. Although this might seem like a very normal position to take in most other places, it set off alarm bells throughout the European Union, including with the competition authorities that closely monitor what might be discriminatory state aid for domestic firms. France also remained at the forefront of calls to strengthen the economic union with an "economic government" with fiscal and sanction powers.

Germany seemed to be going in a different direction. As mentioned earlier, it acted as a brake on initiatives such as a European rescue fund or a single European bond. While it did not hesitate to intervene to bail out some of its banks and automobile firms, it was wary of using public finances to stimulate demand. The German preference was to continue to look to exports to sustain economic growth, and the government continued to resist pressures to address global imbalances, as Germany's current account surpluses persisted throughout the crisis. Moreover, the German postwar model of tight monetary policy, price stability, and control of public finances continued to provide German policymakers with a map for a way out of the crisis for the EU. The ECB was more than willing to steer toward the first two of these goals (in fact, it is mandated to do so), while the approval of a constitutional amendment proposed by the Merkl government committing to a balanced budget assured that public finances would remain under control. So while other members of the eurozone, including France, were announcing plans to breach the terms of the Stability and Growth Pact, Germany was taking important steps in the other direction in the midst of a an economic crisis that was causing strains between members. The danger was that each side could accuse the other of being a free-rider. Those countries that were using public funds to stimulate demand could claim that Germany's export-driven economy would ride on the coattails of demand in other member states. Germany could claim that the credibility of European monetary policy was sustained by its fiscal restraint and that the entire eurozone would face the consequences if any member ran into sovereign debt problems.

The differences between Germany and France, and more generally fissures within the EU, came into relief when the economic crisis entered a second phase in Europe in the final months of 2009. The newly elected Socialist government in Greece announced in December that its budget deficit would equal 12.7 percent of GDP and not 6 percent as forecast by the previous government, well above the 3 percent required by the Stability and Growth Pact. There were more dire reports in the final months of 2009 as rating agencies downgraded Greek sovereign debt, which was projected to reach 124 percent of GDP by the end of 2010. The Greek government introduced emergency budget measures to bring the deficit below 3 percent by 2012, but this met stiff domestic resistance and did little to assuage jittery international markets. By January 2010, there was serious discussion among policymakers and in international markets about the possibility of a Greek default on its sovereign debt. The spread on Greek bonds began to grow precipitously, and there was a very real sense that the Greek economy had entered into a downward spiral that would be difficult to reverse in order to regain investor confidence. It was inevitable that eyes would turn to the EU and the eurozone for help.

Greece constitutes only 2.5 percent of the eurozone economy and, on its own, does not represent a major threat to the stability of the entire currency area. The worry in the first half of 2010 was that the Greek crisis would spread to other parts of the eurozone, especially the heavily indebted members, such as Portugal, Spain, Ireland, and even Italy. The macroeconomic fundamentals for each of the peripheral economies were different, but this did not seem to matter for nervous market operators. For instance, Spain and Ireland did not have particularly heavy public debts, but the fear was that exposure to risky loans by their banks would lead to a sovereign debt crisis. If one of the larger economies of the eurozone, such as Italy or Spain, was to default, then the consequences for the entire currency area would be much more severe.

There were no easy solutions to the Greek crisis for European policymakers. The treaties governing the EU specifically prohibited the ECB from bailing out any member of the eurozone that defaulted on its debt. There were no transfer mechanisms within the EU that would help shift resources from surplus to deficit areas of the eurozone economy. Moreover, there was a heated discussion among policymakers about the risks of spreading moral hazard if aid were provided to Greece. Some argued that this would lead profligate governments to spend even more freely, knowing that they would receive help from the other eurozone members. On the other hand, not intervening in Greece could have led to a loss of credibility for the euro and, perhaps more worrying, serious problems for European banks, especially French and German, who were exposed to sovereign debt in Greece, Spain, and Italy. Additionally, Greece had threatened to seek help from the IMF if none was forthcoming from the EU. It was feared that this would have further eroded confidence in the euro and in the EU as a global economic power. These considerations led many commentators to call for Greece to be removed, or suspended, from the single currency area, while others predicted that the eurozone would not remain intact in the medium term. The speculation may have been premature, but it is a sign that the challenges raised in the past three years are serious.

After numerous unsuccessful attempts to ease concerns about Greece in the first few months of 2010, the EU introduced a series of measures in May. The most important of these is the European Financial Stabilization Facility (EFSF), which draws from a €440 billion fund to help member states facing financial instability. The IMF also provided funding, so that a total of close to €750 billion is available. Importantly, the rescue package includes funds contributed by member states in an effort to ensure that it does not constitute a violation of the no-bail-out restrictions. It remains to be seen whether the package can help retain investor confidence and help avoid any sovereign defaults.

The French government claimed that the package was a great step forward for its objective of creating an economic government for the EU. Interestingly, the English text spoke of economic "governance" rather than government. The differences on what the package means are more than semantic. It faces a challenge in German courts on the grounds that it violates German commitment to price stability, as well as EU law with respect to not bailing out member states that face a sovereign debt problem. Slovakia has resisted providing its share of the fund (€800 million). Moreover, although the dimensions of the package are impressive, some observers feel that it would not be enough if a large economy such as Spain or Italy ran into the same problems as Greece.

Lessons from the Crisis

The responses to the crisis, in both the first phase and the subsequent sovereign debt crisis, brought to the surface some tensions that had probably always been there but became harder to manage in turbulent economic waters. First, it was apparent that the fundamental weakness of macroeconomic governance in the European Union—that is, the lack of coordination across the main policy instruments and between the EU and national levels—would shape and limit its response.[13] Europe's economic project of recent decades was very much focused on the notion that monetary policy would be the basis of economic governance. This was partly because it would have been hard to venture into areas such as fiscal policy without meeting strong national resistance; but it also reflected the view that tight monetary policy and price stability were the engines of economic growth.[14] Governments, even if not always true to the letter of the Stability and Growth Pact, accepted it as the cognitive and normative map on which to base macroeconomic policy.[15] It was possible to imagine, then, that member states could retain almost exclusive control of fiscal policy within a single currency area without creating coordination problems or structural imbalances.

However, the governance structures have not proven always conducive to ensuring that the map leads to the same places for everyone.[16] The debate almost from the inception of the single currency has been about how to deal with the "asymmetrical economic and monetary union," with monetary policy in the hands of the independent European Central Bank and fiscal policy still in the hands of the member states.[17] The problems of coordination were always there but were compounded by the crisis as member states were divided not only on the weight to be given to stimulus packages but also on when to put in place an "exit strategy," that is, when to go back to the centrality of price stability and fiscal restraint. Without recourse to monetary policy, member states could only rely on fiscal measures, with the very real possibility of beggar-thy-neighbor effects. The EU faced the prospect of drawing fire for having set in motion fundamental changes to the governing of European economies in the previous two decades but then not having the capacity to resolve the first major crisis faced by the eurozone countries. As a group of leading EU observers and policymakers noted, "politically, the European Union is at risk of being blamed for having fostered a liberalization agenda in the past rather than being praised for having promoted a coordinated response to the crisis when it struck.[18]

Moreover, the asymmetrical economic union meant that there was no way to deal with policy differences among member states and their consequences. This brings us to one of the major fissures that emerged in the crisis, especially in the analysis and response to the sovereign debt issue. There were very clear differences between surplus countries, primarily Germany, and those member states that had been running large current account deficits. Angela Merkl's government argued that it had accumulated surpluses through a policy of wage restraint and fiscal prudence, while others claimed that this was further proof of Germany free-riding by resisting the stimulation of demand while exploiting strong demand in the rest of the eurozone. Additionally, it became apparent that German voters, who had borne the brunt of wage restraint and fiscal rigor, were not receptive to helping out eurozone members seen to have acted irresponsibly. It was also clear that the hoped-for convergence of macroeconomic fundamentals had not taken place. For most of the decade of the euro's life, all member states enjoyed stability and, in some cases, steep drops in borrowing costs. In the case of Spain, this helped fuel a housing bubble, while in some member states, such as Greece and Italy, it helped put off difficult decisions with respect to fiscal policy. When the global economic crisis hit at the end of the decade, these differences revealed deep structural imbalances within the EU.

Second, it is hard to look at developments in the past three years in the European Union and not conclude that economic nationalism has reared its head. It is likely that it was always there but that national leaders were not willing to use the rhetoric of protecting national firms so freely and that the central institutions of the EU, chiefly, the Commission, were better positioned both politically and institutionally to temper the effects of the pursuit of possibly discriminatory practices.[19] In the feverish months that followed the collapse of Lehman Brothers, as member states rushed to save their banks and banking systems, the Commission was largely a bystander. Matters did not change very much as governments moved from shoring up the financial system to protecting industries and then addressing sovereign debt problems. More important, the position of the German government has begun to reveal a greater willingness to assert its national interest in a way that is not intimately intertwined with that of the EU as a whole.

Third, the financial crisis eclipsed Europe's constitutional and institutional odyssey. The events of the past three years emphasized what was already obvious, that the fate of the Lisbon Treaty paled in comparison to the deeper problems faced by European economies.[20] The introduction of the euro, despite political rhetoric to the contrary, put into question European social models; that is, the macroeconomic and labor regimes that were part of the postwar settlement did not fit neatly with the more competitive single market and global economy. For many members of the EU, loss of monetary policy meant that weaknesses in the competitiveness of product and labor markets could no longer be masked.[21] Proponents of reform argued that the models could survive but needed to be "modernized" in order to respond to global economic pressures as well as greater competition within the EU.[22] Regardless of what position one took in this debate, many European states—and in particular the large continental economies in France and Italy—needed to bring about structural reforms to their labor markets and macroeconomic regimes. France may have emerged relatively unscathed by the current crisis, but it too faces creeping unemployment rates. The eurozone unemployment rate crossed into double digits in 2009 and will likely remain there for some time. At the same time, most member states have introduced fiscal austerity measures in the wake of the Greek crisis so as to avoid having to pay a premium for borrowing in international markets.

Fourth, it also became clear that the lack of coordination in providing a response to the global financial crisis made it more difficult for the EU to present itself as a model for transnational governance of the global economy. There is an argument that claims that the EU's influence in international politics is determined by its "normative power," that is, by its capacity to project norms, values, and ideas to shape outcomes.[23] Part of this normative power rests in the EU as a model for how cooperation, interdependence, and coordination can take place in transnational or supranational institutions. The EU is structurally predisposed to seek out multilateral solutions to common problems, so the search for a more coordinated global response, perhaps with a new institutional architecture, presented an opportunity for the EU to play to its strengths. However, the lack of coordination was not only a major problem internally; it prevented the EU from being a major player in its own right on the global stage, especially as the focus of policy response shifted from the monetary side to fiscal policy. As the international system began to take shape during the crisis, Europe's place was at the "margins of influence."[24] Commentators have suggested that even in those areas where the EU had begun to take a lead, such as human rights and climate change, the lack of internal coordination and cohesion has led to waning influence.[25]

From One Crisis to the Next?

After the high expectations of the period following the Cold War, the EU faces a number of difficult choices and possible scenarios. One solution, although unlikely, is more Europe—that is, not only ambitious plans to enlarge the EU to include parts of the Balkans, Iceland, and maybe even one day Turkey but also a deepening of its penetration into more policy areas. This view is based on an interpretation of the history of integration that sees the EU emerge from each tumultuous period ultimately looking for ways to enhance cooperation and institutionalize the Union. In the wake of the financial and sovereign debt crisis, it means that member states would coordinate, if not harmonize, their exit strategies and would embark on a round of reform that would see them create robust institutions of economic governance and forms of fiscal transfers within the Union. Proposals that have surfaced during the past three years include a European regulatory body that would have prudential powers as well, a joint European sovereign debt instrument, a European rescue fund for banks, and so on. Along with the Lisbon Treaty provisions for a European presidency and the creation of a single foreign-policy representative, these proposals, in this view, would move Europe from the "margins of influence" in the new global economic order to assume a central position. As economic governance in the EU becomes less asymmetrical, the Union could assume a position of dominance and influence in the global order.

Given developments of the past decade and particularly over the past three years, it is not likely that even the least "invasive" of these reforms will have much traction. Moreover, the loss of monetary sovereignty has entrenched more than loosened the member states' grip on fiscal policy. The events of the past three years, when it became evident that there were wide divergences on how to manage the economy despite commitments such as the SGP, are more likely to dampen enthusiasm for more European governance than to lead to a push for closer integration. Resistance from important member states such as Germany and Britain is more than likely, as both political elites and public opinion have resisted any proposal that would lead to fiscal transfers.

Moreover, there does not seem to be any compelling narrative that could serve to rally the twenty-seven member states around a commitment to push for more Europe. What makes this crisis different from others in the past is that the story of European integration as the harbinger of peace and stability no longer captures the imagination of successive generations of Europeans. What became apparent in the past three years was that there was no "European" narrative of the crisis that could provide a cognitive and normative map to define solutions and a way forward. It is not likely that there could be more Europe until a new story is found to give the project meaning across the continent. The introduction of the euro has meant that just muddling through might not be enough and could even be an obstacle to further integration.

A second scenario is one that sees a differentiated Union in which integration proceeds in an uneven way across policy areas and with different member states.[26] It is a notion that is flagged every time that the lack of consensus on major issues stalls the Union, and it has taken many different names: "enhanced cooperation," a core Europe with concentric circles, multispeed Europe, a variable geometry, and so on. We already have versions of this with the various opt-outs that some member states have in different policy areas, most notably in the case of the single currency, with only sixteen of twenty-seven members taking part. The problem here is that it is not clear whether this would change the EU's position at the "margins of influence" in the governing of the global economy. Variable geometry might make it easier for some member states to have "enhanced cooperation" in some areas, but this only formalizes the lack of a "European" narrative on how to respond to the challenges of a global economy. Moreover, it does not solve some of the problems that emerged as a result of existing asymmetries, and it is also clear that some essential features of economic and monetary union that have strained under the pressure of economic nationalism—such as the single market—can function with a variable geometry. The opportunities and incentives for free-riding and beggar-thy-neighbor policies would likely increase.[27]

The third scenario is less Europe—that is, that the cracks that opened during the past few years become more gaping, so that the Union continues to become more intergovernmental and less supranational. A union of twenty-seven that has weakened supranational institutions and commitments will become even harder to coordinate, leading to a slow dismantling of the Union. This is also not likely to happen, as it would be wrong to underestimate the very real accomplishments that the Union has achieved, and there is an institutional architecture that has become entrenched in many areas of European life. Europeans may not understand how the EU works, nor is it likely that they are ready to give it fiscal powers. But it is a club that they want to belong to and that they see as contributing to peace and stability on the continent. Even most of the so-called Euroskeptics do not support its dismantling; they simply want to curtail some of its policymaking powers.

The European Union, then, is not likely to disappear any time soon, nor will it lose any of its members; but it is not going to be anything more than the sum of its parts, and here lie its problems. Although there is not likely to be "less" Europe in the form of the dismantling of the Union, a more likely future is one of diminished expectations and diminished capacities for European institutions. The crisis highlighted that an economic union without a fiscal policy and without the tools to carry out regulatory, prudential, and redistributive actions will remain largely sidelined as member states take the lead. The crisis saw a limited role for the

Union's supranational institutions—the Commission and the European Parliament—especially in sustaining the pillars of economic and monetary union. The problems that surfaced were not just with the European institutions but with the member states themselves. They were divided on a range of issues and had little enthusiasm to provide the EU with greater powers, especially in economic governance. They rarely agreed on a common position on how to respond to global pressures; and when they did, they largely abandoned the commitments that would have met domestic resistance. More important, the EU needed a new narrative, but there seemed little consensus on what this should be or even where the story should start. Events of the past three years have made this task even harder, and it is not likely that things will get any better in the near future, casting Europe adrift.

CHAPTER 7

The Paradox of Faith:
Religion beyond Secularization and Desecularization

Adrian Pabst

Since the nineteenth century, social theorists of religion have claimed that the rise of modernity is synonymous with the decline of religion and the spread of secularism. Since the 1960s, critics have contended that modernization is compatible with faith and that the contemporary resurgence of religion marks the desecularization of the world.[1] While modernity is predominantly secular, it seems that postmodernity (or late modernity) has a significant religious dimension. However, the modern is not simply an exit from religion or theology but in large measure the product of shifts in theological discourse and changes within religious traditions.[2] So given its origins, there is no single modernity but rather alternative, rival modernities (both western and non-western) that are variously more secular or more religious.[3]

If, moreover, the postmodern is an intensification of certain modern trends instead of a new phase of history,[4] then arguably postmodernity cannot be equated with either more secularization or a sustained return to religion but in fact both. This suggests that what we are seeing is not just a growing opposition between a militant secularism and a violent religious fundamentalism (which are nonetheless conceptual mirror images of each other).[5] There is also an increasing bifurcation—within and across different faiths—of traditional, orthodox traditions, on the one hand, and modernizing creeds, on the other hand. Examples of this paradoxical development include the opposition between liberal and nonliberal wings in the Roman Catholic Church and the Anglican Communion or the religious resistance to unbridled "free-market" capitalism and secular liberal democracy that is shared by various faiths.

Closely connected to this are different responses to the economic crisis of 2007–10: while some religions or denominations support the preeminence of state and market over society and religious bodies, others view the "free civil space" between those who rule and those who are ruled as more primary. Whereas the former tend to separate the idea of human contract from that of divine gift, the latter seek to transform state-administered rights or economic-contractual ties by drawing on notions of gift exchange and social bonds. Since the forces of modernity and countermodernity operate globally, the simultaneous expansion of both orthodox traditions and modernizing creeds is likely to continue in future. This encapsulates the paradox of religion in the late modern age: just as the argument that secularization has been the dominant modern reality is hard to deny, so too is the contention that religion never vanished from the public sphere and that it is once more reverting to public prominence.

In this chapter, I argue that the standard models of "secularization" and "desecularization" are theoretically problematic and empirically questionable. By essentializing religion, both theories adopt a secular perspective. This perspective ignores key sociological, anthropological, and philosophical features that can account for the specificities of different religious traditions (section I). Moreover, modernity is not a linear process that progressively replaces the religious past with a secular future. Rather, it is a dialectical process oscillating between a dominant secularism (and a variety of denominational subcultures that are positively linked to modernization), on the one hand, and an increasingly visible revival of traditional faiths that resist and seek to transform the secular outlook of global modernity, on the other hand (section II). Instead of the rather sterile debate in terms of secularization and desecularization, the future will probably consist of a contest of ideas and practices between those traditions that either embrace or challenge secular modernity. This is seen in how religious ideas on reciprocity, mutuality, and relationality are coming to the fore in public discussions on ethics, political economy, and science (section III).

I. Changing the Terms of Debate

1. Deconstructing the "Secularization" and the "Desecularization" Thesis

The standard models of the "secularization" and the "desecularization" thesis are variants of essentially the same set of theoretical assumptions and empirical claims, though with opposite conclusions. Broadly speaking, both suggest that there is a single, linear relationship (either positive or inverse) between modernization and secularization. By producing a more differentiated economy and fragmented society, modernization tears the "sacred canopy" of religion asunder—either loosening the grip of faith or increasing the demand for religion.[6]

This conception is grounded in a historically dubious narrative that can be summarized as follows. On the one hand, public religion was gradually superseded and sidelined. New, progressive ideas of nature, science, technology, states, and markets gradually replaced archaic, obsolete notions of creation, theology, rituals, and the church, as well as the civil economy of guilds and cooperatives. On the other hand, it is contended that religion never really went away and that it has already returned to a position of cultural visibility and political influence. Thus, the same secularizing effects of modernization on faith have produced very different consequences. Either religions have adapted to modernity and become more like secular society, or else faiths have engendered powerful movements of countersecularization and ensured the continuity of religious belief and practice, albeit at the level of individuals and groups rather than society as a whole.

At the risk of caricaturing a little, proponents of the secularization thesis accuse their critics of underplaying the persistence of secularism. Advocates of the desecularization thesis blame the defenders of secularization for reading the whole world through the lenses of secular western Europe. My contention is that both are right about each other but wrong about religion.

2. The Conceptual Limits of Both Theories

Both theories view the historical and social evolution of religion in the modern era through an essentially secular prism that is founded on certain sociological, anthropological, philosophical, and (mostly hidden) theological concepts that are theoretically flawed and empirically questionable (mainly measuring church attendance). Sociologically, the paradigm of (de)secularization is inextricably intertwined with socio-economic modernization and cognate ideas such as industrialization, urbanization, rationalization, bureaucratization, individualization, priva-tization, and disenchantment. Linked to this is the claim that society represents a set of general, social facts and lawlike regularities rather than an association of living communities and groups. This shifts the focus from communal practice to individual belief, defined in terms of private consciousness.

Much of the disagreement between the two theories therefore boils down to empirical evidence. Either the crisis of religious consciousness is proof for the growing secularization of modern societies (Durkheim or Weber),[7] or else the perseverance of religious consciousness in individuals and groups is evidence that modernization is compatible with faith and that it can even lead to desecularization.[8] Since both phenomena are sup-ported by different sets of statistical data, neither theory can fully explain world religions.

Anthropologically, notions such as general social systems and inner consciousness are deeply problematic. Both theories hold to an essential-ist conception of religion that uproots each faith from its unique and specific traditions and reduces all religions to a set of abstract, generaliz-able principles, beliefs, or emotions. These are assumed to be either inner psychological phenomena linked to human nature (rather than the entire cosmos) or outer social phenomena tied to formal institutions and general spiritual exercises (rather than specific communities and practices of wor-ship)—or indeed both.[9] In any case, the secularization and the desecu-larization theses confidently predict that religious principles, beliefs, and emotions will either be swept away or strengthened by the process of modernization.

The conceptual problem is that such and similar conceptions—which underpin influential accounts such as Locke's idea of the rea-sonableness of Christianity and Kant's notion of a universal, moral reli-gion—redefine faith in one of two ways: either as a sort of innate, natural, rationalist (or reasonable) religion or as a blind, fideist belief in an external divinity (and divine, providential intervention). Both theorizations posit a unitary, transhistorical essence of faith that denies two anthropological insights: first, that religions constitute distinct forms of belief and practice irreducible to any other sphere (nature or consciousness); and second, that religious symbols embodying models *of* and *for* reality are inextricably linked to narratives, meaning, and culture. For narratives, meaning, and culture cannot be subsumed under any abstract, disembodied concept representing general laws of natural regularity or human consciousness (or again both at once).

Philosophically, the primacy of these modern, general categories over premodern conceptions of the link between universal principles and particular practices can be traced to a variety of traditions stretching back to the late Middle Ages. In brief, this transition is characterized by the emergence of two dualisms: first, between the secular space of pure, material nature and the sacred sphere of the immaterial supernatural; and second, between experience and reason or empiricism (e.g., Bacon, Boyle, Locke) and rationalism (e.g., Descartes, Leibniz). Taken together, these dualisms undermine the theistic idea of a continuous link between God and the world (e.g., divine love for creation). Either the divine is relegated to a transcendental sphere amenable to abstract reason or blind faith (transcendentalism), or else it is reduced to purely immanent nature and the material world we directly experience (positivism).[10]

Theologically, the centrality of positivism in the sciences and humanities has provoked a robust critique of the secular nature of modern inquiry and the recognition that the origins of modern philosophy and social theory are distinctly theological.[11] The idea that philosophy (subsequently replaced by natural and social science) is the only universal discipline concerned with the data of pure nature is itself the product of redefining theology as a merely regional science investigating the supernatural gift of revelation. (By contrast, St. Thomas Aquinas developed a theory of the subalternation of all disciplines to the supreme science of theology.)

So redefined, modern thought rejects the theistic idea of an analogical participation of immanent reality in the transcendent source of being in God. It also embraces a deistic dualism whereby, first, the sacred is rendered transcendental and confined to the supernatural realm of faith and revelation (divorced from reason and nature), and second, the secular space of society is conceived as a positive "given" and equated with the purely natural sphere of material reality and human agency.[12] Crucially, the patristic and medieval idea of real, embodied relations between persons and groups that somehow mirror relations between the divine persons (albeit partially and imperfectly) is abandoned in favor of nominalist poles of the individual and the collective.[13]

This conceptual change from the Middle Ages to modernity had far-reaching implications for religious practice in Europe and later in North America.[14] Instead of binding together believers in a universal brotherhood, faith was increasingly tied to either individuals or nations (or indeed both). Likewise, society was seen as an autonomous, general set of "facts" and lawlike rules rather than a whole that exceeds its parts—an "association of associations" that links individuals, communities, and groups to one another in organic and reciprocal ways (not either state-administered rights or economic-contractual ties). Since modernity redefines religion itself along secular lines, it is hardly surprising that a number of faith traditions are resisting modernization.

3. Toward an Alternative Account of Religion and Secularism

For all the reasons adduced in the foregoing, secularization and desecularization theories must be discarded in favor of alternative accounts of religion drawing on three disciplines that reject the transcendentalism and positivism in much of the modern sciences and the humanities: first, historicized and comparative sociology; second, comparative and philosophical anthropology; and third, philosophical theology.

The first replaces rather simplistic claims about unitary, ahistorical trends with a historical and comparative analysis of concepts and practices associated with different religions. Some of the key findings of this approach include (a) the profound, lasting differences between Protestant countries, where religion and the Enlightenment tended to converge, and Catholic countries, where they tended to conflict; (b) the importance of religious monopoly and degrees of pluralism, including the modalities of church establishment in the United Kingdom or Scandinavia but also in Muslim states; (c) the fusion of religion with ethnonational identities and the rise of denominational plurality, for example, in parts of postcommunist eastern Europe; (d) the divergence between secularized elites and ordinary believers within and across the growing gulf between urban centers and rural peripheries, for example, in countries with strongly secular constitutions, such as France or Turkey; and (e) the rise of individualism and the privatization of social life, coupled with the resurgence of religion in society (and even politics). Across the world, religions have become significant social and political actors precisely to the extent that they have renounced the complicit collusion with old structures of power (e.g., states/governments, oligarchic elites).[15] All this underscores the difference (already highlighted in the previous section) between those religious strands that embrace modernization and those that repudiate it.

Second, this also points to a different anthropological approach whereby religion is defined in terms of specific communities of believers and all-encompassing practices within a communal body such as the synagogue, the temple, the church, or the mosque—not a set of abstract doctrines, beliefs, or worldviews held by individuals on account of psychological inclinations or social needs. As such, many forms of religion are paradoxically more mediated *and* more holistic than the (de)secularization thesis can capture. This is particularly true of those faiths that reject any accommodation with the secularizing dimensions of modernity that compromise religious orthodoxy (e.g., denying universal truths or replacing religious virtues embodied in practices with abstract, secular values and formal institutions).

Third, the importance of philosophical theology is that it helps reorient the dominant accounts away from the transcendentalist emphasis on the supernatural and the focus on the facticity of "the social" toward a new accentuation of meaning, narrative, culture, and symbol. Thus, religion is no longer essentialized and equated with abstract, generalizable beliefs to which believers give assent based on either pure reason or blind faith or prerational moral sentiments—or indeed all at once. Instead, religion is an integral part of human existence that cannot be deconstructed into psychological or social phenomena but frames individual and societal life by assigning positions and roles of communal, political, and cultural significance. Whether these positions are relatively more hierarchical or more egalitarian, different faiths tend to emphasize the common realm of civic society rather than the purely private sphere in a modern sense. This shifts conventional conceptions away from secular ideas of autonomy and personal choice toward communal sense making and shared interpretations of meaning.

Here one must go further and link these three perspectives more closely to each other. Just as sociology and anthropology add a crucial historical-comparative dimension to philosophical theology, so the latter can reinforce the theological dimension of religious master narratives and highlight the crucial distinction within each faith tradition between orthodoxy and heterodoxy. These terms are fiercely debated but none-theless shared by communities of believers. Taken together, the three perspectives provide a compelling critique of both secular-liberal tri-umphalism and religious-fundamentalist triumphalism, whose uncanny similarity can be traced to their shared modern roots. Notions of com-munity, belief, or faith are of course not identical across different world religions.[16] Nor does it make much sense to speak of a religious perspec-tive "in general." What exactly is this "panreligious," shared faith position? Does it not risk amalgamating rival and perhaps incommensurable con-ceptions of God, theism, or the distinction between religious and political authority? Surely it is conceptually more compelling and practically more persuasive to speak of both similarities and differences within or across different religious traditions from a specific faith stance. But nonetheless, one key divide is between different religions or denominations that either embrace or contest modernity, as the following section also discusses.

II. Beyond the Dialectic of Modernity

In this section, I link the shortcomings of "(de)secularization" to the opposition between modernizing creeds and traditional faiths. Modernity, like secularism, neither has a single line of origination nor is stable in its historical identity. Instead, both these concepts—and the realities they signify—operate through a series of tensions between the sacred and the secular as well as the premodern and the modern. In premodern cultures, for example, the sacred tended to be seen as a cosmic reality that is dif-fusely mediated through signs and symbols in the world inhabited by all. By contrast, modernity views the sacred as an immutable essence and the object of an internal, human experience that Durkheim calls "religious."[17] Likewise, premodern meanings of the secular accentuated the temporal dimension (e.g., the interval between fall and *eschaton* in Christianity)—whereas modern ideas define the secular in spatial terms as an autono-mous domain separate from supernatural sanctity in God.

Thus, the modern opposition between two general categories—a supernatural "sacred" and a natural "secular"—is fundamentally different from the premodern distinctions of the divine and the profane, the temporal and the spiritual, or earthly and heavenly powers. These and other distinctions are hierarchical in the sense that the divine, the spiritual, and the heavenly somehow comprehend or "enfold" the profane, the temporal, and the earthly. Why? Because none of the latter has any existence or meaning except with reference to the former. Crucially, premodern conceptions suggest that the natural only *is* by participating in the supernatural that created it. On the contrary, modern, dualistic conceptions claim that immanent nature can operate independently of its ultimate, transcendent cause.

1. Modern Secularism at the Level of Ideas

Modernity is neither synonymous with secularism nor unrelated to it. Secularism neither marks the wholesale destruction of faith nor represents a simple simulation of religion under a different guise. Rather, modernity—at least in the Christian West—is in continuity with some aspects of the late Middle Ages and also constitutes a radical departure from other medieval traditions. Concretely, the concepts and practices instituting "western" modernity reconfigure the sacred as a wholly transcendental source of authority and also as a positivized, pure space that must not be profaned. Thus, the notion of revelation ceases to signify the objective manifestation of transcendent realities (e.g., first principles and final ends) in the immanent world. Henceforth, revelation becomes an object of transcendental belief to which believers must give assent. In short, God is erased from the workings of the natural world and either relegated to an external cause (e.g., a watchmaker) or an internal force (e.g., moral religion or inner religious consciousness).

Likewise, the meaning of religion shifts from signifying a series of beliefs embodied in practices binding together communities of believers within the social body of the Church ("authorizing doctrine" and "authorized practice") toward a fixed set of abstract beliefs to which the immaterial mind/soul gives assent[18]—while the physical body is handed over to the centralized, modern state.[19] As such, the modern redefines the sacred while also inventing and instituting a number of new structures, such as the sovereign state, the disembedded free market, and the disciplining practices of centralized educational, penal, and medical organizations.[20] This shows that modernity is not confined to desacralization but encompasses a new, secular economy of power and knowledge enforced by new institutions.

One can also contrast (premodern) secularity with (modern) secularism. The principle of secularity is founded on the Judeo-Christian distinction of religious and political authority. Historically, there was a constant tension within Judaism between the prophets and the kings, with the former always calling the latter back to a true righteousness untouched by the corruption of power and avarice. Similarly, the realm of the church was generally demarcated from that of the state. This is evinced by Saint Augustine's (Pauline and Neo-Platonist) juxtaposition of the earthly city and the City of God, Pope Gelasius I's teaching on the two swords, and also Saint John Chrysostom's critique of Christian attempts either to sacralize secular power or to secularize the Church. As such, the shared Catholic and Orthodox principle is to distinguish and relate the religious and political spheres without separating religion from politics or privatizing faith.

On the contrary, the modern age endorsed the partition of church and state, as it was supposed to foster tolerance between rival confessions and to create perpetual peace among the nations. After the violent events of the Protestant Reformation and the "wars of religion," a new constitutional settlement was required. However, from its inception in the sixteenth century to the present day, European secularism has subordinated the religious freedom of individuals and groups to the power of the central state. The Augsburg peace of 1555 and the 1648 Treaty of Westphalia, which helped to establish national states and the modern international system, granted monarchs and their vassals a power monopoly at the expense of the supranational papacy and a transnational network of monastic orders and local churches. By codifying the principle *"cuius regio, eius religio"* (in the prince's land, the prince's religion), it was modern secularism that politicized faith and curtailed the freedom of belief.

Here one can go further and suggest that just as modernity emerged earlier than the seventeenth century, so important strands of the Enlightenment constitute a critical reaction against early modern rationalism and empiricism. This is certainly true of Italian, English, and Scottish thinkers such as Vico, Doria, Genovesi, Shaftesbury, Cudworth, and Hume.[21] In different ways, they retrieve an earlier emphasis on hierarchical mediations and the participatory relation of finite creation in the infinite Creator. At the level of practice, this translates into an accentuation of reciprocity, social sympathy, and gift exchange, which contrasts sharply with the modern social-contract tradition and its focus on self-interest, economic utility, and commercial exchange—"the natural propensity to truck, barter and exchange one thing for another," as Adam Smith wrote in *The Wealth of Nations*.[22] All of which highlights the plural nature of modernity and its contested development.

2. Modern Secularism at the Level of Practice

First, it is imperative to acknowledge the difficulty of accounting for the divergence between theoretical shifts and empirical changes. The secularization of philosophy and political theory—which we can trace to the late Middle Ages, the Renaissance, and the Enlightenment critique of theistic religion[23]—was not matched by an equivalent secularization of (trans)national culture and society. Except perhaps for postrevolutionary France and some other parts of continental Europe, such as the Low Countries and northwestern Germany, Roman Catholicism and cognate denominations such as Eastern Orthodoxy and Anglicanism as well as other world religions such as Islam continued to exert their transnational sway across the globe throughout the modern age—including the Holy Roman Empire of the German Nation, the Byzantine Commonwealth, and the Ottoman Empire.

For example, popular religious practice and the public influence of faith rose steadily and often quite spectacularly in North America throughout a period of accelerating modernization from about 1800 to 1950.[24] Similarly, eighteenth- and nineteenth-century Britain featured a moral economy underpinned by the modernizing creed of Methodism common to elite and populace alike.[25] The secularization of British and American culture is far more recent than commonly supposed and clearly linked to certain strands of Protestantism.[26] For these reasons, this secularizing process is by no means linear or irreversible. Nor should one assume that the same processes will occur in other contexts with other religions.

Second, these contrary trends throughout the modern age are not limited to post-Enlightenment western Europe. Long before the Iranian Revolution of 1979 or the victory of Catholicism over Communism in

Poland (1980–89) or the events of 9/11, world faiths such as Christianity and Islam were an integral part of nineteenth- and early twentieth-century politics, both locally and globally. For example, American Protestant theologians and religious figures played a decisive role in creating the League of Nations after 1919 and the United Nations in 1946. European Christian Democrats from Italy, Germany, the Benelux countries, and even France led the way in setting up the project for European integration and enlargement in the 1950s.[27] They were inspired by Christian social teaching: since the groundbreaking encyclical *Rerum Novarum* (1891) on the Industrial Revolution, the social doctrine of the Catholic Church has viewed the supremacy of the national state and the transnational market over the intermediary space of civic society and civil economy upheld by the Church as contrary to the Christian faith[28]—a position shared by the other episcopally based traditions of Orthodoxy and Anglicanism.[29]

Likewise, Islam was the dominant political and social force in the wider Middle East and beyond until late nineteenth-century colonialism and the dissolution of the Ottoman Empire in 1922. This replaced the caliphate with secular republics (e.g., Turkey) and modern nation-states based on false borders imposed across Arabia. Elsewhere, traditional faiths such as Hinduism pervaded politics and culture before economic and social modernization changed the dynamic in favor of secularism and modern creeds. This is also true for China, where Christianity was instrumental in the transition from the empire to the republic under Sun Yat-sen—only for the Communist Party to marginalize it alongside Confucianism, Taoism, and Buddhism. Even where secularizing modernization was adopted, the radical elites struggled to remake society and the populace in the image of their own secular values—as evinced by cases as different as China, Russia, Turkey, much of Latin America, and most parts of eastern (and even western) Europe.[30]

Contrary to claims about linear secularization, there is thus a spectrum of nineteenth- and twentieth-century religious responses to secular modernity, ranging from resistance by Muslims, Roman Catholics, and the Orthodox (and even some Anglicans) to Jewish acceptance and Protestant support—measured in terms of social integration and degrees of individualization. There is much variation across world religions and within specific traditions such as Sufi Islam, Orthodox Judaism, and Christian evangelicalism (Protestant or Catholic). But fundamental differences between certain strands in relation to secular modernity are borne out by evidence on religious ideas and practices.[31]

Third, one can suggest that the twentieth century, which saw a clash of secular ideologies with unprecedented levels of violence, is arguably an exception to the enduring presence of religion in politics. One defining mark of Communism, Fascism, and National-Socialism is their shared secular messianism, underwritten by religious language.[32] The twentieth century can perhaps be described as the "first and last truly modern century," with more extreme forms of secularism than before or thereafter. If so, then the contemporary global resurgence of religion marks the return to a more "normal" presence of religious ideas in (inter)national politics.[33] However, cultural and social secularization proceeds apace, notably the decline of traditional religious beliefs and practices as well as the rise of secular values and lifestyles with the approval and connivance of modernizing creeds (mostly variants of evangelicalism in Christianity, Islam, and other world religions).

Fourth, this growing split between faith traditions that reject or embrace secular modernity is illustrated by divisions among more and less orthodox strands of Christianity. Those traditions most marked by the Protestant Reformation are also more secularizing than other Christian traditions. This serves to qualify the rather simplistic depiction of American religiosity versus European secularism. The latter is a recent phenomenon.[34] And although the United States is far more religious than Europe in terms of personal observance and political discourse, it is also far more secular in terms of equating faith with private therapy and with a directed, unmediated link between the individual and God. This underplays other key aspects of religion, such as sacramentality and the communal, public character of faith. It also explains why in some important sense even observant believers uncritically embrace secular culture—for example, the idea of a "gospel of wealth" that equates the rich with the elect and sanctifies the pursuit of power and pleasure.[35]

Moreover, America's vague "civil religion" is governed by a post-Christian, gnostic spirituality that bears increasingly little resemblance to creedal Christianity.[36] Its liberal polity—based on a total church-state separation since its inception—is structured by specifically American holidays rather than universal Christian festivals. In addition, America's more strongly privatized public sphere opens up a space for a more explicitly politicized and moralized creed that feeds on the Manichean moralism taught in mainstream churches in order to fuel a sense of national exceptionalism[37]—rather than religious universalism. All of which helps account for the tendency of US Catholics (and Jews) to become more like Protestants—even though strong Catholic immigration from Central and Latin America might change this in the future.

Fifth, what we are seeing more generally is that traditional faiths such as Roman Catholicism, Eastern Orthodoxy, Buddhism, and some strands of Sufi, Shia, and Sunni Islam are intellectually (if not as yet culturally and numerically) revivified and that they are leading the way against the modern hegemony of secularism.[38] Thus, the idea that the secularization of thought and practice has not been the predominant modern reality is just as misguided as the idea that religion ever disappeared from the public realm or that it cannot regain political influence. For all those reasons, modernity is a dialectical process oscillating between a dominant secularism (and a variety of denominational subcultures that are positively linked to secularization), on the one hand, and the revival of traditional, nonmodern faiths that oppose and seek to correct the secular orientation of modernization, on the other hand.

Of course, the contemporary resurgence of Islam, Buddhism, and certain episcopally based Christian churches could represent but a short-lived phase prior to enduring secularization—religion in death throes and faith's last gasp. But leaving aside their current intellectual revival, strong demographic dynamics suggest that traditional, orthodox faiths will continue to grow—and not just modernizing creeds (either more liberal or more fundamentalist). That is because sustained population growth in developing countries produces many more religious people than those lost to secularism elsewhere. Thus, the world is growing more religious even as people in economically developed countries and emerging markets are becoming more secular. Believers already outnumber nonbelievers by about five to one—even though believing is of course quite different from belonging (i.e., affiliation and attendance).[39]

More specifically, in the West and East Asia, the ongoing population decline and aging might even be reversed at some point between 2020 and 2070, as the social conservatism shared by many Christians, Muslims, Jews, and others could combine with immigrants and other minorities to produce a demographical revival. This will be based on pronatalism, endogamy (in-group marriage), and voluntary self-segregation, which conjointly ensure high fertility and high retention rates. The proportion of believers in the total population is bound to increase in the medium and long run. In that process, fundamentalists could gradually squeeze out moderates and ratchet up global "culture wars" with seculars.[40] Since the extremes tend to resemble (and cancel out) each other, the future will largely depend on more traditional faiths that reject the shared modern foundations of both religious fundamentalism and secular extremism. This, alongside other phenomena, is likely to determine the future of religion—as the final section argues.

III. What Is at Stake

1. Conflicts and Contests between Modernizing Creeds and Traditional Faiths

American evangelicalism and its worldwide offspring encapsulate the complex, paradoxical nature of religions embracing global modernity.[41] First, evangelicalism and Pentecostalism are national, global, and local all at once. Their origin is clearly the specific cultures of the Protestant Atlantic North, but Pentecostalist movements have used global society created in the American Protestant image (with elements from the British and Spanish imperial legacy) to reach new territories, where they become rapidly enculturated and intermixed with indigenous subcultures centered on spirit-filled religiosity.

This is also reflected in the Neo-Buddhist Soka Gakkai and a new generation of Muslim televangelists, such as Amr Khaled, speaking to a globalized *ummah*. The processes of globalization facilitate this spread while also acting as a catalyst for ethnoreligious resistance and a violent backlash against foreign, global forces. Here the complex dynamics between majority and minority cultures come to the fore, with charismatic strands of different world religions often appealing to subcultures that resist the domination of local majorities by linking themselves to the transnational identity of evangelical movements.

In turn, this has important implications for individualization and communal fragmentation. The evangelical emphasis on inwardness, individual choice, and direct, unmediated access to God—based on conversion by a personal transference of emotional attachment—allows believers to escape local structures such as extended kin or religious communities and the sacramental mediation of divine grace administered by the priest-hood. Depending on culture and other factors, evangelical movements can mitigate or exacerbate the communal fragmentation caused partly by the individualizing effects of their creed. Hence, social atomism, which is a problem associated with modernization, affects evangelical and secular groups much more than the adherents of traditional, orthodox faiths.

Second, evangelical and Pentecostal movements across different faith traditions exhibit a series of striking paradoxical tensions such as central authority and personal participation, formal patriarchy and infor-mal matriarchy, work discipline and crass consumerism, and group soli-darity and individual wealth. The latter is linked to the idea of a gospel of the immaterial spirit that consecrates the pursuit of material wealth. As such, evangelicalism and Pentecostalism are a harbinger of global moder-nity, though they nonetheless reject a number of key modern phenomena, including the total privatization of religious practice, the absolute indi-vidualization of belief, and the complete separation of spiritual inward-ness from an outward orientation to the material world. Evangelical and Pentecostal movements can be termed postmodern in that their embrace of secular modernity is highly selective.

Linked to this is the prospect of rapid religious conversion coupled with growing secularization. China is a case in point. Its Protestant popu-lation has grown from less than 1 million in 1949 to something between 100 and 150 million today.[42] On current trends, it could reach up to 250 million by 2050—making China the (second) most populous Christian country in the world and providing (qualified) support for the expan-sion of the sort of secularizing capitalism that is currently promoted by the Chinese Communist Party to undermine the social relations hold-ing together religious communities in Tibet and the Muslim-dominated northwestern province of Xinjiang. Meanwhile, the number of Chinese Catholics and Muslims has risen less spectacularly but no less steadily, with levels of about 20 million and 22 million, respectively, and projec-tions of strong growth in the future—such that China might be the larg-est Christian and possibly also the largest Muslim country by 2100. Thus, the Middle Kingdom could be a prime theater for conflicts and contests between modernizing creeds and traditional faiths, with Pentecostals broadly endorsing the socioeconomic modernization generally opposed by Muslims and Catholics.

Moreover, Pentecostalism rejects the Weberian and Calvinist routes to modernity by eschewing rationalization, bureaucratization, and iconoclasm[43] in favor of social and cultural practices (including audiovisual and electronic media)—encompassing "story and song, gesture and empowerment, image and embodiment, enthusiastic release and personal discipline."[44] This confirms the point made repeatedly throughout this chapter that modernity is not monolithic but contested by different religious traditions.

Third, more traditional faiths, such as Roman Catholicism and Islam, have in different ways either resisted or adapted to the advance of global evangelicalism and its diverse manifestations. This has taken various forms: either an attempt to reverse the earlier centralized control of local churches, which opened up a space occupied by Pentecostals, or else the creation of Christian (or Muslim) charismatic movements such as the Catholic Charismatic Renewal, wherein there is a shift of emphasis from sacramental participation and episcopal authority to a kind of reduced mediation and authority, both of which are concentrated in charismatic leadership—a description that partly applies to influential European movements and lay fraternities such as Comunione e Liberazione. These and other responses to evangelicalism operate both inside and outside the mainstream churches and seek to mobilize against aggressive secularism (including by giving a greater role to the laity), while also borrowing heavily from the secular ideas of evangelical modernity.

The contest of ideas between modernizing creeds and traditional faiths is already changing public debates on political economy and science, as discussed in the next section.

2. After Liberalism: Religion and Political Economy

Twenty years after the collapse of state communism, the crisis of free-market capitalism that has plunged much of the world into the worst economic turmoil since the Great Depression of 1929–32 offers a unique opportunity to chart an alternative path. Broadly speaking, the modern age marks the progressive subordination of civil society institutions, actors, and practices to the administrative and symbolic order of the national state and the transnational market. In the complex and nonlinear process of modernization, civil society came to be seen either as an extension of the state or as being synonymous with the market. Concomitantly, social relations were redefined either as state-controlled links based on sovereign power and individual rights or as economic-contractual ties based on commercial exchange. Often this occurred with the approval and connivance of actual religions that supported absolutist (monarchical) regimes and feudal arrangements on the basis of unequal landholding and the exploitation of wage laborers.

However, there is a religious alternative that is once more coming to the fore. Historically, the Judeo-Christian distinction of religious from political authority created a "free space" between the rulers and those who are ruled. Together with other religious communities and civic bodies, the Church often defended civil society from both political coercion and economic commodification. This gave rise to the idea that the "intermediary institutions" of civil society—such as professional associations, manufacturing and trading guilds, cooperatives, trade unions, voluntary organizations, universities, educational establishments, communal welfare, and religious communities—are more primary than either the national bureaucratic-authoritarian state or the transnational "anarchic" market. Instead of operating on the basis of either state-administered rights or economic-contractual relations, these structures are governed by social bonds of reciprocal trust and mutual assistance. Such bonds of reciprocity and mutuality are not confined to the third, "voluntary" sector but can extend to the public and private sectors, helping to "reembed" both the state and the market into the complex web of social relations. Now that the growing convergence of state and market has failed so conspicuously, the crisis of 2007–9 has the potential to eschew the bipolar order of the communist east and the capitalist west in favor of a genuine "third way" beyond centralized bureaucratic statism and unbridled free-market capitalism.

Moreover, the main world religions view the dominant models of democracy and capitalism as secular. Broadly speaking, their argument is that democratic and capitalist systems subordinate the sanctity of life and land to abstract, disembodied standards such as representation, formal rights, or commercial exchange. The religious critique goes further than the Weberian thesis about rationalization, bureaucratization, and disenchantment. Arguably, the modern state and the "free market" redefine the sacred by gradually secularizing the public realm and sacralizing the politicoeconomic sphere. This double process tends to sideline religious conceptions of hierarchical virtues and truths in favor of abstract values and fetishized commodities. For this reason (and building on the work of Walter Benjamin), liberal democracy and modern free-market capitalism can be termed "quasi-religions."[45]

In response, religious leaders combine a critique of modernity with alternative ideas aimed at transcending the false divide between the purely secular and the exclusively religious. In our "postsecular" era, religious and other bodies should be able to express themselves directly in their own terms within the public square.[46] However, for most liberals, the norms to regulate this debate must ultimately remain secular and liberal (procedural and majoritarian). For religious figures, by contrast, there must be a plural search for a shared common good, which is not merely pregiven in natural law and abstract reason—for that is part of modern rationalism rejected by more traditional faiths.

In the case of Catholicism, a reinvention of constitutional corporatism in a more pluralist guise against modern liberalism is linked to an insistence on the dignity and autonomy of persons, communities, and associations. By upholding real relations, these intermediary institutions provide an indispensable mediation between the modern, nominalist poles of the individual and the collective. Equally, such a nonsecular political economy is linked to the argument that education as the transmission and exploration of truth is as fundamental a dimension of politics as is the will of a democratic majority or the authority of the executive. Secularists, by contrast, defend variants of liberalism that maintain a secular separation of state, market, and civil society.[47]

The modern political Right has always focused on the absolute power of "the one" and the prerogative to decide on the state of exception (Carl Schmitt), while the modern Left has insisted on an equally absolute right of "the many" to give and withdraw legitimacy (Michel Foucault).[48] Both uproot state and market from the social relations that (should) embed them. Therefore, the Left and the Right ignore the primacy of real, embodied relations and also the mediating role of "the few" concerned with truth and virtue—not some privileged socioeconomic class but rather a meritocratic hierarchy committed to an ethos of excellence across all spheres of human activity.

A political economy focused on the latter would be at once more mediated and holistic, defining the secular realm as concerned with things in time and with necessary coercion. So defined, the secular is linked to the sacred through an outlook toward transcendent norms. Only such norms can supply ultimate standards beyond the will either of "the one" or of "the many." Different religious leaders are asking nothing less than whether the politics of "right" and "left" remain caught within shared secular, liberal axioms. These axioms are *also* those of theocratic fundamentalisms since they equally deal in a politics of the indifferent will, inherited (as is also the case in the end for liberalism) from the late medieval and early modern focus on volition (rather than the intellect).[49] There is a parallel with the contemporary centrality of individual will, self-determination, and personal taste—a predicament that Joseph Ratzinger, shortly before his election as Pope Benedict XVI, described as "dictatorship of relativism that does not recognize anything as definitive and whose ultimate goal consists solely of one's own ego and desires."[50]

A nonsecular political economy is a quest for a way that cannot be charted on our current conceptual map. Instead of formal representation and commercial exchange, the emphasis shifts toward notions of real relationality, the common good, and principles that can determine appropriate "mixtures" of government as between a whole variety of instances: "the one," "the few," and "the many"; the center and localities; political government and prepolitical society; international community and nations; education in time and government in space; absolute right and free decision; economic freedom and just distribution—and finally, secular and religious authorities.

The task for religions is not to embrace particular modes of political or economic governance but rather to promote models that protect the sacredness of life and uphold hierarchically ordered virtues. Notions of goodness and justice trump individual freedom, negative liberty, and the pursuit of happiness reduced to utility, power, or pleasure. Thus, different faiths dispute the secular claim to universal validity and seek to change the terms on which public debates about political and economic choices are conducted.

3. Science, Atheism, and Religion

Today's militant atheists brand religious faith as repressive, irrational, and fundamentalist. Although these cultured despisers of religion are once again making strident appeals to secular values and unmediated reason, they do not realize that the religious absolutism they denounce is but a variant of their own fundamentalism returned in a different guise.[51] For true faith is never separate from proper reason, as all world religions hold. In Pope Benedict's controversial 2006 Regensburg address, he defends the "grandeur of reason" against the fanatical faith of religious fundamentalists and the crude rationalism of secular extremists. Extending Pope John Paul II's 1998 encyclical *Fides et Ratio*, Benedict argues that faith and reason require each other and are mutually augmenting. Theologically, just as faith habituates reason to see transcendence at the heart of immanence and thus broadens the scope of rationality, so reason binds faith to cognition and thereby helps believers explore the intelligible dimension of revelation—faith seeking understanding (St. Anselm's Augustinian dictum *fides quaerens intellectum*). Politically, without each other's import, both principles can be distorted and instrumentalized at the service of egoism or absolute power. Just as rationality acts as a controlling organ that binds belief to knowledge, so faith can save reason from being manipulated by ideology or applied in a partial way that ignores the complexity of the real world. Without each other's corrective role, distortions and pathologies arise in both religion and secularism—either religious extremism that uses faith as a vehicle of hatred or the secular, totalitarian ideologies of the twentieth century that legitimated genocide and total warfare.

Moreover, faith and reason are intimately intertwined in beneficial ways. Faith can reinforce trust in the human capacity for reasoning and understanding. Secular rationality can help religious belief make sense of its claims and give coherence to its intuitions. Crucially, reason and faith can assist each other's search for objective principles and norms governing both personal and political action. What binds rationality to belief is the shared commitment to universal standards of truth, even if these are never fully known and always deeply contested. As such, the relatedness of reason and faith is not merely a concern for religion but in fact lies at the heart of politics, the economy, and society.

By contrast, contemporary atheists defend an account of reason that is conceptually impoverished. Richard Dawkins's philosophically illiterate polemic *The God Delusion* declares that religion is irrational without ever explaining the source of rationality. Sam Harris's diatribe *The End of Faith* has to falsify history by claiming that Hitler and Stalin were religious to make its case for the malign influence of faith. The attacks on religion are becoming ever more shrill and desperate, a clear sign of atheist anxiety about the status of their first principles and explanatory frameworks.

This atheist apprehension is well founded, as the latest developments in biology, physics, philosophy, and ethics open the door to a revivified theology and a renewed import of religion in debates on the universe and human nature. Hitherto, it had been assumed by most mainstream scientists that forms of life are the product of essentially natural, random processes—such that if we ran evolution again, life would look very different.[52] However, there is increasing evidence to suggest that evolution shows biological convergence and is not random: if it ran again, the world would look much as it does.[53] Here one can go beyond old divides (creation versus atheism; intelligent design versus natural evolution) and argue that recent research sheds new light on the teleology (or finality) of life. Natural selection is no longer thought to be the main driver of biological change. Rather, life displays a certain kind of inherency, such that the beings that come about are *also* a product of their own, intended integrity—intimating the possibility of being linked to transcendent principles and finalities.

All of which means that there is no necessary conflict between evolution and religion. In fact, different religious traditions provide a defense of evolution against the atheism of certain Darwinists and the fundamentalism of creationists.[54] Arguably, evolution is no more purely naturalistic than God is totally deterministic—both can be shown to be compatible in the sense that the process of evolution does not conclusively refute the idea of an absolute beginning and a final end in a creative source. Just as creationists cannot reject scientific evidence on natural evolution, so scientists such as Dawkins cannot pretend that evolution justifies atheism.

Similarly, in cosmology and physics, the idea that the world was produced by chance has long been dismissed. The extreme precision of the gravitational constant that allows a universe such as ours to exist requires an explanation in terms of first principles and final ends. But rather than exploring the world as an intended creation, secular physics posits infinite numbers of multiverses existing alongside our own. The sheer uniqueness of our universe is qualified by the existence of all other possible universes. This supposition sounds no more reasonable than the religious idea of creation *ex nihilo.*

Moreover, positing this secular-scientific paradigm leads to the *Matrix* hypothesis that we are only a virtual simulation run by other universes more powerful and real. So religion finds itself in the position of defending a certain account of reality against those who suggest that nature and humanity are either purely material or almost entirely virtual—or once again somehow both. Of course, there will also be gaps between theistic and naturalistic accounts of the world. But equally there are eminent scientists such as Simon Conway Morris and others who see no contradiction between religious conceptions of a Creator God and scientific accounts of evolution deriving from Darwin. This changes the terms of debate on science and religion and also casts doubt on secular claims to reality and universal validity.

Different world faiths, in particular Christianity and Islam, can draw on the historical links between theology and science to correct purely secular interpretations of evolution and to argue for a broader account of reason beyond the boundaries of immanent finitude. Ultimately, this challenges the modern claim that nature is divorced from the supernatural—a foundational assumption that underlies the (de)secularization thesis and misinforms much of the public understanding of religion.

Conclusion

In this chapter, I have argued that the secularization and desecularization theses are self-reflexive, secular theories that are inescapably wedded to the dominant secular logic of modernity. Neither can conceptualize the religious roots of the modern or the nature of the "postmodern" religious revival. By reducing religions to an ahistorical essence, both ignore the differences between faiths and the specificities of each tradition—different conceptions of the nature of God, relations between the divine and the human, or links between religious virtues and social practices.

Christianity and Islam are a case in point. Christian accounts of God stress the relations between the three divine persons of the Holy Trinity. Therefore, the belief that we are all made in the image and likeness of a personal, "relational" Creator God translates into an emphasis on the strong bonds of mutual help and reciprocal giving within civil society. By contrast, the Muslim God is disembodied and absolutely one. This accentuation of unity is reflected in a priority on absolute unitary authority (compared with intermediary institutions) and a premium on territorial conquest or control, while also imposing strong norms on economic exchange (including bans on speculation and similar practices).

For this reason also, neither secularization nor desecularization can explain how or why certain religions embrace the sort of modern secularism rejected by others. Since modernity is itself the product of theological shifts and changes within religious traditions, it is unsurprising that some faiths are integral to modernization, such as certain strands of Calvinism, Puritanism, and Pentecostalism. By contrast, more traditional, orthodox faiths, such as Roman Catholicism, Eastern Orthodoxy, and certain Muslim traditions such as Sufi Islam, resist modernization and seek to transform the secular outlook of global modernity.

Thus, the master narratives about the universal validity of secular values that dominated the modern age are breaking down. We have already entered a phase of history that is not properly captured by labels such as "postmodern" or "postsecular." The false universalism of secular principles is not merely being contested, as was the case throughout the modern period. Nowadays religious ideas and practices are changing the terms of public debate and putting forward concrete alternatives in virtually all spheres of human activity. Notions of reciprocity, mutuality, and relationality are coming to the fore in public discussions on ethics, political economy, and science. We are witnessing a real intellectual return to religion that cannot be reduced to the spread of fanaticism. "Programmatic secularism" that relegates faith to the private sphere or co-opts it as part of secularizing modernization reinforces rather than overcomes both religious fundamentalism and militant atheism.

The false opposition between secularization and desecularization opens the way for an alternative account that rejects their shared modern logic and analyzes religion on terms beyond the false divide between a purely secular and an exclusively religious perspective. There is in fact a "middle" position: faith can lead to a strong notion of the common good and a belief that human behavior, when disciplined and directed, can start to act more charitably. There can also be secular intimations of this:

the more faith-inspired practices are successful even in narrow secular terms (e.g., more economic security, more equality, more sustainability), the easier it will be for nonreligious institutions to adopt elements of such an overarching ethical framework without, however, fully embracing its religious basis.

The paradox of faith is this: Not only is secularity a religious invention, linked as it is to the Judeo-Christian distinction between secular and religious powers and authorities. After the failure of modern secularism, it is also clear that religions are indispensable in upholding "secular" values of freedom and happiness by relating them to transcendent, final standards of truth and goodness in God.

Chapter 8

Global Governance after the Analog Age:
The World after Media Piracy

Ravi Sundaram

The spectacular terror attacks on world cities beginning with the events of September 11, 2001, in New York and continuing in London, Madrid, and Mumbai have been marked by cycles of war and counterterror that have spread across Europe, Asia, and Africa. In many ways, the events of September 11 and the decade following have disclosed the global shift that seems to be underway: the crisis of US power and the consequent impact on twentieth-century governmental institutions. Debates on these issues, and the future of global governance, have reverberated across continents, in newspaper columns, public discussions, and new scholarly research.

An important part of the new situation is transformation of media, as it has been experienced and governed for much of the twentieth century. Until the 1980s, media forms included print, television, cinema, and radio. For the most part, these were institutionally managed by regulators; censors; film, radio, and television companies; newspaper houses; states; and a host of intellectual-property laws dating back to the nineteenth century. In retrospect, what was remarkable about this world was its apparent geographical stability. Consumers would typically access media content in cinema halls, on television sets, in print, and on radios. Production took place in radio, television, and film studios and in printing shops, and then the products were retailed by distributors. When disputes took place, they were settled in law courts and by legislative and regulatory bodies.

Over the past three decades, this situation has changed dramatically. With the arrival of personal gadgets such as video and audio recorders, the computer, and the Internet, the old media worlds have been thrown into flux. The coming of the digital age has made media production more widespread across the world. What was usually the monopoly of production houses has entered everyday life. Populations worldwide now have access to low-cost new media through local distributors and Internet platforms. The cinema theater and the television set have not disappeared, but they have to contend with media sharing between individuals and groups, outside the older regulatory systems. A growing media-connected population now links to social-networking sites such as Facebook and Orkut and uploads video and photographs on Internet platforms such as YouTube and Flickr.[1] Through peer-to-peer (P2P) websites, books, television shows, movies, software, and music produced by companies are shared between users at no cost. In the non-Western world, more of this media circulates through neighborhood markets and informal distributors, who retail commercially.[2] This circulation of media also happens through computers and cellular phones, the latter a low-cost option in poorer parts of the world. In short, we are seeing a transformed media ecology, where new systems of use, production, and circulation have come into play. Media today straddles legal and nonlegal domains; covers multiple technological objects, from iPads and cellular phones to televisions; involves formal and low-cost informal production; and is subject to constant technological innovation. The seamlessness of media use with everyday life has been a great engine of growth of the past few decades and has also been a mounting challenge for the international system. This is a situation that global governance never anticipated three decades ago.

In an influential book on the coming of the printing press to Europe in the early modern age, Elizabeth Eisenstein suggests that the transmission of ideas without any "loss of precision"[3] produced new collaborative knowledge communities across national boundaries.[4] Print culture destabilized knowledge monopolies around scribal authority. In a similar way, the coming of the digital age has also destabilized the knowledge systems of media clustered around states and corporations. New practices have mixed leisure with politics, social communication, and counterculture; the divisions between work time and leisure time are equally fuzzy.

Most consumers also produce some media, with vast amounts of user content and shared media making their way to Internet sites. In short, the digital age has generated a whole new series of situations that challenge the basic premises of the media model of twentieth-century governance. Populations have moved from being seen as "recipients" of media in cinema halls and in front of radio sets and televisions.[5] Populations now participate as producers, consumers, and proliferators of media, a mobile set of practices that disrupts all major twentieth-century cultural references: the media industry, the system of regulation, and even radical counterculture, which placed itself outside the commercial realm.

Media piracy is a fundamental component of this changed scenario. As more and more media circulates outside old regulatory and control systems, media corporations have designated a good part of that traffic as piracy, or as violating intellectual property law. These practices range from young people sharing music through P2P networks; to websites sharing PDFs of academic books; to small media companies making versions of material once in copyright; to commercial pirates in Asia, Africa, and Latin America; to artist interpretations of cultural material—the list is endless.[6] Debates over media piracy reverberate in interstate disputes, in bodies such as the WTO, and in media discourse worldwide. Media piracy is indicative of the growing vulnerabilities of corporations and states in their ability to control information in the digital age. As the online disclosure of the Afghan war logs demonstrated in July 2010, the most powerful of states is not immune to this scenario; the "leak" seems indicative of a permanent condition of our digital times. Contemporary media piracy is expressive of this postdigital scenario in its complexities and also allows us to reflect on it.

Media piracy has been in existence since the beginnings of European print culture, but the purchase of postdigital media piracy is greater.[7] Contemporary media piracy involves millions of people sharing media and information, often radically bypassing the control systems of the twentieth century. In this chapter, I use media piracy as a heuristic device to understand the transformations of global media governance through the twentieth century. I first look at the relationship between technology and culture to clarify concepts of the digital and the analog. I then examine the rise of US power in this media system, which became organized around what I call an "analog empire," with specific production and control systems. I then look at the challenges and eventual break-down of this regime after the rise of video and the significance of media piracy as a component of the new digital media ecology.

Definitions: Technology, Culture, and Materiality after the Digital Age

In a recent book, the film theorist D. N. Rodowick ponders the arrival of the digital age for film culture.[8] With the coming of the digital age, says Rodowick, the twentieth-century world created by celluloid seems difficult to sustain. Part of the idea of cinema, says Rodowick, is "already dead," with a future difficult to predict.[9] The new media territory that has emerged is "a landscape without image." Rodowick goes on to foreground the confusion for scholars and film researchers: "On electronic screens, we are uncertain that what appears is *an* 'image,' and in its powers of mutability and velocity of transmission, we are equally uncertain that this perception has a singular or stable existence either in the present or in relation to the past."[10] In Rodowick's writing, as in that of many others, there is also a renewed focus on the technical medium itself, as the digital is read through the transformation of surface, storage, and the relationship between spectator and screen. Rodowick's discussion is dominated by celluloid, the quintessential form of analog cinema. Analog film technology, for example, involves the combination of discrete units (still images) and is based on celluloid film and editing in professional studios. Analog photography combines individual dots, and video uses scan lines. This is a simple rendering of a more complex process: the important point is that analog media required an infrastructure of pro-duction and lost quality when it was reproduced. By contrast, digital media can be reproduced without loss of quality.[11] Digital processing transforms media signals into numerical representations of zeros and ones, making it flexible and programmable. Media became less depen-dent on specific materials (such as celluloid) to circulate; this also allowed radical combinations. Software programs were developed by companies to provide interfaces for businesses and individual users to rearrange and combine processes that seemed separate in analog media: text, video, images, audio.[12] Today's social-networking websites such as Facebook and Orkut routinely have their millions of users do this rearranging on a daily basis, tasks that would have been unimaginable in the analog era. Corporations and individuals routinely carry out multiple processes, across space and time: "multitasking" has been the digital era's unique addition to the English language.

Digital technology has evoked a series of widely contrasting responses. When digital media first arrived, some media scholars argued that standardized processing into binary numbers erased all differences between individual media, producing a paralyzing effect of "immateriality" for users. The German writer Friedrich Kittler complained that "with numbers anything goes."[13] With the dissolution of specific media in the digital age, the argument went, human experience lost its material reference to the affective qualities of "tangible" objects such as the photograph, the printed book, and the celluloid reel. The art historian Jonathan Crary suggested, that "we [are] seeing the emergence of a world where visual images, now millions of bits of information, will no longer have reference to an observer in a 'real' optically perceived world."[14] In complete contrast, the "digital" has been held out as the new prime mover of our time by corporations, media companies, and transparency campaigners and hackers (antiestablishment activists).[15] If techno-utopians dream of egalitarian communities on the Internet, managers of corporations and states push digital technology for modernization, innovation, and surveillance. Technology is yet again the independent variable that could modernize the international regime and revitalize contemporary global capitalism. Both the dystopian and enthusiastic reactions to the digital recall the responses to older technologies such as the telegraph and the cinema. Critics saw the new technologies as devaluing the human senses and putting humans in abstract relationships. On the other hand, Walter Benjamin welcomed the arrival of cinema in the 1920s, as its techniques of shock and montage offered a new, critical relationship to technology.[16] For Benjamin, technological media disrupted categories of distance, originality, citation, and time and stable models of authenticity.

In contrast to a techno-centered approach, I want to suggest that digital media works through a *materiality*.[17] Contemporary digital media works through technological infrastructures of electricity and communication and also through cultural economies of circulation. Materiality inheres not just in specific media objects (computers, iPods, TVs) but also in the connections that are made between them. Video, initially an analog technology, played an important part in undermining the control structures of the dominant media industries in the 1980s. Populations around the world interact with the new environment of media on an everyday basis; this involves a combination of cultural transactions and economies of production and circulation. Media materiality links infrastructures, affective worlds, monetary transactions and electronic traffic, and local and regional geographies. New media increase these material connections in manifold ways, producing constant innovations and also challenging efforts to manage them. Like never before, this constellation has brought expanded media infrastructures to the non-Western world.

Piracy is a component of this global media materiality; it combines economy, culture, and the "recombination" of the digital in a dynamic process. It resides in the material circuits of the digital and the techno-cultural infrastructures that are integral to it. Both the strengths and vulnerabilities of the digital are mobilized by media piracy.

The Twentieth-Century Analog Apparatus: Hollywood on a World Scale

It is now a truism that twentieth-century media modernity was dominated by the power of cinema; Hollywood has been the most powerful international cultural force of our recent times. In the strategies of Hollywood, we can discern the paradigmatic link between the rise of US cultural power, the global control regime for media, and structures of cultural production.

Early cinema in the 1900s was dominated by French and European producers who had pioneered the technology of celluloid. By the outbreak of World War I in 1914, European exports dominated US film exhibition. US companies soon fought back by deploying intellectual property rules and lobbying for limits on foreign entry into the US market. With the transformation of film into intellectual property,[18] US firms began to dominate film-stock production and the motion-picture business itself. The emergence of the film-studio system in the United States paved the way for a powerful industrial form, which connected production, global distribution, and lobbying within Congress for Hollywood majors. The devastation of European film industries during World War I placed the United States in a powerful position to leverage a hegemonic position in the film industry.[19] The shift from the 1900–14 period was dramatic. As the authors of a recent book on Hollywood's global expansion point out, "Between 1915 and 1916, US exports rose from 36 million feet to 159 million feet, while imports fell from 16 million feet before the First World War to 7 million by the mid-1920s."[20] The Hollywood presence expanded rapidly in Latin America, Europe, and Asia, with studios buying out local distributors, and foreign-language versions of US films expanded the reach of the industry. With the arrival of sound, the silent era in cinema came to an end. The Hollywood studios were able to mount lavish production sets, initiate a star system, and develop film genres such as biopics, Westerns, musicals, and comedies.[21] This was Hollywood's "Golden Age," which produced the dream worlds of cinema that made it irresistible the world over, from Europe to India. Victoria de Grazia places Hollywood's success within a wider context of Americanism in European culture, where US modernity became attractive to mass publics drawn to dream worlds of consumption and technological power.[22] This model was successful from the 1930s onward, as European studios such as the German UFA struggled to hold their ground against the increasing popularity of US cinema. After the European devastation in World War II and the postwar expansion under US hegemony, Hollywood spread its wings further. Hollywood's power over European markets was supreme, something that was also apparent in Latin America and many parts of Asia and Africa.

In the context of US hegemony on a world scale, Hollywood's cultural power was attacked by Third World intellectuals and European cultural elites for much of the 1970s. Theories of cultural imperialism were part of public discourse in many countries. Hollywood's cultural script and the link to US power was addressed by many institutions, such as UNESCO, in the 1970s.[23] Despite all the attacks by critics and radicals, the power of US media industries on a world scale seemed unassailable for the first three decades after World War II. If Hollywood dominated content, near total control over film stock and processing underlined US hegemony over all cultural production; US corporations also ran film exhibition chains worldwide. US media industries, represented by their powerful Motion Picture Association of America (MPAA), were able to lobby and leverage lucrative deals with relative ease, despite periodic local opposition in many countries and criticisms of Hollywood's "cultural imperialism."

US power was also an analog media empire. This was not inherent to the technology but an expression of its 1930s historical form. Early analog cinema had a more open-ended ownership pattern; it also allowed a range of audience interventions.[24] By the 1930s, however, analog technological models were embedded in large socioeconomic structures of accumulation in the West, which controlled production and distribution. Mid-twentieth-century analog structures prevented easy reproduction and required significant infrastructures of production and distribution: film stock, processing, television studios, large investment in telecommunication cables, film theaters. US studios imagined a mass audience referenced by streamlined film genres and dependent on culture industries for content. This combination of the analog empire with commodification and mass culture led Guy Debord in his famous polemic in 1968 to posit the existence of a "society of spectacle." Conjuring the vision of a once-unmediated life, Debord said that the everyday has become a "mere accumulation of spectacles." Detached from life, images become autonomous, producing a reality that is but pseudo-real. For Debord, the society of spectacle was the reigning image of a paralyzed memory and of a paralyzed history.[25] This argument echoed a running theme in twentieth-century modernity discussed earlier, that is, the destruction of authentic human experience by technology.[26] Debord's innovation was to combine this older thematic with a radical theory of postwar capitalism and mass consumption. Debord's essay took on cult status in the political atmosphere of the 1970s and was read by many people as a response to global Americanism. In the society of the spectacle, mediation was necessarily filtered through the media-industrial structure of US hegemony. Debord's fundamental flaw was to confine all representation to this status, holding out the avant-garde and counterculture as the only possible alternatives to the analog model. Paradoxically, at the very moment that Debord's *Society of the Spectacle* was pronouncing the seamless image-capital combination in the analog empire, that very empire was showing significant strains.

Video and the Analog Empire

Hollywood's global regime of content drew sustenance from US power in the global system. US hegemony suffered a significant setback after its military defeat in Vietnam and the collapse of the Bretton Woods system—a process of secular decline that unfolded for the next three decades. The global crisis of 1968–73 accelerated the rise of newly industrialized countries (NICs) and East Asia, as production structures shifted from the core countries of historical capitalism to new areas of stable accumulation.[27] This radical transformation of the world's economic geography and production structures fundamentally undermined the cultural-industrial structure I have called the analog empire and the hegemony of US media industries. The first sign of this decline was the introduction of the home VHS player and video cassettes in the late 1970s, which set in motion many of the unstable media geographies of the digital age. This was a geography where media flowed with indifference to authorized places of production and distribution. New sites and connections emerged across regions and in transnational circuits. Video expanded globally, disrupting the stable exhibition and distribution system that Hollywood had set up in the preceding few decades. Exhibitors, cinema houses, and national control were destabilized as millions of people all over the world flocked to the VHS experience: in private homes, in pirate video halls, and in video clubs that evaded the copyright and censorship regimes. Nowhere was this clearer than in the societies of Asia, Africa, and Latin America, usually on the periphery of the capitalist world system.

Writing in the Australian media journal *Continuum* in the early 1990s, Tom O'Regan mapped out the three global sites of video: the VCR as part of the personalized home-entertainment market of the West; the semiunderground TV service in eastern Europe and the postcolonial world where national monopolies controlled television content; and a third hybrid that was part pay service and part alternative TV, as in the Persian Gulf.[28] Piracy was identified as a major force all over the world, with lesser effects in the West, where major studios initially moved to control distribution chains and video outlets.[29] In the event, the VCR disturbed national sovereignty and media monopolies, more so in the non-Western world. In the long run, O'Regan forecast accurately that video would provide lucrative markets for media industries with distribution, control, and even more integration of media industries.[30] In the non-Western world, the 1980s saw video as a mode of *disassembly*—of space and of audiences—as if foreshadowing the digital era. Research from Mexico, Nigeria, and India shows parallel but diverse processes underway after the arrival of the video recorder.

In Mexico, Néstor García Canclini reported that video clubs played a significant role in disrupting the older cultural citizenship that had emerged in post–World War II Mexican society.[31] In a report tinged with nostalgia for a disappearing age of the old cinema hall, Canclini suggested that video took place in a "present without memory."[32] The integrity of the cinematic release was dissipated in a flood of video releases, a seemingly endless mediatized present. Old arrangements of genre were ignored in video clubs, as was information about directors, in favor of a culture of the instant. "Immediacy and the value of the instantaneous are reflected in what young videophiles seek. The numbers of images that succeed each other by fractions of a second are the beginning of a challenge to time that does not correspond to time."[33]

In India, the early years of video saw viewers engage in a similar play against time: the rush for the latest movie, to beat the circuits of distribution, even obtaining a film before the official release. This limitless desire became a significant part of the pirate assemblage, mutating into networks that spanned global and regional temporal zones. The video explosion stood out in Indian media history for the rapidity of its expansion. Booming makeshift video theaters and thriving cassette libraries sprang up in small towns and villages all over the country. Showing the latest releases from Hindi and regional cinema, as well as a reasonable selection of pornography, video drew people from all walks of life—youth, working people, businessmen, women, and children. Libraries and theaters sourced the latest movies from an international circuit almost immediately, bypassing local laws and film-industry prohibitions. The films were then distributed through low-cost VHS cassettes in local video libraries and makeshift theaters. New, parallel infrastructures of distribution arose rapidly—cable networks, video libraries, and small theaters. A rapid expansion of the media public was underway, while older cinema theaters and exhibition spaces declined. Drawing from a growing infrastructure of small enterprise and an emerging class of entrepreneurs, video let loose a series of conflicts around piracy, between large and small companies, between pirates and copyright-enforcement detectives, and between large and small pirates.[34]

If the Mexican researchers had perceived the emergence of video as disturbing national cultural citizenship, reports from Nigeria underlined a more democratic proliferation of video culture:

Video rental clubs rent [pirated] videos for a very modest [price]; such businesses at the lower end are very informal affairs, run out of someone's room in a compound with no signboard to advertise their presence. There are also one-room video parlors, equipped with ordinary televisions and VCRs, which cater at low prices to a poorer clientele. Cassettes are sold out of modest shops and stalls on the street very much a part of the ubiquitous West African petty trading. Traders and market women are said to be major consumers of video films.[35]

Internationally, video blurred the strict divisions between the consumer and the producer of media content. As millions began using video recorders to tape home video, the US film industry recognized that this constituted a significant blow to its content monopoly and decided to pursue legal action. The most celebrated case in the 1970s was that of *Sony Corporation of America v. Universal City Studios*,[36] in which the media industry claimed "that a contributor infringement" had occurred in the taping of television shows by private individuals. The media industry sought to impose liabilities on Sony and makers of VCRs. In a case that went all the way to the US Supreme Court, the final judgment held that home taping, "time shifting" of programs, and private video libraries fell under the category of "non-infringing fair-use" and were not illegal. The importance of this event was twofold. It exposed a new, emerging media public of user-producers, and it highlighted the conflict around intellectual property law for immaterial works such as video media.

Copyright, Piracy, and the Unmaking of the Analog Empire

Copyright's own pasts are deeply contradictory—the current regime has emerged out of conflicts between authors, publishers, corporations, states, and legal philosophies and statutes. The broad legal consensus is that the "origins" of copyright can be traced back to the Statute of Anne in England in 1710. That statute ended the system of royal privileges and print monopolies that had developed in Europe in the early modern period. In the last few decades of the seventeenth century, this system of monopolies was largely held by the Stationers Company, a printer's guild, which combined monopoly with censorship of prohibited works.[37] By the early eighteenth century, this monopoly was under attack, and the 1710 act removed printed monopolies in the name of "authors," who were now granted rights over their work for a total period not exceeding twenty-eight years.[38] To be sure, "authors'" rights in a growing capitalist society meant that writers typically assigned their rights to publishers; at best, the statute tried to balance private monopoly with a rough notion of public purpose.[39] Thus, overall, copyright doctrine since the Statute of Anne has seen the confused and conflictual coming together of three streams:

1. The Anglo-American utilitarian legal model that modified the Lockean theory[40] of property into a system of incentives for cultural goods, setting up statutory limits on eternal property rights in print and other media to help authors and creators to contribute to "public good." This economic concept allowed early modern states to give limited protection to authors and inventors, as the United States did in its Constitution, for the progress of "the science and the useful arts" (Article I, section 8). The federal Copyright Act of 1790 went further, opening the door for the piracy of materials of non-US origin: "Nothing in this act shall be construed to extend to prohibit the importation or vending, reprinting, or publishing within the United States, of any map, chart, book or books, written, printed, or published by any person not a citizen of the United States, in foreign parts without the jurisdiction of the United States."[41]

2. The idea of the moral rights of the author, drawing from German idealist and expressivist traditions in which the idea of copyright is an expression of the personality of the author. The collusion between the idea of literary property that drew from Anglo-American utilitarianism and a nineteenth-century Romantic notion of creative authorship[42] played a significant role in the rhetorical discourse around copyright law, if not its substance.[43]

3. The concept of an abstract authored work, which laid the grounds for immaterial control and exploitation irrespective of the media (print, music, image, etc.). This was summarized in the Berne Convention of 1886, which opened the contemporary discourse on

copyright doctrine. The Berne Convention was revised many times to accommodate the spread of newer media such as photography and cinema. Abstract authorship, perfected under the TRIPS agreement of the WTO in 1994, has now moved firmly into the global arena, with copyright and patent compliance becoming the legal requirement for membership in the world economy.

For over a century, the United States refused to sign the Berne Convention of 1884. All this changed in the 1990s with the rise of the information industries. In 1998, the industry-friendly Sonny Bono Copyright Extension Act and the Digital Millennium Copyright Act were passed, ushering in a new era of international enforcement and zero tolerance for any deviation, including piracy.[44] Thus, the post-WTO era has seen a new discourse of globalization emerging worldwide. Intergovernmental organizations have joined advocacy and enforcement organizations for the US and regional media industries in the campaign against "piracy" and the push for "compliance." The best known organization is the International Intellectual Property Alliance (IIPA), formed in 1984 to represent the US copyright-based industries.[45] The IIPA's members include all the major US media industries, the Association of American Publishers (AAP), the Business Software Alliance (BSA), the Entertainment Software Association (ESA), the Independent Film and Television Alliance (IFTA), the Motion Picture Association of America (MPAA or MPA), the National Music Publishers' Association (NMPA), and the Recording Industry Association of America (RIAA). Of these, the MPAA, the BSA, and the RIAA have been the most active in the international campaign against piracy, lobbying national governments, conducting workshops for police and judges, and leading punitive raids against "pirates." For its part, the IIPA issues periodic country reports that detail its version of compliance with the international legal copyright regime; the reports also recommend to the US trade representative (USTR) that various countries be placed on "priority watch lists" for alleged noncompliance.[46] For 2007, the US trade representative put Argentina, Chile, Egypt, India, Israel, Lebanon, China, Russia, Thailand, Turkey, Ukraine, and Venezuela on the priority watch list.[47] The IIPA, the MPA, and the BSA have all been active worldwide, with local offices and advocacy initiatives with local police and the local media and information industries.

The spread of media technologies in the postdigital era has vastly expanded the potential scope of the copyright regime and the ambitions of international media industries. The Sony case was a turning point in this respect. Since the 1980s, and particularly after the early 1990s, US media industries have shifted to designating defense of intellectual property in knowledge industries as one of the key markers of global control. Since production outlets of hardware were gradually shifted to East Asia, control over the more "immaterial" elements of media (i.e., elements that are not "tangible" objects) has been central to media industries. These elements include knowledge industries such as software, design, and information. Knowledge is now central to the dramaturgy of global trade wars and antipiracy campaigns.

Global media industries have been on the offensive since the 1990s, hammering away at legislators, courts, and national governments to widen the scope of copyright protection. The campaign has also been aimed at limiting that bundle of public-access rights known as "fair use." Fair-use doctrine emerged primarily from US case law, in which the use of copyrighted material was allowed without permission for creative purposes.[48] In theory, fair use is intended to strike a balance between private ownership of media and social use. James Boyle points out that fair use is "part of the implicit *quid pro quo* of intellectual property; we will give you this extremely valuable legal monopoly.... In return, we will design the contours of your right so as to encourage a variety of socially valuable uses."[49] The shrinking fair-use regime and the public domain in general has been the focus of the left-liberal critique of the contemporary media property regime (John Frow, James Boyle, Yochai Benkler, Laurence Lessig). Curiously, the campaign against piracy has paralleled this transformation of older notions of copyright, which left open the domain of individual use for noncommercial purposes. As legal scholar Jessica Litman points out, the campaign against piracy has incorporated domains that were perfectly legitimate under the label of fair use:

> They've succeeded in persuading a lot of people that any behavior that has the same effect as piracy must *be* piracy, and must therefore reflect the same moral turpitude we attach to piracy, even if it is the same behavior that we all called legitimate before. Worse, any behavior that *could potentially cause the same effect* as piracy, even if it doesn't, must also be piracy. Because an unauthorized, unencrypted

digital copy of something *could* be uploaded to the Internet, where it *could* be downloaded by two million people, even making the digital copy is piracy.[50]

High-speed networks of the 1990s have led to the deployment by the media industry of tracking and controlling architectures to manage piracy. These efforts combine technological fantasies of constant encryption, the mobilization of local law enforcement authorities, and advocacy for more stringent laws.

These efforts have been paralleled by some of the most draconian laws against piracy, leading to legal cases against individuals[51] and small shops and violent raids by enforcement agencies against "infringers." The discourse against piracy as both morally reprehensible and illegal is in large part produced by this campaign. A spectral zone of infringement statistics[52] and the supposed link between terrorism and piracy are retailed by the antipiracy campaign on a global scale.[53] By all accounts, the success of this campaign has been mixed. The very expansion of contemporary copyright's power has been challenged at each step—by hackers, who break every digital encryption used by the industry; by peer-to-peer networks, which dodge enforcement and provide a platform for users to share media files;[54] and most important, by hundreds of millions of ordinary buyers of pirated media, who seem not to share the media industry's vision of the world today. I want to suggest that there is more to piracy than its illegality or economic potency, its destructiveness or radical alterity.[55] This position draws from, but also departs from, Western liberal critiques of the copyright regime.

Western debates have focused on authorship and the shrinking public domain in the intellectual property regime. In critiques of the current property regime, public-domain theorists have variously mobilized the category of the information commons, the right to share and reinterpret cultural material, and a domain of creative authorship through collaborative P2P networks.[56] Piracy's absence in this debate is significant, perhaps because it fundamentally disrupts the categories of private property, capitalism, personhood, and the commons that have moved the debate in the past decade. Piracy cuts across the creative and the everyday, the legal and the illegal, the national and the transnational. By proliferating in a media ecology that spreads across the spheres of the social and the media,[57] piracy has evaded the conventional models of control and expulsion used by early opponents of print technology.

The Postanalog World

In the first decade after the emergence of the digital era, the focus was on emerging media-industry monopolies that were leveraging to take advantage of the new constellation. With the example of the AOL–Time Warner merger in the 1990s and the rise of software giants such as Microsoft, many observers argued that the digital epoch changed little; it provided the US media industry a greater opportunity to make new profits and reconsolidate its control on the newer platforms. Media centralization in the West and the digital divide in the South constituted the overarching discourse of the 1990s.[58] This seemed almost obvious at that time: DVDs and online platforms provided huge profits to US media companies, and Microsoft's power seemed unassailable. A decade later, the AOL–Time Warner merger is now a business disaster,[59] Microsoft is facing aggressive competition from competitors using open-source platforms, and low-cost electronic infrastructures in the South have come from China, not California. Many initial West-centered reactions after the 1990s tended to elide significant material transformations on a world scale, many of which are now coming into view today. These include the shift of many production structures to Asia and the emergence of new networks of circulation that bypass those of property and capital. These changes are particularly powerful in zones outside the West. This changed geography allows us to reflect on the problematic of power and management in a postdigital world.

The vast expansion of the production of world media commodities to Asia in the past two decades and the turbulence of the speculative economies of the 1990s that drew millions into the cycle of money, consumption, and mediatization both offer images of a transformed world. Media goods are produced in China and East Asia, and low-cost technological infrastructure (cameras, VCRs, mobile phones, microprocessors, and computer hardware) has spread to the periphery of capital (Africa, Asia, Latin America) through circuits ranging from the bazaar to pirate networks. Older models of control have melted away, as significant urban populations (including the poor) now access low-cost, even used techno-logical infrastructure in the digital era. In the past, such infrastructures were more vulnerable to incorporation by the state or large capital. Since the 1980s, these networks have often taken on a life of their own, refusing to follow the mandates of legal accumulation.

The digital age is part of a larger destabilization of the media form beginning with video in the 1980s. Since then, more often than not, contemporary media has emerged as a bad object, materializing itself in unstable assemblages that do not fit conventional accounts of media and modernity. Media piracy is an important part of this new arrangement between the old zone of the social and the mediatized worlds, and it offers us interesting insights into the current crisis.

Piracy works through digital and mechanical reproduction, but it takes on a life of its own. The most visible traffic of piracy is through P2P online networks, connecting all those who have good Internet access. P2P data was the largest form of Internet traffic in 2010, an indication of the scale of online media piracy today.[60] In Asia, Africa, and Latin America, piracy has also became a larger mode of replication for low-cost urban technological infrastructure. The world of piracy involves not just immaterial media goods of all kinds (software, movies, music) but also most mass-market commodities, ranging from counterfeits to the "unbranded," the "greymarket," or the local commodity. Piracy is not a form of resistance, though it clearly offers creative solutions outside the property regime to subaltern populations.[61]

Contemporary media piracy's space-disrupting techniques recall comparable practices of early cinema in the analog age. Jane Gaines writes in her work on copying in early cinema, "Copying literally followed the first logic of the motion picture apparatus itself, which is, 'to produce is to reproduce.' Stories crossed national boundaries shipped in cans, duplica-tion factories were hooked up to the beginnings of distribution routes, only barely imagined as the global networks they would become."[62] This was a world that soon came to an end with the rise of the Hollywood studio system and US global hegemony. In the digital age, dispersal of production centers, global communication networks, and the decline of the United States have ensured that the current moment will not go the way of early cinema.

Conclusion: Media Piracy and the Global System

Media piracy after the end of the twentieth century illuminates two inter-related features of the current global system. First, the world is increasingly embedded in a media ecology that is fairly fundamental to our daily lives. We are all media practitioners in some way now, when we write, photograph, share, and reproduce on a daily basis. There are crucial variations and inequalities on a world scale, including differing infrastructures, from low-cost phones in poorer parts of Africa and Asia to permanent online connectivity in other areas. The current global regime was not designed to acknowledge this media ecology or the vast world of new knowledge production that has emerged today. States are more dependent than ever before on information systems and digital media for economic modernization and war; this also renders them vulnerable on a daily basis. The vast security apparatus cannot protect constant "leaks" in the system, which seems to be a feature everywhere. These leaks can come from anyone: personal digital images taken by jailers and soldiers, Facebook updates posted by government officers, or vast daily sets copied and shared by dissident soldiers, as in the recent WikiLeaks case. In technologized populations, endless circulation is the engine of the contemporary world. Piracy is a crucial component of this media ecology, and its mass following is puzzling only to those who fail to recognize that we are in the midst of a constitutive shift in the terms of the contemporary world.

The second contribution of media piracy has been its attention to the inequities of the global knowledge system, ruled by an intellectual property regime that is more restrictive every day. Limits on fair use of digital material in every form, criminalization of the sharing of personal media in digital forms, and rights management are all expressions of a media industry that wants to profit from the new media ecology at all levels and to filter all forms of media exchange through property.[63] The big problem for the US media industry, apart from the high levels of piracy, is that the United States' power in the world economy is on a secular decline and the current knowledge regime lacks a long-term guarantor. The criticisms of the current intellectual property regime have been growing worldwide for some time,[64] and the occasion is just right for a thoroughgoing reappraisal.

The conceptual move may be more fundamental. The nineteenth century saw powerful theoretical moves in the human sciences to stabilize global modernity. Interpretive frameworks for the management of populations conceptually differentiated humans from machines, natural science from culture, leisure from work. For most purposes, this architecture of the social has persisted, with various updates in the past hundred years. Today's media ecology illuminates the limits of this framework; nineteenth-century separations are routinely violated by both states and populations worldwide. Bruno Latour, the well-known philosopher of science, has been calling for the "reassembling" of the nineteenth-century model; this is a good time to heed his call.[65]

CHAPTER 9

From Full to Selective Secrecy:
The Offshore Realm after the Crisis

Vadim Volkov

"Secrecy secures, so to speak, the possibility of a second world along-side of the obvious world, and the latter is most strenuously affected by the former," wrote the sociologist Georg Simmel in a 1906 essay.[1] The shifting of boundaries between what is concealed and what is revealed shapes human history, he suggested. "The historical development of society is in many respects characterized by the fact that what was formerly public passes under the protection of secrecy, and that, on the contrary, what was formerly secret ceases to require such protection and proclaims itself."[2] When people seek to secure what they value, they tend to conceal it. Secrecy is a synonym of security. Social and economic life, then, involves multiple methods and practices of restricting access to whatever is regarded personally valuable or strategically significant by individuals and communities.

In modern times, secrecy has become institutionalized. States manage secrecy relating to their operations and at the same time seek information about their citizens as well as about other states. Investments in secrecy regimes and intelligence are huge. Inasmuch as states claim monopoly of violence and taxation, they also tend to monopolize both the right to secrecy and the right to knowledge. People outside the state apparatus, in turn, are endlessly inventive in protecting their private space and valuables through restricting the state's access to them. The asymmetry game goes on, and Simmel may be right in observing that when boundaries of secrecy shift, the world changes.

Some states specialize in producing heightened secrecy as a special service. Banking secrecy and protection of account holders' names is legally guaranteed in certain jurisdictions. Together with very low or zero taxes, this protection creates what are known as tax havens and offshore financial centers, which since the 1980s have become the key nodal points of financial ex-territorial capitalism. As soon as the financial crisis struck in 2008, the legitimacy of this secret realm began to be questioned at the highest levels by governments of developed countries. Territorial states seek to restrict the secrecy of tax havens and to extend regulation to offshore financial centers in order to avoid financial crises in the future. How far can the attack on the offshore sector go? If, as some scholars have argued, the offshore sector is a structural element of contemporary transnational capitalism, then the elimination of secrecy can potentially change its basic architecture. Are governments prepared to go that far? And even if they are, do they have the capacity to implement such a change?

This chapter rests on the premise that the issue of the offshore sector of the world economy is a central one in formulating the postcrisis policy agenda and is also indicative of the degree of determination to pursue real changes. The chapter looks into the origins and driving forces behind the rise of the offshore sector, its scale as well as its interpretations within two opposing ideological frameworks, neoliberalism and social justice. It argues that the two ideologies represent two conflicting models of capitalism, one that is attached to a territory and its resources and an ex-territorial one. A key feature of ex-territorial capitalism as represented by the offshore sector is the production and marketing of low-cost legal entities protected by heightened secrecy. These entities serve as vehicles of global commerce outside state regulation and as instruments for dissociating finance from territorial assets. The effort by governments of the world's leading countries to eliminate the secrecy regime have so far caused minor changes, leading to the establishment of a regime of selective secrecy that benefits privileged OECD countries with strong fiscal services while making no difference for the rest.

Conceptions of the Offshore

During the first thirty years of the twentieth century, personal income and corporate taxes as well as numerous new regulations were introduced on both sides of the Atlantic. The United States went through the Progressive era, the period of trust busting, and the New Deal, all of which contributed to the strengthening of federal authority. Under the pressure of working-class movements and mutual military threats, European states further increased their extractive and redistributive capacities. European fascism demonstrated the weakness of owners of capital vis-à-vis the state, while the Soviet experiment conveyed the idea that development could proceed without them and could be directed by the state alone. The vulnerability of individual and corporate wealth within national boundaries drove a strong impulse to search for asset-protection mechanisms.

Several small states that remained on the periphery of the new global conflicts and developmental experiments invented business models whereby the demand for private-asset protection could be commercialized. In the 1930s, Switzerland turned asset protection and tax evasion into a national business model. Instead of living off taxation, as did other territorial states, it preferred to sell secrecy and legal entities to nonresidents, earning income from servicing accounts and transactions. The secrecy regime, introduced in Switzerland in 1934, protected all information about any accounts, including those of noncitizens, and made any disclosures subject to criminal charges. The laws dissociating legal incorporation from physical activity (residence) allowed private businesses to move company registrars and accounts to Swiss cantons while conducting their physical operations in other countries. Such laws had already been in place in the United States in Delaware and New Jersey, leading to the concentration in these states of holdings that owned companies operating in other states. For decades, these laws allowed big trusts to conceal their ownership of companies in other US states and to successfully avoid anti-monopoly regulations. The United Kingdom adopted the same principle but applied it to national rather than internal borders, allowing companies to be incorporated at home and act in other countries. According to Ronen Palan, the author of a comprehensive study of the subject, such a division of legal entities between different jurisdictions was the origin of the offshore sector.[3]

So while states intensified regulation, a number of smaller jurisdictions, such as Switzerland, Luxembourg, Lichtenstein, Monaco,
Gibraltar, and the Channel Islands, refused to move with the times, preserving the laws from the previous laissez-faire era. They boasted their
unique status and history, commercializing their oddity. The Bahamas,
which adopted English 1866 corporate laws, became the haven for
American capital unwilling to accept Roosevelt's New Deal and the
income sharing that it implied.

In the mid-1960s, the Western world took another left turn. In
1964, Labour came to power in the United Kingdom with plans to
increase taxes and nationalize large segments of the economy. Student
protests following 1968 promised to spark a revolution across Europe,
and labor and civil rights movements in the 1970s urged the US government to increase taxes and adopt welfare-state policies. In response to
these developments, a group of lawyers set up new offshore havens in
the Caribbean basin islands, notably the Cayman Islands and the British
Virgin Islands.[4] This came together with the invention of new convenient
legal shells, such as tax-exempt trusts and the International Business
Company (IBC), which provided sufficient protection at low costs and
offered wide opportunities for international trade and investment. The
neoconservative restoration of the 1980s allowed the multiplication of
offshore havens that emulated successful British jurisdictions. By virtue
of having tax treaties with major havens and offering a wide range of
financial services to potential clients, London became the main gateway
to the offshore world; Amsterdam (linked to the Netherlands Antilles)
followed suit. The Caribbean region was the primary beneficiary of the
second wave of growth of the offshore sector, which became the substitute
for the more traditional banana industry in a number of countries, such as
Dominica and the Windward Islands. By 1999, the Caribbean segment
of the offshore sector commanded over one-third of the US\$5–6–trillion
global offshore-services sector.[5]

The third wave of growth of the offshore sector was driven by the
need to harbor finances of former socialist enterprises and to secure privatized assets after the collapse of state socialism and the disintegration of
the Soviet Union. Political instability and weak but arbitrary states represented the familiar set of incentives for using offshore havens. The emerging Russian oligarchs had only to apply the already widely established

schemes to move offshore the finances of Russian enterprises that were involved in transnational business. Unstable ownership and recurrent redistributions of assets made offshore jurisdictions indispensable participants in frequent and often hostile mergers and acquisitions in Russia and the former Soviet satellites. The rise of Cyprus to global offshore status owed to the double-taxation treaty that it concluded with Russia in 2001, after which it became the major supplier of accounts and legal shells for Russians who previously wired profits out of the country and then back in, but as foreign direct investments. Cyprus continuously occupies first place on the list of sources of foreign investments in the Russian economy. In a similar vein, the Chinese elite began to use the offshore sector, in particular Macao, for covert privatization of assets, despite its declared commitment to socialism.[6] The financial deregulation of the 1990s technically facilitated international financial flows, while the neoliberal hegemony, with its contempt for the nation-state, helped to legitimate the use of offshore financial centers by transnational companies.

Ideology

The interdependency between the policies of nation-states and the use of offshore havens by owners of capital has long been conceptualized in two opposing and somewhat symmetrical fashions. Not surprisingly, the use of offshore tax havens is endorsed within the liberal economic framework and is treated critically from the standpoint of social responsibility and justice.

The liberal vision of the offshore sector associates it with just competition and market efficiency. In a widely cited passage, Milton Friedman states, "Competition among national governments in the public services they provide and in the taxes they impose is every bit as productive as competition among individuals or enterprises in the goods and services they offer for sale and the prices at which they offer them."[7] According to the liberal argument, small states that do not have the physical resources and populations available to large territorial states simply invented a competitive advantage in the form of friendly regulation and efficient legal services that draw companies to register firms and open accounts in their jurisdictions. As with any other free competition, tax competition enables better allocation of resources; it pushes governments toward greater efficiency and puts limits on arbitrary taxation. In response to the G20 attack on offshore havens, the Cato Institute's senior fellow Daniel Mitchell widely publicized the liberal arguments, claiming, for instance, that the existence of offshore havens has led to the reduction of average income tax by 25 percent since the 1980s. "So-called offshore financial centers have contributed to this wave of economic liberalization. By providing tax-efficient platforms for global commerce, they enable investors and entrepreneurs to allocate capital in ways that boost economic growth. And, because of cross-border competition, they encourage so-called onshore jurisdictions to implement—or maintain—reasonable tax and regulatory policies."[8]

The welfare-state view, championed by the OECD Global Tax Justice Network and Financial Action Task Force (FATF), focuses on the adverse side of the offshore sector. The jurisdictional competition is unfair because it privileges large global companies over small and medium ones and owners of movable financial assets over those who own stationary ones because in both instances the latter have to bear the full burden of taxation. Offshore havens undermine democracy, so the argument goes, by helping rich individuals to avoid their social responsibility vis-à-vis territories and their populations. The secrecy regime undermines efforts by national law enforcement, allows money laundering, and helps to sustain global organized crime.[9] In this perspective, the offshore sector is an equivalent of the shadow economy for large transnational businesses. According to the conventional understanding of the shadow economy, it emerges and expands when taxes become too high and entrepreneurs respond by distorting financial information regarding their business or by avoiding formal registration altogether. The shadow economy, then, is the result not so much of companies' absolute growth but of changes in the legal status and accounting practice of companies responding to the regulatory policy of the state.

The development of offshore havens made the classic shadow economy look anachronistic. The offshore sector allows residents of one jurisdiction to conduct business operations behind the façade of foreign companies and to avoid being identified. As these companies are registered as subsidiaries of other companies registered in ostensibly respectable places, such as London or Amsterdam, parts of national economies are now safely placed outside national boundaries and protected by special jurisdictions, some of which are independent political units, and some, dependencies of other states. Now operations and incomes of the same business enterprise can be divided between different legal entities and between different jurisdictions for accounting purposes. In effect, the distribution of economic activities between different legal entities means deciding which parts of profits to show and which to hide, depending on the national tax regime. One problem of the classic shadow economy is that its scale is limited by the size of social networks, because participants cannot use formal laws and have to rely on informal contracting and personal relations. The invention of the offshore sector resolved this problem by supplying sophisticated legal environments compatible with legal systems of several countries. It is thus the large business that gets the biggest advantage from the offshore sector, as it can fully utilize the advantages of flexibility and scale of transactions. Unlike the shadow economy, which expands when taxes and restrictions intensify and shrinks when they decrease, the offshore sector does not react in the same way to global waves of regulation and liberalization. It tends to benefit from both, capitalizing on the growing demand for safe havens during welfare turns, as in the 1930s and '70s, and increasing international financial mobility and investment during periods of conservative liberalizations, as from the 1980s on.

The Size of the Offshore Economy

Attempts to define and measure the offshore economy have been made since the 1970s. According to the IMF review that summarizes these attempts, the offshore financial centers (OFCs), as they are routinely called, share three key features: (1) a primary orientation of business toward nonresidents, (2) a favorable regulatory environment (low supervisory requirements and minimal information disclosure), and (3) the low- or zero-taxation schemes.[10] The IMF operational definition that sets an OFC apart from other countries rests on the idea that their essential feature is the export of financial services.[11] Therefore, the key indicator is the ratio of net exports of financial services to GDP, which, the IMF established, is extraordinarily high for twenty-three countries.[12]

Besides numerous financial centers and corporate registers, there are other offshore varieties. They include flags of convenience that specialize in low-cost maritime registration, among which the leaders are Panama and Liberia; special export-processing zones with relaxed custom duties, such as Mexico, Puerto Rico, Taiwan, and Hong Kong; offshore insurance centers, such as Bahrain, the Isle of Man, and Bermuda; centers of e-commerce; offshore casinos; and even specialized telephone sex centers.[13]

There is no shortage of numeric estimates of wealth "hidden" in the murky domain. They are, understandably, rough; otherwise the offshore sector would not fulfill its major promise. In 1998, Meryl Lynch/Cap Gemini's World Wealth report estimated that one-third of the wealth of the world's high-net-worth individuals (HNWIs) was held offshore. This share was about the same in 2003, equaling US$8.5 trillion. In 2000, the IMF estimated the amount of cross-border asset transactions involving tax havens at US$5.1 trillion, or 52.7 percent of all cross-border bank claims in the world. In 1994, tax havens accounted for only 1.2 percent of world population and 3 percent of world GDP, but they already accounted for 26 percent of the assets and 31 percent of the profits of American multinationals.[14] Now their share of the world's population has dwindled to 0.49 percent, while the share of wealth remains about the same. Summarizing different sources, the Tax Justice Network gave the following estimates for 2005: Approximately US$11.5 trillion of assets are held offshore by HNWIs; the annual income that these assets might earn amounts to US$860 billion annually; and the tax not paid as a result of these funds being held offshore might exceed US$255 billion each year. About half the wealth of Latin America, over 40 percent of the wealth of the countries in Asia and the Middle East, and up to a quarter of European assets are supposedly held offshore.[15]

The Onshore Strikes Back

The dissolution of the neoliberal hegemony, that is, the weakening of the authority of ideas of free trade and deregulation, has left the offshore sector less protected against the world's leading states as they have faced increasing budget deficits and have avariciously looked for additional sources of tax revenue. According to the OECD, the amount of unpaid taxes from incomes generated offshore equals US$250 billion annually.

The argument that the very existence of the offshore sector was closely linked to the financial crisis strengthened the determination to revise regulation policies. According to Germany's finance minister Peer Steinbrueck, "Tax havens are also places where unregulated financial market deals are made."[16] Former Malaysian prime minister Mahathir Mohamad later made a more specific claim, linking the activity of off-shore hedge funds referred to as "leveraging" with global financial insta-bility. Hedge funds borrowed money from banks in amounts twenty to thirty times higher than their own assets in order to buy and sell large numbers of shares so that their market price would be affected and the clients of hedge funds could make more money. "The investments by the hedge funds and their leveraging (borrowings) are mysterious. It seems that they need not report to the Government on their activities. Besides, by operating from offshore tax-free havens, they needed to submit reports to no one. Investors in hedge funds were thus able to make huge profits."[17] The fact that offshore financial centers also spe-cialize in the creation and promotion of derivatives and other high-risk financial instruments directly linked this realm in the minds of its critics to the moving springs of the 2008–10 financial crisis. Hedge funds are almost entirely an offshore phenomenon—79 percent of all hedge funds are registered in the Caribbean islands, of which 67 percent are in the Cayman Islands.

The Tax Justice Network analysts summarized the role of offshore havens in conditioning the financial crisis: "A key feature of the crisis is that the financial system became frozen as a result of mutual mistrust and impenetrable complexity making it impossible for actors to understand the financial positions of their partners. The secrecy jurisdictions, by giv-ing companies incentives to festoon their financial affairs across multiple jurisdictions, and by covering these affairs in a veil of secrecy, played a major part."[18]

In the United States, Barack Obama has campaigned against offshores since 2007, when he sponsored, together with Senator Carl Levin, a Stop Tax Haven Abuse Act that grants the Treasury Department authority to take special measures against foreign jurisdictions and finan-cial institutions impeding US tax enforcement. Back then, the act did not enjoy much legislative support. In 2009, however, after the financial crisis struck and Obama was elected to the presidency, Levin put it forward again, hoping to turn it into law. At the same time, the US Justice Department struck at the heart of Swiss private banking, accusing UBS Bank of helping US citizens to avoid taxes and demanding access to information on fifty thousand US clients. The bank agreed to pay US$780 million and name some of its clients to resolve the criminal fraud charges against it.[19]

At the April 2009 G20 summit in London, governments of the world's leading states turned attention to offshore tax havens and financial centers. Backed by the collective authority of the OECD, France and Germany led the assault. This time, even the United Kingdom and the United States, two countries that have long been intimately linked to the offshore web, could not help but join the choir. "The era of banking secrecy is over," stated the joint communiqué.[20] The G20 leaders agreed to take action against noncooperative jurisdictions. The ground for that action had already been prepared by the OECD Global Forum on Transparency and Exchange of Information, which, since 2000, had worked to compel eighty-four countries and, especially, secret-protected offshore jurisdictions to sign bilateral treaties or at least to commit to standards of transparency and exchange of information. Both the OECD and the FATF used the method of blacklisting, threatening government sanctions. By 2008, many countries had chosen to sign agreements, while some had only expressed official commitment; but eleven notoriously secretive jurisdictions—Andorra, Switzerland, Monaco, Jersey, Guernsey, the Marshall Islands, Costa Rica, Belgium, Luxembourg, Singapore, and Macao—refused to cooperate. The financial crisis and the political pressure of the G20 governments compelled those remaining on the blacklist to change their minds. The OECD stated in its last progress report (2009) that all eighty-four countries have in one form or another agreed to implement transparency standards.[21]

Exterritorial Capitalism

The offshore sector deserves attention not just because of the amount of wealth that is hidden there from national public agencies. No less important are opportunities for transnational capital accumulation and mobility that have become the modus operandi of contemporary capitalism. For many countries, developed as well as developing, such as Brazil, Russia, India, and China, the offshore financial centers have become the major sources of investments, at least de jure, and this fact may compel governments to treat them with caution. Vital though not immediately apprehensible is the offshore sector's function of creating and reproducing the structuring distinctions that constitute the present-day economic system, such as the distinction between how much profit is made and how much profit is shown, between physical assets and their legal shells. The onshore and the offshore sectors correspond to territorial and exterritorial capitalism.

Thinking of the possible futures of the offshore sector, one should therefore look beyond the immediate interests of national governments in repairing their tax base and even beyond the collective interests of nation-states in controlling financial risks. There is always a risk that if efforts to "tear away the offshore cloak of secrecy will continue," as Senator Levin has promised, some core mechanisms of reproduction of capitalist economies may be disrupted and governments may find it wise to back down. It is reasonable to ask whether changes in regulatory regimes, and especially those related to secrecy, will have a deep impact on the global economic system. How far can states go, and what new cleavages may emerge? Will the unveiling of the offshore sector affect the onshore economic institutions and, if so, in what directions?

The liberal view that explains and justifies the offshore sector in terms of international tax competition and the social critique that equates it with the shadow economy both capture important aspects but do not reach far enough in understanding the systemic significance of the offshore sector and its key mechanisms for contemporary global capitalism. Palan suggests that the offshore sector has been, from the very beginning, not a parallel institution that sought to undermine sovereignty but a domain integral to the capitalist dynamic. It emerged as a creative solution to the growing contradiction between the regulation of the economy confined to the territorial boundaries of nation-states and the internationalization of capitalism. Palan also invokes the nice term "commercialization of sovereignty," and one may attempt to further specify how it works and what it does.[22]

It is in the nature of our world that a state jurisdiction corresponds to a territory. First of all, states tax and regulate immovable assets that are visible and within reach of authorities. Production sites, trading facilities, and the population are the primary objects of taxation and governance. Likewise, the need to maintain the infrastructure that makes territory economically productive requires public spending and redistributive mechanisms. Hence, nation-states support territorial capitalism, where value is attached to physical units. To facilitate taxation, states have long supported monetization. Later, they invented legal entities that were both subjects with legal rights and objects of taxation. Legal entities and accounting rules became the main instruments of "seeing like a state," to use John Scott's famous phrase—that is, the means enabling states to govern their domains.[23]

As territorial states increased taxation and intensified regulation, capital invented methods of exterritorialization: leaving the territory to avoid regulation. The key principle of taxation, following from its being a monopoly, is that any entity can only be taxed once and within one jurisdictional territory. The combination of legal entities for nonresidents, tax treaties with some major onshore countries, and zero tax constitutes the toolkit of the business model of offshore jurisdictions. It is also the mechanism that turns territory into an abstraction. When this happens, two other abstractions, finance and legal entity, cease to serve the territorial state and become powerful vehicles of transnational, exterritorial capitalism.

For the offshore sector, elementary geography matters a lot. Most havens are micro- or even nanostates. A lot of them are warm tropical islands. At least twelve of about thirty major offshore havens have territory that covers less than one thousand square kilometers, and fourteen have a population of less than one million. Yet they legally hold about US$16.28 trillion, or 29 percent of the total wealth of the world's HNWIs. Offshore banks hold about US$6 trillion worth of cash deposits, which is 17 percent of all global deposits. If the IMF estimates are correct, over 50 percent of all international financial transactions go through these tiny spots on the world map. Minimum physical territory, maximum wealth is the first formula of the offshore sector.

There are a number of simple points to start from when dealing with this phenomenon. Owing to their compact size and warm climate, most offshore jurisdictions require fewer funds for territorial maintenance and policing than other jurisdictions (with exceptions such as Switzerland, Cyprus, Singapore, and a few more). This allows for the reduction of public spending to a minimum and the maintenance of a zero-taxation policy. Because they make the most of the sovereign right to make laws and capitalize on this right, territorial maintenance beyond the necessary minimum would be a net loss for them. What really matters is the sovereign right to make laws, including regarding secrecy, and the capacity to produce legal entities that follow from this right. Legal entities are then sold to "nonresidents." Once these nonresidents have acquired legal shells from an offshore jurisdiction, at home onshore, they can become foreign companies. So technically they are nowhere.

The central element of the political economy of the offshore sector is the production, marketing, and maintenance of legal entities. Many offshore havens have a special legal provision forbidding nonresidents to conduct business on their territory, so they are "export-only" regimes for legal entities. These legal entities are protected by secrecy and by the law and, in many cases, by access to British courts. But the costs of their maintenance are low, since few or no accounting reports are required and low or no taxes are paid. Unburdened by public spending but enjoying sovereignty rights and legal protection (mostly British laws and courts, since about one-third of offshore jurisdictions are British dependencies), offshore havens and financial centers benefit from exporting low-cost but well-protected legal entities in large numbers. The economies of scale in the production of legal entities and the servicing of bank accounts allow offshore havens to generate profits sufficient to waive direct taxation. The tiny principality of Lichtenstein, for instance, has about seventy-four thousand registered companies, which is twice its number of citizens. The Cayman Islands are home to 279 banks and over six hundred thousand companies.[24] President Obama cited a single building in the Cayman Islands, called Ugland House, which notionally houses eighteen thousand corporations but employs just 241 people.[25]

The large-scale production of low-cost legal entities is the main business of the offshore sector. According to my estimates, the total number of legal entities produced by offshore jurisdictions, including banks, insurance companies, and business corporations, for 2003 was 1.76 million, which is about the same as the number of registered enterprises in Germany, more than in Japan, and about half the number of enterprises

Figure 9.1: The number of enterprises registered, 2003

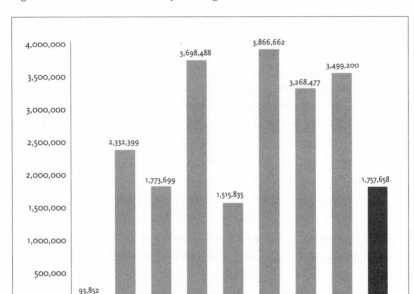

Sources: OECD, "Structural and Demographic Business Statistics (SDBS), OECD," March 2010, http://www.oecd.org/document/17/0,3343,en_2649_34233_36938705_1_1_1_1, 00.html; Bureau of International Narcotics and Law Enforcement Affairs, US Department of State, "Offshore Financial Centers: International Narcotics Control Strategy Report," March 2004, http://www.state.gov/p/inl/rls/nrcrpt/2003/vol2/html/29918.htm; and IMF, "Financial Sector Assessment Program (FSAP): FSSA Country Reports," www.imf.org/external/np/fsap/fsap.asp.

in the United States (see figure 9.1). Minimum territory, maximum legal entities is the second formula of the offshore sector.

It is true that the offshore sector helps individuals to hide their incomes from onshore taxation authorities. But the economy of the offshore sector is based less on hiding money than on providing means for dissociating finances from territories and for concentrating them in places beyond the reach of territorial governments. On-site production facilities and other stationary assets that territorial governments tax and regulate are part of international companies' production chains and, as such, cannot be dispensed with by national or transnational companies. But what can be done to avoid the regulatory power of states is separating enterprise finances from fixed assets and concentrating them in exterritorial legal shells. The financialization so evident over the past decade would have been impossible without the massive production of legal entities in jurisdictions that accumulate and reinvest enterprise finance so that these funds function autonomously from fixed assets, to which they relate through a sophisticated web of ownership.

The overproduction of legal entities underlies the overproduction of finance, and this, in turn, has become possible because of exterritorial sovereignty. So any policy aimed at tightening financial regulation is bound to take into account the offshore sector.

The Secrecy Regime: Minor Changes?

Now the leading territorial states have declared the end of banking secrecy and have displayed their determination to undermine the offshore sector. This correlates with the general ideological shift away from neoliberalism and toward a new regulation policy. At the time of the 2009 London summit, there were three policies for dealing with offshore havens on the G20 agenda. The most liberal one, advocated by the United Kingdom, was to focus on bilateral agreements between OECD and offshore jurisdictions about transparency standards and information disclosure. This is a soft measure because it foresees the provision of information on clients and their firms/accounts upon request only, and this requires justifications and adherence to complex procedures. It puts the burden of costs and investigative efforts on national regulatory authorities. A more radical solution proposed by German government experts was the automatic disclosure of information about assets and account holders. This would mean that local secrecy laws would be overridden by transparency demands by the international community. The full-transparency option would strongly reduce the degree of protection and undermine the sovereignty of offshore jurisdictions. Following the radical position of French authorities, one of the primary engines behind OECD efforts, French experts suggested going as far as compelling G20 countries to sever taxation treaties with offshore havens, which would mean, in effect, taxing nonresidents at the same rates as residents—which, for businessmen operating under offshore registration, would eliminate their advantages. This measure is especially sensitive for the United Kingdom and the Netherlands, which have double-taxation agreements with most of the developed countries, on the one hand, and with many offshore jurisdictions, on the other hand, which constitutes them as gateways to the offshore world.

In fear of the worst scenario, the offshore jurisdictions have cooperated with the OECD and have actually signed treaties on transparency standards and exchange of information. Exchange of information upon special request is the best deal that offshore jurisdictions could get given the circumstances. As the treasury and budget minister of Luxembourg noted, "banking secrecy is not incompatible with OECD standards."[26] As many offshore governments expect, the "information upon request" formula will give them time to adapt and will not lead to the elimination of secrecy since it will require OECD members to make a strong case in order to demand information disclosure with regard to particular clients.

The new emerging regime is that of selective secrecy. It is selective in a twofold sense. First, only selected companies and individuals may be disclosed on the grounds of suspected wrongdoing. Second, this regime will be limited to the OECD. This means that other countries, notably BRIC and developing countries, the biggest net losers of taxes and capital, will still face the same problems that motivated the OECD to take action. While OECD countries have improved their position, for nonmembers, things have stayed largely the same. In terms of the global economic order, the change is minor. Once the G20 countries come up with new standards for financial regulation, they may demand that offshore jurisdictions accept them. So far, there has been a 10–15–percent drop in the number of offshore-registered companies, but it is unclear whether this drop occurred because of new regulations or the financial crisis.

At the G20 meeting in Pittsburgh, the offshore issue was barely mentioned. World leaders indicated satisfaction with OECD progress, meaning that the liberal solution still prevailed. Exterritorial capitalism withstood the attack. The advantages for transnational corporations with regard to investments and capital mobility will be preserved, and government actions stood short of radical measures. The fate of the offshore sector, therefore, will be determined by decisions of individual governments and their efforts at collecting information and making requests to disclose financial information on individual accounts and company registers kept offshore. In order to collect and process complex financial information, authorities have to be equipped with a highly professional tax apparatus capable of tracking financial flows on a global scale. This means that at present, only strong and efficacious states will be able to monitor the offshore sector and to prevent abuse, whereas weaker states will remain at a disadvantage. To a large extent, Mohamad's pessimism in summarizing the outcome of the crisis is justified: "The leaders of the West are still in a state of denial. What is more likely is that they are aware of how the financial market operations have brought about the crisis but are unwilling to do away with them because they have made so many of their investors rich and have contributed much to per capita and GDP growth in their countries."[27]

Notes

Notes to the Introduction

1. Michael Likosky, *Obama's Bank: Financing a Durable New Deal* (Cambridge: Cambridge University Press, 2010); and on the international dimensions of similar issues, see Michael Likosky, *Law, Infrastructure, and Human Rights* (Cambridge: Cambridge University Press, 2006).

2. Immanuel Wallerstein, "Dynamics of (Unresolved) Global Crisis," in *Business as Usual: The Roots of Global Financial Meltdown*, ed. Craig Calhoun and Georgi Derluguian (New York: NYU Press, 2011), chapter 2.

3. Nancy Fraser, "Marketization, Social Protection, Emancipation: Toward a Neo-Polanyian Conception of Capitalist Crisis," in Calhoun and Derluguian, *Business as Usual*, chapter 5.

4. Manuel Castells, "The Crisis of Global Capitalism: Toward a New Economic Culture?" in Calhoun and Derluguian, *Business as Usual*, chapter 7.

5. See also Mary Kaldor, *New and Old Wars: Organized Violence in a Global Era* (Stanford, CA: Stanford University Press, 1999).

Notes to Chapter 1

1. David Held, "Reframing Global Governance: Apocalypse Soon or Reform!" *New Political Economy* 11, no. 2 (2006): 157–76.

2. See David Held and Anthony McGrew, *Globalization/Anti-globalization* (Cambridge: Polity, 2002), 78–84.

3. Mathias Koenig-Archibugi, "Understanding the Global Dimensions of Policy," *Global Policy* 1, no. 1 (2010): 16–28.

4. For a full explication of these and other deficiencies within the system of global governance, see David Held, *Global Covenant* (Cambridge: Polity, 2004).

5. See David Held, *Democracy and the Global Order: From the Modern State to Cosmopolitan Governance* (Cambridge: Polity, 1995), chapters 5 and 6.

6. Brian Barry, "International Society from a Cosmopolitan Perspective," in *International Society: Diverse Ethical Perspectives*, ed. D. Mapel and T. Nardin (Princeton, NJ: Princeton University Press, 1998), 34–35.

7. See Held, *Global Covenant*, chapter 6.

8. For an overview, see Howard Davies and David Green, *Global Financial Regulation: The Essential Guide* (Cambridge: Polity, 2008).

9. Robert Wade, "The First-World Debt Crisis of 2007–2010 in Global Perspective," *Challenge* 51, no. 4 (2008): 23–54; Gerald A. Epstein, ed., *Financialization and the World Economy* (Cheltenham, UK: Edward Elgar, 2005); and Jan Toporowsky, "The Economics and Culture of Financial Inflation," *Competition and Change* 13, no. 2 (2009): 145–56.

10. See Paola Robotti, "Mapping the Regulatory Debate on Hedge Funds: A Political Analysis" (FMG Discussion Paper, Financial Markets Group at the London School of Economics, London, 2006); and Eric Helleiner and Stefano Pagliari, "The End of Self-Regulation? Hedge Funds and Derivatives in Global Financial Governance," in *Global Finance in Crisis: The Politics of International Regulatory Change*, ed. Eric Helleiner, Stefano Pagliari, and Hubert Zimmerman (London: Routledge, 2010).

11. Jakob Vestergaard, *Discipline in the Global Economy: International Finance and the End of Liberalism* (London: Routledge, 2009); Dieter Kerwer, "Governing Financial Markets by International Standards," in *New Modes of Governance in the Global System: Exploring Publicness, Delegation and Inclusiveness*, ed. Mathias Koenig-Archibugi and Michael Zürn (London: Palgrave, 2006), 77–100; Daniel Ho, "Compliance and International Soft Law: Why Do Countries Implement the Basel Accord?" *Journal of International Economic Law* 5 (2002): 647–48; and

Alexander Kern, Rahul Dhumale, and John Eatwell, *Global Governance of Financial Systems: The International Regulation of Systemic Risk* (Oxford: Oxford University Press, 2006), 227–38. See also Hyoung-Kyu Chey, "Explaining Cosmetic Compliance with International Regulatory Regimes: The Implementation of the Basle Accord in Japan, 1998–2003," *New Political Economy* 11, no. 2 (June 2006): 271–89; and Andrew Walter, *Governing Finance: East Asia's Adoption of International Standards* (Ithaca, NY: Cornell University Press, 2008).

12. See Tony Porter, "Technical Collaboration and Political Conflict in the Emerging Regime for International Financial Regulation," *Review of International Political Economy* 10, no. 3 (2003): 538; and Davies and Green, *Global Financial Regulation*, 84.

13. Ngaire Woods, "Global Governance after the Financial Crisis: A New Multilateralism or the Last Gasp of the Great Powers?" *Global Policy* 1, no. 1 (2010): 51–63; David Rapkin and Jonathan Strand, "Reforming the IMF's Weighted Voting System," *World Economy* 29, no. 3 (2006): 305–24; J. Lawrence Broz and Michael Brewster Hawes, "Congressional Politics of Financing the International Monetary Fund," *International Organization* 60, no. 2 (2006): 367–99; and Peter Evans and Martha Finnemore, "Organizational Reform and the Expansion of the South's Voice at the Fund" (G-24 Discussion Paper no. 15, United Nations Publications, New York, December 2001).

14. See Fernando J. Cardim Carvalho and Jan Kregel, *Who Rules the Financial System?* (Rio de Janeiro: Ibase, 2007).

15. Stephany Griffith-Jones and Kevin Young, "Institutional Incentives and Geopolitical Representation in Global Financial Governance: Explaining the Puzzle of Regulatory Forbearance before the Crisis" (paper presented at the Task Force on Governance, Transparency and Accountability Meeting on National and International Financial Institutions, Columbia University, New York, April 28, 2009).

16. This institution has since 2006 included central bankers from Mexico and China on its board of directors. This is historically significant, but the precise impact of this change in participation is ambiguous.

17. See Jan Kregel, "From Monterrey to Basel: Who Rules the Banks?" in *Social Watch Report 2006: Impossible Architecture* (Uruguay: Instituto Del Tercer Mundo, 2006), 26–28; and Randall Germain, "Globalising Accountability within the International Organization of

Credit: Financial Governance and the Public Sphere," *Global Society* 18, no. 3 (2004): 217–42.

18. See Stijn Claessens, Geoffrey R. D. Underhill, and Xiaoke Zhang, "The Political Economy of Basel II: The Costs for Poor Countries," *World Economy* 31 no. 3 (2008): 313–45; and Stephany Griffith-Jones and Avinash Persaud, "The Pro-cyclical Impact of Basle II on Emerging Markets and Its Political Economy," in *Capital Market Liberalization and Development*, ed. Joseph Stiglitz and José Antonio Ocampo (Oxford: Oxford University Press, 2008).

19. World Bank, *Global Monitoring Report 2009: A Development Emergency* (Washington, DC: IBRD/World Bank, 2009); World Bank, "New Risks from Global Crisis Create Development Emergency, Say World Bank, IMF," press release, April 24, 2009, http://go.worldbank.org/6UJ27933Z0; International Labour Organization, "Migrant Working Girls, Victims of the Global Crisis," press release, June 10, 2009; and International Labour Organization, "The Economic Crisis in Asia: It's about Real People, Real Jobs," press release, June 26, 2009.

20. Supachai Panitchpakdi, speech at the Executive Session of the Trade and Development Board on Financing for Development 45th Executive Session, Geneva, November 13, 2008.

21. In this regard, Dimitris Stevis provides an excellent historical overview of environmental problems, and Peter Brimblecombe provides an excellent historical overview of the near-universal problem of air pollution and its globalization. See Dimitris Stevis, "The Globalizations of the Environment," *Globalizations* 2, no. 3 (2005): 323–33; and Peter Brimblecombe, "The Globalization of Local Air Pollution," *Globalizations* 2, no. 3 (2005): 429–41.

22. The effort to outline environmental sustainability criteria for international trade negotiations is a case in point. The creation of the WTO Committee on Trade and the Environment and the Hong Kong Ministerial round of WTO negotiations, for example, saw some of the most extensive discussions on this matter to date. More recently, the collaboration between the WTO and the United Nations Environment Program (UNEP) on trade and the environment at UNEP's Global Ministerial Environment Forum in Nairobi in February 2007 represents a further step in this direction.

23. For an excellent critique in this regard, see Nick Mabey, "Sustainability and Foreign Policy," in *Progressive Foreign Policy: New*

Directions for the UK, ed. David Held and David Mepham, (Cambridge: Polity, 2007); see also Robert Keohane and Kal Raustiala, "Toward a Post-Kyoto Climate Change Architecture: A Political Analysis" (Discussion Paper 2008-01, Harvard Project on International Climate Agreements, Cambridge, MA, July 2008).

24. See David King, "Climate Change Science: Adapt, Mitigate, or Ignore?" *Science* 303, no. 5655 (2004): 176–77.

25. On the problem of less-developed countries' capacity to engage in climate-change issues, see Björn-Ola Linnér and Merle Jacob, "From Stockholm to Kyoto and Beyond: A Review of the Globalization of Global Warming Policy and North-South Relations," *Globalizations* 2, no. 3 (2003): 403–15.

26. The Reducing Emissions from Deforestation and Forest Degradation (REDD) initiative is a UN-led effort to generate financial value from the carbon stored in forests of developing countries, with the aims to give developing countries an incentive to reduce their emissions and to trigger a flow of funds from rich countries to poor ones.

27. See Robert Keohane and David Victor, "The Regime Complex for Climate Change" (Harvard University John F. Kennedy School of Government Discussion Paper 10-33, January 2010); and Robert Falkner, Hannes Stephan, and John Vogler, "International Climate Policy after Copenhagen: Towards a 'Building Blocks' Approach," *Global Policy* 1, no. 3 (2010): 252–62.

28. See Anthony Nyong, "Climate Change Impacts in the Developing World: Implications for Sustainable Development," in Lael Brainard, Abigail Jones, and Nigel Purvis, *Climate Change and Global Poverty: A Billion Lives in the Balance* (Washington, DC: Brookings Institution, 2009); and Nicholas Stern, *The Economics of Climate Change: The Stern Review* (Cambridge: Cambridge University Press, 2006).

29. See Abigail Jones, Vinca LaFleur, and Nigel Purvis, "Double Jeopardy: What the Climate Crisis Means for the Poor," in Brainard, Jones, and Purvis, *Climate Change and Global Poverty;* and United Nations Development Program, *Human Development Report 2007/8* (New York: Palgrave Macmillan, 2008).

30. See United Nations Development Program, *Human Development Report 2007/8,* 41, 43–44. While countries such as China and India are increasing their per-capita carbon footprint at a considerable rate (especially given their large populations and projected level of

industrialization), the historical picture is sobering—with the mass of responsibility lying with already industrialized states such as the United States and Britain. For example, the cumulative total of per-capita emissions for the history of the United States and Britain has been estimated to be eleven hundred tons of carbon dioxide but just sixty-six tons for China and twenty-three tons for India.

31. See SIPRI, *2009 SIPRI Yearbook* (Oxford: Oxford University Press, 2009).

32. The global financial crisis has not had an effect on military spending by the major powers, though it has for some small economies. See SIPRI, *2010 SIPRI Yearbook* (Oxford: Oxford University Press, 2010), 9, 177.

33. G. John Ikenberry, *After Victory: Institutions, Strategic Restraint, and the Rebuilding of Order after Major Wars* (Princeton, NJ: Princeton University Press, 2000).

34. See George Soros, *The Age of Fallibility: The Consequences of the War on Terror* (New York: Public Affairs, 2006).

35. Carnegie Commission on the Prevention of Deadly Conflict, *Preventing Deadly Conflict: Final Report* (Washington, DC: Carnegie Corporation of New York, 1997), 142.

36. James S. Sutterlin, "The Past as Prologue," in *The Once and Future Security Council*, ed. Bruce Russett (New York: St. Martin's, 1997), 10.

37. Jonathan Kirshner, "Keynes, Capital Mobility and the Crisis of Embedded Liberalism," *Review of International Political Economy* 6, no. 3 (1999): 313–37.

38. See Helleiner and Pagliari, "End of Self-Regulation?"

39. For an outline of the new governance arrangements of the FSB, see Financial Stability Board, "Financial Stability Board Holds Inaugural Meeting in Basel," press release no. 28, June 27, 2009, http://www.financial stabilityboard.org/press/pr_090627.pdf.

40. On the IMF's declining role prior to the crisis, see Bessma Momani and Eric Helleiner, "Slipping into Obscurity? Crisis and Reform at the IMF," in *Can the World Be Governed? Possibilities for Effective Multilateralism*, ed. Alan Alexandroff (Waterloo, Ontario: Wilfred Laurier University Press, 2008).

41. See World Bank, "New Risks from Global Crisis."

42. In this regard, see Group of Twenty-Four, "Intergovernmental

Group of Twenty-Four on International Monetary Affairs and Development," communiqué, April 24, 2009.

43. See Eric Helleiner and Stefano Pagliari, "Crisis and the Reform of International Financial Regulation," in Helleiner, Pagliari, and Zimmerman, *Global Finance in Crisis*, 1–17.

44. For a discerning overview and critique of such problems more generally in the network of global financial governance institutions, see Amar Bhattacharya, "A Tangled Web," *Finance and Development*, March 2009, 40–43.

45. See, for example, Financial Services Authority, *The Turner Review: A Regulatory Response to the Global Banking Crisis* (London: Financial Services Authority, 2009); and Nout Wellink, "Basel Committee Initiatives in Response to the Financial Crisis" (speech before the Committee on Economic and Monetary Affairs of the European Parliament [ECON], Brussels, March 30, 2009). Even more critical academic scholarship has observed such tendencies—see, for example, Heikki Patomäki, "What Next? An Explanation of the 2008–2009 Slump and Two Scenarios of the Shape of Things to Come," *Globalizations* 7, no. 1 (2010): 79.

46. Joint Forum, *Review of the Differentiated Nature and Scope of Financial Regulation—Key Issues and Recommendations* (Basel: Joint Forum on Financial Conglomerates, 2010).

47. BCBS, "LGD Floors," *Basel Committee Newsletter* 14 (December 2009).

48. BCBS, "Basel II Capital Framework Enhancements Announced by the Basel Committee," news release, July 13, 2009.

49. For a concise summary and justification of Basel III shortly after its endorsement by the G20 leaders summit in Seoul in November 2010, see Hervé Hannoun, "The Basel III Capital Framework: A Decisive Breakthrough" (Bank of Japan, BIS High Level Seminar on Financial Regulatory Reform, Hong Kong, November 22, 2010).

50. See Helleiner and Pagliari, "End of Self-Regulation?"; European Commission, "Proposal for a Regulation of the European Parliament and of the Council on Credit Rating Agencies" (2008/0217, April 30, 2008); European Commission, "Proposal for a Directive of the European Parliament and of the Council on Alternative Investment Fund Managers and Amending Directives" (2004/39/EC and 2009/EC, April

30, 2009); US Department of the Treasury, "Administration's Regulatory Reform Agenda Moves Forward: Credit Rating Agency Reform Legislation Sent to Capitol Hill," July 21, 2009; US Department of the Treasury, "Administration's Regulatory Reform Agenda Moves Forward: Legislation for the Registration of Hedge Funds Delivered to Capitol Hill," July 15, 2009; and Joint Forum, *Review of the Differentiated.*

51. See International Monetary Fund, *A Fair and Substantial Contribution by the Financial Sector: Interim Report for the Meeting of G20 Ministers* (Washington, DC: IMF, 2010).

52. Randall Germain, "Global Financial Governance and the Problem of Inclusion," *Global Governance* 7 (2001): 411–26; and Randall Germain, "Reforming the International Financial Architecture: The New Political Agenda," in *Global Governance: Critical Perspectives*, ed. Rorden Wilkinson and Steve Hughes (London: Routledge, 2002).

53. See Robert Wade, "Wheels within Wheels: Rethinking the Asian Crisis and the Asian Model," *Annual Review of Political Science* 3 (2000): 85–115.

54. Nuria Molina and Nora Honkaniemi, "IFI and Global Finance Reforms Advance at a Snail's Pace at the Spring Meetings," Eurodad— European Network on Debt and Development, press release, May 5, 2010, http://www.eurodad.org/whatsnew/articles.aspx?id=4118.

55. Although it is still very early to provide a systematic analysis of change within the IMF's policies, some recent research suggests that for low-income countries—that is, the most vulnerable and in need of external assistance—there has been little fundamental change in approaches to macroeconomic policies. Policy space has arguably expanded—higher fiscal deficits have been allowed—but this has been short lived and lasted only through the brunt of the crisis, reflecting what Van Waeyenberge et al. have called "crisis Keynesianism." The emphasis on price stability (and hence restrictive monetary policies) has returned as a focus. See Elisa Van Waeyenberge, Hannah Bargawi, and Terry McKinley, *Standing in the Way of Development? A Critical Survey of the IMF's Crisis Response in Low Income Countries* (Brussels: Eurodad and Third World Network, April 2010).

56. See Edward C. Luck, "The UN Security Council: Reform or Enlarge?" in *Irrelevant or Indispensable? The United Nations in the 21st Century*, ed. Paul Heinbecker and Patricia Goff (Waterloo, Ontario: Wilfred Laurier University Press, 2005); and Bardo Fassbender, "On the

Boulevard of Broken Dreams: The Project of a Reform of the UN Security Council after the 2005 World Summit," *International Organizations Law Review* 2 (2005): 391–402.

57. See Zhou Xiaochuan, "Reform the International Monetary System" (speech at the People's Bank of China, Beijing, March 23, 2009), http://www.pbc.gov.cn/english/detail.asp?col=6500&id=178; see also Daniel Drezner, "Bad Debts: Assessing China's Financial Influence in Great Power Politics," *International Security* 34, no. 2 (2009): 7–45.

58. See Eleni Tsingou, "Regulatory Reactions to the Global Credit Crisis: Analyzing a Policy Community under Stress," in Helleiner, Pagliari, and Zimmerman, *Global Finance in Crisis,* 21–36; also see Charles Dallara, "Structure of Regulation: Lessons from the Crisis; A View from the Institute of International Finance (IIF)," *Journal of Financial Stability* 4 (2008): 338–45.

59. Eric Helleiner and Tony Porter, "Making Transnational Networks More Accountable," in *Re-defining the Global Economy,* ed. Sara Burke (New York: Friedrich Ebert Stiftung Occasional Paper no. 42, 2009), http://library.fes.de/pdf- files/iez/global/06293.pdf.

60. The G24 is arguably increasingly assertive in demanding further changes to institutions, such as the IMF's lending and surveillance and the World Bank's role in lending to developing countries in the wake of the crisis. See Bhumika Muchhala, "G24 Ministers Call for Deeper Governance Reforms and More Tailored Lending Instruments for Developing Countries," Third World Network Info Service on Finance and Development, press release, April 30, 2010; and Group of Twenty-Four, "Intergovernmental Group of Twenty-Four on International Monetary Affairs and Development," communiqué, April 22, 2010.

61. Richard Falk, "A Radical World Order Challenge: Addressing Global Climate Change and the Threat of Nuclear Weapons," *Globalizations* 7, nos. 1–2 (March–June 2010): 138.

62. On the equivalence principle, see Inge Kaul, Pedro Conceição, Katell Le Goulven, and Ronald U. Mendoza, eds., *Providing Global Public Goods* (Oxford: Oxford University Press, 2003), 27–28.

63. See David Held and Kevin Young, "The Equivalence Principle," in *Responses to the Global Crisis: Charting a Progressive Path* (London: Policy Network, 2009), 37–39.

Thanks to Andrew Blau, Craig Calhoun, Jenny Johnston, Robby Mockler, Dorothy Wall, and Erik Olin Wright for their comments on earlier drafts of this chapter.

1. There is considerable scientific debate about the speed of global warming and the precise nature of its effects. However, there is broad consensus that global temperatures are rising, that human activities (particularly the emission of greenhouse gases) bear a large part of the responsibility for this rise, and that even a small increase in average surface temperature of the earth will have significant effects on human societies. For a good layperson's summary of the state of the scientific debate about climate change, see "The Clouds of Unknowing," *Economist,* March 18, 2010, http://www.economist.com/displaystory.cfm?story_id=15719298.

In terms of how our argument connects to current scientific definitions of possible emissions/climate futures, we believe that modernist economic growth principles correspond to the "A1" family of marker scenarios developed by the Intergovernmental Panel on Climate Change (IPCC). (IPCC marker scenarios: Special Report on Emissions Scenarios website, "A1 Marker Scenario," http://sres.ciesin.columbia.edu/OpenProcess/htmls/storyline_families.html.) The world we are currently living in, which entails no significant limits on GHG emissions and relies on coal- and oil-intensive energy production, specifically corresponds to the "A1F1" marker scenario. A1F1 suggests that we may hit 1550 ppm of CO_2 by 2100 (IPCC, *Climate Change 2007,* Fourth Assessment Report [Geneva: IPCC, 2007]). (It should be noted that the A1F1 scenario is *not* the worst case imaginable, though it is the worst case considered by the IPCC in its scenarios. Even worse scenarios revolve around positive climate feedback mechanisms; see K. M. Walter, S. A. Zimov, J. P. Chanton, et al., "Methane Bubbling from Siberian Thaw Lakes as a Positive Feedback to Climate Warming," *Nature* 443 [September 7, 2006]: 71–75.) If A1F1 is the business-as-usual scenario, then the most climatically optimistic high-growth scenario is the "A1T" scenario. A1T envisages both high levels of global economic growth and major emissions-reduction technology breakthroughs—in other words, the high-modernist dream. However, even in this scenario, we are likely to hit 700 ppm of CO_2 by the end of the twenty-first century, with a corresponding temperature rise of 2.5°C—with far worse to come. Note that *this is the best-case scenario,* given business-as-usual modernist growth and development commitments. The actual outcome is more likely to be closer to 1100 ppm.

What would the climate look like with a CO_2-equivalent of 1100 ppm? In this scenario, according to Joseph Romm, "average temperatures over much of the inland United States would be a scorching 20°F hotter. Soil moisture would drop 50 percent or more over much of the country. Prolonged drought would ravage much of our cropland, turning breadbaskets into dust bowls. Sea-level rise of 80 feet or more would be inevitable. We would exceed global temperatures [like those] before the Antarctic ice sheet formed, when sea levels were 70 meters (230 feet) higher on our planet." Romm, *Hell and High Water: Global Warming—the Solution and the Politics—and What We Should Do about It* (New York: William Morrow, 2006), 94. In other words, any A1 scenario—that is, any scenario that keeps faith with high-modernist dreams of growth and consumption commitments—involves a commitment to nightmarishly dangerous levels of CO_2.

We believe that whereas economic modernists might be able to live with any of the A1 scenarios, the other marker scenarios (A2, B1, B2) represent limitations to growth that are politically unacceptable (indeed, unimaginable) to economic modernists. The producerist republicanism that we propose in this chapter as an alternative to carbon-intensive economism imagines the reincarnation of a political tradition that would permit us to move away from the A1 scenarios and toward a world more akin to the IPCC B2 marker scenario, which has significantly less dire outcomes for atmospheric chemistry and climate.

2. Nils Gilman, Doug Randall, and Peter Schwartz, "Impacts of Climate Change: A System Vulnerability Approach" (GBN white paper), http://www.gbn.com/consulting/article_details.php?id=61; Jeffrey Mazo, *Climate Conflict: How Global Warming Threatens Security and What to Do about It* (London: Routledge, 2010); and Nils Gilman, Doug Randall, and Peter Schwartz, "Climate Change and National Security: An Analytic Framework," in *The Oxford Handbook of Climate Change and Society,* ed. John Dryzek (Oxford: Oxford University Press, forthcoming 2011).

3. James Lovelock, *The Vanishing Face of Gaia: A Final Warning* (London: Allen Lane, 2009); and Joel E. Cohen, *How Many People Can the Earth Support?* (New York: Norton, 1996).

4. Thomas Pogge, *Politics as Usual* (Cambridge: Polity, 2010); Branko Milanovic, *Worlds Apart: Measuring International and Global Inequality* (Princeton, NJ: Princeton University Press, 2005); see also Mike Davis, *Planet of Slums* (New York: Verso, 2006); UNDP, *Human Development Report 2007/08: Fighting Climate Change: Human Solidarity in a Divided World* (New York: Oxford University Press, 2007); and Diane E. Davis, "Non-State Armed Actors, New Imagined Communities, and Shifting Patterns of Sovereignty and Insecurity in the Modern World," *Contemporary Security Policy* 30, no. 2 (2010): 221–45. As Mike Davis says: "For thirty years, cities in the developing world have grown at breakneck speed without counterpart public investments in infrastructure, housing or public health.... Sheer demographic momentum... will increase the world's urban population by 3 billion people over the next forty years, 90 per cent of whom will be in poor cities. No one... has a clue how a planet of slums with growing food and energy crises will accommodate their biological survival, much less their aspirations to basic happiness and dignity." Davis, "Who Will Build the Ark?" *New Left Review* 61 (January–February 2010): 39–40.

5. See Richard Heinberg, "Temporary Recession or the End of Growth?" *The Oil Drum* (blog), August 8, 2009, http://www.theoildrum.com/node/5638; and Steven Solomon, *Water: The Epic Struggle for Wealth, Power, and Civilization* (New York: HarperCollins, 2010).

6. Typical in this respect is Anthony Giddens, *The Politics of Climate Change* (London: Polity, 2009), a book filled with sage advice about the governmental policies that ought to be implemented but with almost nothing to say about the political obstacles to achieving these policies, much less how those obstacles might be overcome. Even those who stress the need for fundamental change in our civilization typically do not take on the question of the political requirements—or even highlight the centrality and magnitude of that issue, beyond one-sentence acknowledgments. See, for example, the otherwise admirable Nick Brooks, Natasha Grist, and Katrina Brown, "Development Futures in the Context of Climate Change: Challenging the Present and Learning from the Past," *Development Policy Review* 27, no. 6 (2009). Thomas Homer-Dixon goes further than most in explaining that politics is a big part of the problem, without making this point central to his overall argument; see Homer Dixon, *The Upside of Down* (Washington, DC: Island, 2006), 214–19.

7. Pew Global Attitudes Project, "Global Warming Seen as a Major Problem around the World: Less Concern in the U.S., China, and Russia," December 2, 2009, http://pewglobal.org/commentary/display.php?AnalysisID=1066.

8. Gwynne Dyer, "Copenhagen: Let the Failure Be Clear," December 4, 2009, http://www.gwynnedyer.com/articles/Gwynne%20Dyer%20article_%20%20Copenhagen.txt. The need for industrial countries to cut emissions by 80 percent is the IPCC consensus, though some people suggest that we need to cut emissions by more. On the debate over the "safe" level of CO_2, see Lauren Morello, "Is 350 the New 450 When It Comes to Capping Carbon Emissions?" *New York Times,* September 28, 2009, http://www.nytimes.com/cwire/2009/09/28/28climatewire-is-350-the-new-450-when-it-comes-to-capping-c-6627.html; also see Gar Lipow, "We Need to Cut Emissions Faster than 80 Percent by 2050, but How Fast?" *Grist,* January 25, 2009, http://www.grist.org/article/How-soon-do-we-need-to-cut-greenhouse-gas-emissions/N20/.

9. Dyer is more pessimistic in his just-published *Climate Wars: The Fight for Survival as the World Overheats* (Oxford: Oneworld, 2010).

10. The claim that all the necessary technology already exists is put forth so often, and with so little justification, that it seems unfair to pick on any particular promoters of this perspective. But here are a few high-profile ones: Sir John Houghton, "Overview of the Climate Change Issue" (presentation to Forum 2002, St. Anne's College, Oxford, July 15, 2002), http://www.jri.org.uk/resource/climatechangeoverview.htm; Katie Fehrenbacher, founding editor, Earth2Tech, in the *Economist,* August 21, 2008, http://www.economist.com/debate/days/view/208; and the European Green Party, "Climate Change Facts," February 10, 2006, http://www.greens-efa.org/cms/default/dok/134/134192.climate_change_facts@en.htm.

11. As noted earlier, it does not much matter whether we believe the safe limits are 450 ppm or 550 ppm, or whether we think we have twenty-five or forty years to accomplish the necessary transformation in the global energy system; ultimately, these are rounding errors, given the magnitude of the required changes.

12. Of course, the choice between technological improvements and production cutbacks is not strictly either/or but could come via some combinatory mix of both. But even if technology can make up half of

what needs to be done, that still implies a 40 percent cut in production and consumption across the global economy—presumably most of which will need to be borne by wealthy economies. Such a drop in industrial output is far greater than any industrialized economy has ever experienced, even during the Great Depression.

13. How much per-capita decline is required depends on global population growth. The "official future" calls for global population to max out (and then stabilize) around nine billion around 2050. It is worth noting, however, not only that population projections over that time span have a notoriously poor track record for accuracy but also (and not coincidentally) that the theory of the demographic transition is entirely tied up with modernization theory; see Simon Szreter, "The Idea of Demographic Transition and the Study of Fertility Change: A Critical Intellectual History," *Population and Development Review* 19, no. 4 (1993): 659–701.

14. Griffith, quoted in Stewart Brand, *Whole Earth Discipline: An Ecopragmatist Manifesto* (New York: Penguin, 2009), 14.

15. Griffith himself believes that, while a monumental undertaking, such a remaking of the world's energy infrastructure is technically feasible, were the political will and funding forthcoming (which we regard as so highly unlikely as to be utopian—and note that we have not included the additional task of transitioning the world's vehicle fleet from hydrocarbons). Political issues aside, there is significant debate about the theoretical and practical feasibility of current/emerging green technologies as full replacements for existing conventional energy-generation infrastructure. What is striking is how hedged even the most optimistic arguments are. Consider the reasonable case made by Mark Z. Jacobson and Mark A Delucchi, "A Plan to Power 100 Percent of the Planet with Renewables," *Scientific American,* November 2009. To make the numbers work, Jacobson and Delucchi make sanguine assumptions about efficiency gains during the conversion process. They also concede that dire new-materials shortages are likely to arise (uranium, as well as various rare earth elements required to build batteries, gears, and photovoltaic cells) and wring their hands about the political challenges associated with trying to replace the large majority of the world's energy generation, transmission, and consumption infrastructure. For more, see Benjamin K. Sovacool and Charmaine Watts, "Going Completely Renewable: Is It Possible (Let Alone Desirable)?" *Electricity Journal* 22, no. 4 (2009): 95–111.

16. Nicholas Stern, *The Economics of Climate Change* (Cambridge: Cambridge University Press, 2007), xv. This is not to mention the even more optimistic views of William Nordhaus and Freeman Dyson: see Nordhaus's book, *A Question of Balance: Weighing the Options on Global Warming Policies* (New Haven, CT: Yale University Press, 2008); Dyson's review of the book in the *New York Review of Books,* June 12, 2008; and the subsequent exchange in William Nordhaus, Dimitri Zenghelis, Leigh Sullivan, and Freeman Dyson, "'The Question of Global Warming': An Exchange," *New York Review of Books,* September 25, 2008. Stern now acknowledges that things look worse than he formerly expected, but he still insists on optimism. See his review of *Eaarth: Making a Life on a Tough New Planet,* by Bill McKibben, *New York Review of Books,* June 24, 2010.

17. Paul Krugman, "Building a Green Economy," *New York Times Magazine,* April 5, 2010.

18. Michael Hoexte, "Carbon Pricing Is Just One Piece of the Puzzle: Towards a Comprehensive Climate and Energy Policy—Part 2," *Green Thoughts,* February 4, 2009, http://greenthoughts.us/2009/02/04/carbonpricing2/.

19. The Manhattan Project, the ultimate high-modernist technological triumph, is regularly invoked as a supposed model for developing breakthrough green technologies—despite the radical differences between building a weapon and remaking the entire global energy system. (See, for example, Susan Kraemer, "Energy Push Rivals Manhattan Project, Says WSJ," *Scientific American,* December 3, 2009, http://www.scientificamerican.com/article.cfm?id=energy-push-rivals-manhattan-projec-2009-12.) On the feebleness of the Manhattan Project analogy, see Megan McArdle, "Manhattan No More," *Megan McArdle* (blog), *Atlantic,* November 12, 2008, http://www.theatlantic.com/business/archive/2008/11/manhattan-no-more/4348/.

20. See Weinberg's essay "Can Technology Replace Social Engineering?" *Bulletin of the Atomic Scientists* 22, no. 10 (December 1966): 4–8.

21. Techno-salvationists are constantly proliferating optimistic scenarios, most of which are more or less in the realm of science fiction. For example, various people have proposed that massive programs of carbon sequestration could help; they would indeed, except that the technology

does not yet exist. More recent discussions have centered on "geo-engineering" options—for example, putting up shields in outer space to block incoming solar radiation or somehow fixing carbon from the atmosphere on a massive scale. Even if these solutions were to become technologically viable, the political obstacles to implementing them would remain vast—a point that the engineers usually only remark on in passing. See David Biello, "What Is Geoengineering and Why Is It Considered a Climate Change Solution?" *Scientific American,* April 6, 2010; and David G. Victor, M. Granger Morgan, Jay Apt, John Steinbruner, and Katharine Ricke, "The Geoengineering Option: A Last Resort against Global Warming," *Foreign Affairs,* March/April 2009.

22. Kenneth Boulding, "The Economics of the Coming Spaceship Earth," in *Environmental Quality in a Growing Economy,* ed. Henry Jarrett (New York: Harper and Row, 1966), 3.

23. John Michael Greer, *The Long Descent: A User's Guide to the End of the Industrial Age* (Gabriola Island, BC: New Society, 2008).

24. For the basic story, which only touches on Kuznets and neglects the Soviet antecedent, see Timothy Mitchell, "Fixing the Economy," *Cultural Studies* 12, no. 1 (1998): 82–101.

25. See William Barnes, "Development Theory and Ideology: The Triumph of the Modern Middle Class in Theory and Practice" (PhD dissertation, University of Michigan, 1979).

26. The dominant view in the 1990s—brilliantly encapsulated by Francis Fukuyama in his essay "The End of History?" (*National Interest* [Summer 1989]: 3–18)—was that the late modernity of the advanced capitalist world, and the United States in particular, supplied a general model and goal culture for all future human development, with the expectation that sooner or later this modernity would be universalized across the planet. For dissenters from the late 1950s through the 1970s, see Howard Brick, *Transcending Capitalism* (Ithaca, NY: Cornell University Press, 2006); Robert M. Collins, *More: The Politics of Economic Growth in Postwar America* (New York: Oxford University Press, 2002); Daniel Horowitz, *The Anxieties of Affluence: Critiques of American Consumer Culture, 1939–1979* (Amherst: University of Massachusetts Press, 2005); and Andrew L. Yarrow, *Measuring America: How Economic Growth Came to Define American Greatness in the Late Twentieth Century* (Amherst: University of Massachusetts Press, 2010).

27. See Bjorn Hettne, *Development Theory and the Three Worlds: Towards an International Political Economy of Development* (London: Longman, 1995).

28. Kevin Drum, "The Rationing Canard," *Kevin Drum* (blog), *Mother Jones*, August 28, 2009, http://motherjones.com/kevin-drum/2009/08/rationing-canaard.

29. Walt Whitman Rostow, *The Stages of Economic Growth: A Non-Communist Manifesto* (New York: Oxford University Press, 1961).

30. Minxin Pei, "Communist China at 60," Carnegie Endowment for International Peace, September 30, 2009, http://www.carnegie endowment.org/publications/index.cfm?fa=view&id=23922.

31. The basic ideas of "ecological modernization" have become commonplace over recent years, but the term itself is not well known outside the academic field of environmental sociology. Ecological modernization theory first appeared among German and Dutch environmental sociologists and social theorists in the early 1980s, in response to neo-Marxist theories of the irremediable ecological destructiveness of advanced capitalism. By the mid-1990s, ecological modernization was a flourishing academic field with a broad literature. See Gert Spaargaren and Arthur P.J. Mol, "Sociology, Environment, and Modernity: Ecological Modernization as a Theory of Social Change," *Society and Natural Resources* 5, no. 4 (1992): 323–34; M.A. Hajer, *The Politics of Environmental Discourse: Ecological Modernization and the Policy Process* (Oxford: Oxford University Press, 1995); P. Christoff, "Ecological Modernization, Ecological Modernities," *Environmental Politics* 5, no. 3 (1996): 476–500; Arthur P.J. Mol and David A. Sonnenfeld, eds., *Ecological Modernization around the World* (London: Cass, 2000); D.R. Fisher and W.R. Freudenburg, "Ecological Modernization and Its Critics: Assessing the Past and Looking toward the Future," *Society and Natural Resources* 14 (2001): 701–9; and Arthur P.J. Mol, Gert Spaargaren, and David A. Sonnenfeld, eds., *The Ecological Modernisation Reader* (London: Routledge, 2009). The school of thought had precursors among policy intellectuals in the mid-1970s, reacting to the 1973 energy crisis and the growing First World environmental movement of the time, such as the work of Amory Lovins on "soft energy paths" and "natural capitalism." See Lovins, "Energy Strategy: The Road Not Taken," *Foreign Affairs*, October 1976; and Paul Hawken, Amory Lovins, and Hunter

Lovins, *Natural Capitalism: Creating the Next Industrial Revolution* (New York: Little, Brown, 1999).

32. Ecological modernization theory dovetails with (and indeed implicitly replies on) the neomodernization theory of Ronald Inglehart and the "creative class" theory of Richard Florida. See Inglehart and Christian Welzel, *Modernization, Cultural Change and Democracy: The Human Development Sequence* (Cambridge: Cambridge University Press, 2005); and Florida, *The Rise of the Creative Class: And How It's Transforming Work, Leisure, Community, and Everyday Life* (New York: Basic Books, 2004). Inglehart posits that a turn away from high-carbon "more" toward post-materialist values is a natural and inevitable feature of a maturing modernity. The "creative class" as depicted by Florida is made up of highly educated knowledge workers committed to social tolerance and diversity and an upscale, neobohemian lifestyle that includes positive appreciation of nature. Florida casts the creative class as a vanguard that will lead an ecofriendly technological revolution that will make economic growth endlessly sustainable.

33. Arthur P.J. Mol, Gert Spaargaren, and David A. Sonnenfeld, "Ecological Modernisation: Three Decades of Policy, Practice and Theoretical Reflection," in *The Ecological Modernisation Reader*, ed. Mol, Spaargaren, and Sonnenfeld, 1–23.

34. See also Roger Pielke, Jr., *The Climate Fix: What Scientists and Politicians Won't Tell You about Global Warming* (New York: Basic Books, 2010). In fact, the world of environmentalism is broader, more diverse, and more complexly internally conflicted than we can explain here. A crude summary maps three coalitions, overlapping at the margins: (1) New Age Greens, romantic left antimodernists, radical antiglobalists, and anarchists; (2) centrist, high-modernist science-and-technology enthusiasts, policy intellectuals, and green capitalists, who see themselves as the only pragmatists; and (3) an "in-between" grouping of critical-modernist radical reformists, largely in academia and nongovernmental organizations. Nordhaus and Shellenberger are of the second grouping; Bill McKibben straddles the first and third; many of the major environmental organizations have been moving from the second toward the third in recent years.

35. Ted Nordhaus and Michael Shellenberger, "Why Americans Vote Their Values: In a Post-material Era, People Seek Status, Purpose,

and Happiness—and Cast Their Ballots Accordingly," Democratic Leadership Council, July 22, 2006, http://www.dlc.org/ndol_ci.cfm?ka id=127&subid=173&contentid=253983.

36. The contemporary "Third Way" refers to the 1990s compromise between New Right Reagan/Thatcher neoliberalism, on one hand, and New Deal/Social Democratic welfare-state left-liberalism, on the other—a compromise incarnated by Tony Blair and New Labor in Great Britain and by the Clinton and Obama administrations in the United States. The founding theorist, Anthony Giddens, discusses ecological modernization in *The Third Way: The Renewal of Social Democracy* (Cambridge: Polity, 1998), 54–68.

37. Michael Shellenberger and Ted Nordhaus, *Break Through: Why We Can't Leave Saving the Planet to Environmentalists* (Boston: Mariner Books, 2009), 125. See also Robert Brulle, J. Craig Jenkins, and Riley E. Dunlap, "The Break Through Illusion: A Social Science Critique of Nordhaus and Shellenberger," in *Post-Environmentalism: Debating and Extending the Death of Environmentalism Thesis,* ed. Bill Chaloupka, Jay Odenbaugh, and Jim Proctor (Cambridge, MA: MIT Press, forthcoming).

38. The aspiration to share in that affluence, the "psychic mobility" that makes it possible to see one's own future in those terms, is an essential part of what modernization theorists (including contemporary ecological modernization theorists) think it means to be modern. This understanding of modernization and modernity, based in Talcott Parsons's and Edward Shils's translation of Durkheim and Weber into social systems theory, is at the heart of Ron Inglehart's influential revitalization of modernization theory over the past twenty years. See Barnes, "Development Theory and Ideology"; and Nils Gilman, *Mandarins of the Future: Modernization Theory in Cold War America* (Baltimore, MD: Johns Hopkins University Press, 2003).

39. Arguments in favor of the existence of a so-called environmental Kuznets curve (which posits that people demand a cleaner environment when they reach a certain level of affluence) suffer from methodological and category errors. Yes, people demand a cleaner local environment, but this result is generally accomplished by shipping environmental contaminants "over the horizon"—either literally, by moving polluting factories to the Global South, or temporally, by substituting processes that create greater environmental problems down the road (e.g., catalytic

convertors reducing tail exhaust at the expense of fuel efficiency)—with little if any net reduction in total global environmental insults. See Cutler Cleveland and Matthias Ruth, "Indicators of Dematerialization and the Materials Intensity of Use: A Critical Review with Suggestions for Future Research," *Journal of Industrial Ecology* 2, no. 3 (1998): 15–50.

40. David Brooks, *Bobos in Paradise: The New Upper Class and How They Got There* (New York: Simon and Schuster, 2001). By this, we do not mean to reject the "creative class" upscale, neobohemian lifestyle as being without existential integrity. But since this way of life cannot but be limited to a privileged minority, its pursuit—by anyone anywhere—violates norms of justice.

41. Wendy L. Wall, *Inventing the American Way: The Politics of Consensus from the New Deal to the Civil Rights Movement* (New York: Oxford University Press, 2008); Simon Fraser and Gary Gerstle, eds., *The Rise and Fall of the New Deal Order, 1930–1980* (Princeton, NJ: Princeton University Press, 1989); and Robert M. Collins, *More: The Politics of Economic Growth in Postwar America* (New York: Oxford University Press, 2000).

42. John K. Galbraith, *The Affluent Society* (New York: Houghton Mifflin, 1958); Vance Packard, *The Hidden Persuaders* (New York: Pelican, 1962); and Paul Goodman, *Growing Up Absurd* (New York: Random House, 1960).

43. For strong arguments in this vein, see Nick Brooks, Natasha Grist, and Katrina Brown, "Development Futures in the Context of Climate Change: Challenging the Present and Learning from the Past," *Development Policy Review* 27, no. 6 (2009): 741–65, and the literature cited therein.

44. See Patrick Heller's chapter on Kerala in Richard Sandbrook, Marc Edelman, Patrick Heller, and Judith Teichman, *Social Democracy in the Global Periphery: Origins, Challenges, Prospects* (Cambridge: Cambridge University Press, 2007); and Patrick Heller and T. M. Thomas Isaac, "Decentralization, Democracy and Development: People's Campaign for Decentralized Planning in Kerala," in *Developing Democracy: Institutional Innovations in Empowered Participatory Democracy,* ed. A. Fung and E. O. Wright (London: Verso, 2002).

45. Banyan, "Asia's Alarming Cities: How Asian Cities Are Built Will Determine the Prospects for Global Carbon Emissions. Oh Dear,"

Banyan's Notebook (blog), *Economist,* July 1, 2010; and Mike Davis, "Who Will Build the Ark?" *New Left Review* 61 (January–February 2010): 29–46.

46. Mark Selden, *The Yenan Way in Revolutionary China* (Cambridge, MA: Harvard University Press, 1971); Richard Sandbrook, Marc Edelman, Patrick Heller, and Judith Teichman, *Social Democracy in the Global Periphery: Origins, Challenges, Prospects* (Cambridge: Cambridge University Press, 2007); and Heller and Isaac, "Decentralization, Democracy and Development."

47. Major recent works describing this tradition include Robert D. Johnston, *The Radical Middle Class: Populist Democracy and the Question of Capitalism in Progressive Era Portland, Oregon* (Princeton, NJ: Princeton University Press, 2003); Charles Postel, *The Populist Vision* (New York: Oxford University Press, 2007); Doug Rossinow, *Visions of Progress: The Left-Liberal Tradition in America* (Philadelphia: University of Pennsylvania Press, 2008); and Robert Westbrook, *Democratic Hope: Pragmatism and the Politics of Truth* (Ithaca, NY: Cornell University Press, 2005). Important earlier works include Lawrence Goodwyn, *Democratic Promise: The Populist Moment in America* (Oxford: Oxford University Press, 1976); Nick Salvatore, *Eugene V. Debs: Citizen and Socialist* (Urbana: University of Illinois Press, 1982); Christopher Lasch, *The True and Only Heaven: Progress and Its Critics* (New York: Norton, 1991); and Leon Fink, *Workingmen's Democracy: The Knights of Labor and American Politics* (Urbana: University of Illinois Press, 1985).

48. Johnston, *The Radical Middle Class,* 267.

49. See the discussions of the "social economy of Quebec" and the Mondragon cooperative conglomerate in Spain in Erik Olin Wright, *Envisioning Real Utopias* (London: Verso, 2010); on transition towns, see Stephen Hale, "The New Politics of Climate Change: Why We Are Failing and How We Will Succeed," *Environmental Politics* 19, no. 2 (2010): 255–75.

50. See John Judis, "Tea Minus Zero: The Tea Party Menace Will Not Go Quietly," *New Republic,* May 5, 2010. As John Barry says, "Emphasising the republican strains native to the political cultures of western liberal democracies could help to create a political environment more conducive to green politics and policy, and allows greens to offer an 'immanent critique' of the current unsustainable development paths being followed by western societies in a language comprehensible to

the majority of its citizens." Barry, "Towards a Green Republicanism: Constitutionalism, Political Economy, and the Green State," *Good Society* 17, no. 2 (2008): 5.

51. Davis, "Who Will Build the Ark?" 45, quoting *UN Human Development Report 2007/2008* (New York: Oxford University Press, 2007), 19.

Notes to Chapter 3

I wish to thank Helen Tilley for providing to me her various work on Africa as a laboratory for science, Craig Calhoun for his critical reflections on an earlier version of the chapter, and Jeremy Walker for making available his and Melinda Cooper's important paper "Genealogies of Resilience."

1. World Bank, *World Development Report* (Washington, DC: World Bank, 2008), 135; Welthungerhilfe, International Food Policy Research Institute, and Concern Worldwide, *2009 Global Hunger Index* (Bonn: Welthungerhilfe, 2009);.

2. L. Cotula, S. Vermeulen, R. Leonard, and J. Keeley, *Land Grab or Development Opportunity? Agricultural Investment and International Land Deals in Africa* (London: IIED, 2009).

3. See D. Smith and J. Vivekananda, *A Climate of Conflict* (Geneva: International Alert, 2007).

4. A. Roy, *Poverty Capital: Microfinance and the Making of Development* (London: Routledge, 2010).

5. See, for example, United Nations, *Millennium Development Goals 2009* (Washington, DC: United Nations, 2009).

6. There is, it must be said, a counternarrative that paints a rather different picture. A controversial paper by Pinkovskiy and Sala-i-Martin argues that since 1970 poverty rates have fallen rapidly, that the post-1995 economic-growth spurt has reduced income inequality, and that the MDG income goal will be achieved on time. See M. Pinkovskiy and X. Sala-i-Martin, "African Poverty Is Falling Much Faster than You Think" (working paper, Department of Economics, MIT, 2010). A new McKinsey Global Institute report also paints a rosy picture of almost 5 percent GDP growth rates between 2000 and 2008 (a continental GDP of US$1.6 trillion, equivalent to the GDP of Brazil or Russia) and the prospect of

future growth driven by "the global race for resources" and "internal social and demographic trends." See McKinsey Global Institute, *Lions on the Move* (Johannesburg: MGI, 2010). In fact, the picture is very uneven and complex, marked by striking interregional and interstate differences and a typology of African economies (oil exporters, diversified, transition, in McKinsey's lexicon) that suggests a heterogeneous geography of accumulation and stagnation. At the very least, one has to express considerable skepticism over the national accounts data deployed and the extent to which both reports, for example, have nothing to say about the ecology of livelihoods and the impact of climate change; and they offer a dubious set of claims about land availability and the prospects of a green revolution.

7. H. Tilley, *Africa as a Living Laboratory: Empire, Development, and the Problem of Scientific Knowledge, 1860–1960* (Chicago: University of Chicago Press, 2010).

8. See S. Malette, "Foucault for the Next Century: Eco-governmentality," in *A Foucault for the Twenty-First Century*, ed. S. Binkley and J. Capetillo, 222–39 (Cambridge: Cambridge University Press, 2009); A. Agrawal, *Environmentality: Technologies of Government and the Making of Subjects* (Durham, NC: Duke University Press, 2005); and T. Li, *The Will to Improve* (Durham, NC: Duke University Press, 2007).

9. R. Grove, "Early Themes in African Conservation," in *Conservation in Africa*, ed. D. Anderson and R. Grove (Cambridge: Cambridge University Press, 1987).

10. M. Foucault, *Security, Territory, Population* (London: Palgrave, 2007); and M. Foucault, *The Birth of Biopolitics* (London: Palgrave, 2008).

11. See also M. Schabas, *The Natural Origins of Economics* (Chicago: University of Chicago Press, 2005).

12. J.-A. Goodie, "The Invention of the Environment as a Legal Subject" (PhD dissertation, Murdoch University, 2006), 37.

13. Malette, "Foucault for the Next Century," 228–31.

14. J. W. Moore, "Capitalism as World-Ecology: Braudel and Marx on Environmental History," *Organization and Environment* 16, no. 4 (2003): 431–58.

15. E. Dussel, "Beyond Eurocentrism: The World-System and the Limits of Modernity," in *The Cultures of Globalization*, ed. Frederic Jameson and Masao Miyoshi, 3–31 (Durham, NC: Duke University Press, 1998).

16. D. Chavkrabarty, *Provincializing Europe* (Princeton, NJ: Princeton University Press, 2000).

17. Tilley, *Africa as a Living Laboratory.*

18. Malette, "Foucault for the Next Century," 228.

19. H. Arendt, *Imperialism* (New York: Harcourt, 1985).

20. H. Tilley, "Global Histories, Vernacular Science and African Genealogies" (ISIS report, Birckbeck College, University of London, 2009), 2.

21. Grove, "Early Themes in African Conservation," 23. The path-breaking work by Kjekshus and Vail on the sleeping-sickness catastrophe in late-nineteenth-century East Africa explores the ways in which that epidemic was a sort of perfect storm in which the impact of commodity production and colonial resettlement produced exceptionally corrosive effects on systems of local adaptation. See H. Kjekshus, *Ecology Control and Economic Development in East African History* (London: Heinemann, 1977); and L. Vail "Ecology and History: The Example of Eastern Zambia," *Journal of Southern African Studies* 3 (1977): 129–55. In the case of the Cape in South Africa, Grove was able to show how a debate about conservation—rooted in the fate of the forests along the southern coast—emerged in the first half of the nineteenth century and in the appointment of a colonial botanist in 1858 (and an ordinance to preserve large game in the same year). The conservation structure in place in the Cape by 1880 was the product of three forces: the scientific botanists, the white-settler farming community, and the government's being fearful of external security considerations (and in need of supporting a robust settler economy threatened by drought). It took another half century before similar concerns could be expressed in South Africa and elsewhere by experts on behalf of peasants and African smallholders.

22. Tilley, "Global Histories, Vernacular Science," 5.

23. P. Rabinow, *French Modern* (Cambridge, MA: MIT Press, 1989); Grove, "Early Themes in African Conservation"; and R. Grove, *Green Imperialism: Colonial Expansion, Tropical Island Edens and the Origins of Environmentalism, 1600–1800* (Cambridge: Cambridge University Press, 1995).

24. Tilley, "Global Histories, Vernacular Science," 413.

25. W. Beinart and L. Hughes, *Environment and Empire* (Cambridge: Cambridge University Press, 2007).

26. J. MacKenzie, *The Empire of Nature: Hunting, Conservation and British Imperialism* (Manchester: Manchester University Press, 1988).

27. See W. Beinart, K. Brown, and D. Gilfoyle, "Experts and Expertise in Colonial Africa Reconsidered," *African Affairs* 108, no. 432 (2009): 413–33.

28. Tilley, "Global Histories, Vernacular Science," 4.

29. M. Watts, *Silent Violence* (Berkeley: University of California Press, 1983).

30. S. Shapin, *The Social History of Truth* (Chicago: University of Chicago Press, 1994).

31. H. Tilley, "Africanizing Science" (paper delivered at the Agrarian Studies Seminar, Yale University, 2008), 433, http://www.yale.edu/agrarianstudies/real/archive.html.

32. D. Meadows, J. Randers, and W. Behrens, *The Limits to Growth: A Report on the Predicament of Mankind* (London: Earth Island, 1972).

33. P. Taylor, "What Can Agents Do?" in *Advances in Human Ecology*, vol. 8, ed. L. Fresse, 125–56 (Greenwich, CT: JAI, 1999); see also A. C. Picardi, "A Systems Analysis of Pastoralism in the West African Sahel," in *A Framework for Evaluating Long-Term Strategies for the Development of the Sahel-Sudan Region*, ed. W. W. Seifert and N. Kamrany (Cambridge, MA: MIT Press, 1974).

34. G. Hardin, "The Tragedy of the Commons," *Science* 162 (1968): 1243–48.

35. Taylor, "What Can Agents Do?" The contours of the crisis were an echo of similar debates conducted within the ranks of the British and French colonial offices during the 1930s. West Africa had its own Dust Bowl experience in which advancing deserts, rapid deforestation, and declining soil productivity were driven by the poor land-use practices of African peasants and the dead hand of population pressure. Colonial scientists, nonetheless, were deeply divided in the 1930s as to whether and how fast desertification may have been taking place in the West African Sahel.

36. See Foucault, *Security, Territory, Population*; and D. Nally, "That Coming Storm," *Annals of the Association of American Geographers* 98, no. 3 (2008): 714–41.

37. K. Polanyi, *The Great Transformation* (Boston: Beacon, 1947).

38. Foucault, *Security, Territory, Population*, 41–42.

39. See M. Dean *Governmentality* (London: Sage, 1999); J. Vernon, *Hunger* (Cambridge, MA: Harvard University Press, 2007); and Nally, "That Coming Storm."

40. Watts, *Silent Violence.*

41. M. Davis, *Late Victorian Holocausts* (London: Verso, 2001).

42. Nally, "That Coming Storm."

43. See Vernon, *Hunger.*

44. E. Berg, *Marketing, Price Policy and Storage of Food Grains in the Sahel,* vol. 2 (Ann Arbor: CRED/University of Michigan, 1977).

45. A. Mbembe, *On the Postcolony* (Berkeley: University of California Press, 2001), 67.

46. J. Roitman, *Fiscal Disobedience* (Princeton, NJ: Princeton University Press, 2005).

47. See Watts, *Silent Violence*; and P. Richards, *Indigenous Agricultural Revolution: Ecology and Food Production in West Africa* (London: Unwin, 1985).

48. A. Sen, *Poverty and Famines* (Oxford: Oxford University Press, 1980).

49. J. Scott, *The Moral Economy of the Peasantry* (New Haven, CT: Yale University Press, 1976).

50. See M. Leach and R. Mearns, *The Lie of the Land: Challenging Received Wisdom on the African Environment* (Portsmouth, NH: Heinemann, 1996).

51. Melissa Leach and James Fairhead showed how in Guinea, French colonial officials and a cadre of experts interpreted the patches of forest to be found in the savannah zone as evidence of deforestation and framed their policies accordingly. Leach and Fairhead argued that locals provided a different "reading" of the forest landscape. Forest islands were not the residuum of destructive farming practice but were self-consciously formed by farmers themselves. J. Fairhead and M. Leach, *Misreading the African Landscape: Society and Ecology in a Forest-Savanna Mosaic* (Cambridge: Cambridge University Press, 1996).

52. R. Grove, "Scottish Missionaries, Evangelical Discourses and the Origins of Conservation Thinking in Southern Africa 1820–1900," *Journal of Southern African Studies* 15, no. 2 (January 1989): 15, 153–87.

53. See P. Robbins, *Political Ecology* (Oxford: Blackwell, 2004).

54. In genealogical terms, the sort of "limits modeling" of the 1960s and early 1970s reappears in the general atmospheric circulation

models (GCMs) of the 1990s, which made visible the mechanics of the carbon emissions.

55. N. Stern, *The Economics of Climate Change* (London: HM Treasury, 2006), http://www.occ.gov.uk/activities/stern.htm.

56. See "Getting Warmer," *Economist*, December 5, 2009, 3. Kyoto was of course a failure in large measure because of the nonsignatory states such as the United States. It is due to expire in 2012, and implementing a new treaty is expected to take three years. Much therefore rested on the Copenhagen Conference held in December 2009. As the *Economist* put it, "without a new global agreement there is not much chance of averting serious climate change" (ibid.). Earlier in 2009, the G8 agreed that increase in global temperatures should be no more than two degrees Celsius above preindustrial levels. According to IPCC calculations, this would involve cutting global emissions to half their 1990 levels by 2050 (which would involve for richer countries a reduction to two tons of carbon per head, from levels above ten in Europe and twenty-four in the United States). IPCC figures suggest the Global South must cut emissions by 25–40 percent by 2020. It is not a pretty prospect.

57. M. Paterson, "Global Governance for Sustainable Capitalism?" in *Governing Sustainability*, ed. N. Adger and A. Jordan (Cambridge: Cambridge University Press, 2008), 105.

58. Ibid., 107.

59. Ibid.

60. N. Klein, *Shock Doctrine* (New York: Picador, 2007); and G. Monbiot, *Heat* (Toronto: Doubleday, 2006).

61. The EU's Emissions Trading Scheme (ETS), which started in 2005, is the only large-scale attempt to set a carbon price (EU countries receive national allocations parceled out to firms in five dirty industries). The ETS makes up the lion's share of the global market, at US$122 billion, but the price ($22 per ton) does not encourage much of an energy transition. The US Congress is proposing $12 a ton, which will not encourage any investment. Most experts believe that onshore wind energy needs a carbon price of $38 and solar cells of $196 per ton, respectively.

62. I. Boal, *Globe, Capital, Climate* (Berkeley, CA: Retort, 2009).

63. Al Gore, "We Are Facing a Planetary Emergency," *Salon*, March 22, 2007, http://www.salon.com/news/feature/2007/03/22/ primary_sources.

64. Boal, *Globe, Capital, Climate*, 5.

65. As Iain Boal puts it, "at COP15 it would be fair to say that versions of a secularised neo-catastrophism will be the dominant paradigm among climate scientists and laity alike." Ibid., 3.

66. F. Lentzos and N. Rose, "Governing Insecurity," *Economy and Society* 38, no. 2 (2009): 236.

67. Foucault, *Security, Territory, Population,* 45.

68. Lentzos and Rose, "Governing Insecurity," 232.

69. Ibid., 243.

70. World Resources Institute, *Roots of Resilience* (Washington, DC: World Resources Institute, 2008); see World Bank, "Social Resilience and State Fragility in Haiti: A Country Social Analysis" (Caribbean Country Management Unit, ESSD Sector Management Unit, Latin America and the Caribbean Region Report no. 36069-HT, April 27, 2006).

71. See Lentzos and Rose, "Governing Insecurity," 233.

72. J. Barnett and N. Adger, "Security and Climate Change: Towards an Improved Understanding," *Political Geography* 6 (2007): 1–21.

73. As Lentzos and Rose put it, "because of this plurality of planes and vectors, and the plurality of agencies and forces involved, strategies of security cannot be those of a single, all-seeing and all-controlling State: they must give a high priority to mechanisms of coordination, the linking together of very diverse agencies, involving the invention of novel ways of thinking, calculating, acting and intervening." Lentzos and Rose, "Governing Insecurity," 243.

74. N. Adger, I. Lorenzoni, and K. O'Brien, eds., *Adapting to Climate Change* (Cambridge: Cambridge University Press, 2009); C.S. Holling, "Resilience of Ecosystems: Local Surprise and Global Change," in *Sustainable Development of the Biosphere,* ed. W.C. Clark and R.E. Munn (Cambridge: Cambridge University Press, 1986); and C.S. Holling, "Understanding the Complexity of Economic, Ecological and Social Systems," *Ecosystems* 4 (2001): 390–405.

75. Foucault, *The Birth of Biopolitics,* 297.

76. N. Rose, *Powers of Freedom* (Cambridge: Cambridge University Press, 1999).

77. See L. Schipper and I. Burton, *Adaptation to Climate Change* (London: Earthscan, 2009).

78. C. Toulmin, *Climate Change in Africa* (London: Zed Books, 2010); and Intergovernmental Panel on Climate Change, *IPCC Fourth Assessment Report: Climate Change 2007* (Geneva: Intergovernmental Panel on Climate Change, 2007). This is partly why the African delegations were so demonstrative at the Copenhagen COP15 meetings about resources being made available in order to honor their commitments to a problem they did little to create.

79. See N. Adger, "Vulnerability," *Global Environmental Change* 16 (2006): 268–81; and K. Hahn Folke, P. Oslo, and J. Norberg, "Adaptive Governance of Socio-Ecological Systems," *Annual Review of Environment and Resources* 30 (2005): 441–73.

80. See Holling, "Resilience of Ecosystems."

81. C. S. Holling, "Resilience and Stability of Ecological Systems," *Annual Review of Ecology and Systematics* 4 (1973): 21.

82. See L. Gunderson and C. S. Holling, eds., *Panarchy: Understanding Transformations in Human and Natural Systems* (Washington, DC: Island, 2002).

83. Holling, "Understanding the Complexity."

84. F. A. Hayek, "The Pretence of Knowledge" (Nobel Prize speech, Salzburg, December 11, 1974), http://nobelprize.org/nobel_prizes/economics/laureates/1974/hayek-lecture.html; and M. Cooper and J. Walker, "Genealogies of Resilience," *Security Dialogue* 14, no. 2 (2011).

85. F. A. Hayek, *The Fatal Conceit: The Errors of Socialism—Collected Works of F. A. Hayek*, vol. 1 (London: Routledge, 1988); and Cooper and Walker, "Genealogies of Resilience," 14.

86. See Cooper and Walker, "Genealogies of Resilience"; and P. Mirowski and D. Plehwe, eds., *The Road to Mont Pèlerin: the Making of the Neoliberal Thought Collective* (Cambridge, MA: Harvard University Press, 2009).

87. See A. Gamble, *Hayek: The Iron Cage of Liberty* (Boulder, CO: Westview, 1996).

88. World Resources Institute, *Roots of Resilience*, ix.

89. Cooper and Walker, "Genealogies of Resilience," 32.

90. A. Agrawal and N. Perrin, "Climate Adaptation, Local Institutions and Livestock," in Adger, Lorenzoni, and O'Brien, *Adapting to Climate Change*, 350–68; and A. Agrawal, "Common

Property Institutions and Sustainable Governance of Resources," *World Development* 29, no. 10 (2001): 1649–72.

91. World Resources Institute, *Roots of Resilience,* ix.

92. Cooper and Walker, "Genealogies of Resilience," 37.

93. Lentzos and Rose, "Governing Insecurity," 233.

94. Foucault, *The Birth of Biopolitics,* 226.

Notes to Chapter 4

I would like to thank Matt Baltz, Rob Jansen, and Hazem Kandil for helpful comments and research assistance during the original drafting of this chapter and Matt for further valuable help in revising it. Thanks also to Matt Desmond, Craig Calhoun, and an anonymous reviewer for their comments.

1. "The Return of Economic Nationalism," *Economist,* February 5, 2009.

2. Ban Ki-moon, statement to Durban Review Conference, Geneva, April 20, 2009, http://www.un.org/durbanreview2009/coverage/press/pr_20-04-09.shtml.

3. See Nicholas Kulish, "Greek Crisis Churns Up Centuries of Bad Feelings," *International Herald Tribune,* March 8, 2010; for the images, see "Boycott Call in Greece: Greeks Threaten to Stop Buying German Goods," *Bild.com,* February 26, 2010, http://www.bild.de/BILD/news/bild-english/world-news/2010/02/26/greece-boycott-call/greeks-threaten-to-stop-buying-german-goods.html.

4. The contributions in Eric Helleiner and Andreas Pickel, eds., *Economic Nationalism in a Globalizing World* (Ithaca, NY: Cornell University Press, 2005), though not concerned with economic crisis, usefully define economic nationalism as a broader phenomenon than protectionism.

5. Andreas Wimmer, *Nationalist Exclusion and Ethnic Conflicts: Shadows of Modernity* (Cambridge: Cambridge University Press, 2002), chapter 3.

6. Rogers Brubaker, *Citizenship and Nationhood in France and Germany* (Cambridge, MA: Harvard University Press, 1992), ix–x; and Ayelet Shachar, *The Birthright Lottery: Citizenship and Global Inequality* (Cambridge, MA: Harvard University Press, 2009). In EU states, of course,

only non-EU citizens can be routinely excluded; but the effect in sustaining global patterns of inequality is the same. Needless to say, states are not hermetically sealed. But the routine exclusion of billions of the global poor from prosperous countries is one of the dominant facts of our time.

7. Anti-Semitism was pervasive not only in Europe but also in the United States. Leonard Dinnerstein, "Antisemitism in Crisis Times in the United States: The 1920s and 1930s," in *Anti-Semitism in Times of Crisis*, ed. Sander L. Gilman and Steven T. Katz (New York: NYU Press, 1991).

8. The blurring of lines between national and international is not a new theme. As Robert Reich wrote nearly twenty years ago, it is no longer clear "who is 'us'": "as almost every factor of production...moves effortlessly across borders, the very idea of an American economy is becoming meaningless." Robert B. Reich, *The Work of Nations: Preparing Ourselves for 21st-Century Capitalism* (New York: Vintage Books, 1992), 8. On the intra-European web of indebtedness, see Nelson Schwartz, "In and Out of Each Other's European Wallets," *New York Times*, April 30, 2010, http://www.nytimes.com/2010/05/02/weekinreview/02schwartz. html, as well as the accompanying graph, http://www.nytimes.com/ interactive/2010/05/02/weekinreview/02marsh.html.

9. Ian Bremmer and Robert Johnston, "The Rise and Fall of Resource Nationalism," *Survival* 51, no. 2 (2009): 149–58, http://www. informaworld.com/10.1080/00396330902860884.

10. Richard Baldwin and Simon Evenett, "Introduction and Recommendations for the G20," in *The Collapse of Global Trade, Murky Protectionism, and the Crisis: Recommendations for the G20*, ed. Baldwin and Evenett (London: VoxEU.org, 2009), 1, http://www.voxeu.org/reports/ Murky_Protectionism.pdf; Harold James, *The End of Globalization: Lessons from the Great Depression* (Cambridge, MA: Harvard University Press, 2001); and Jan Kofman, *Economic Nationalism and Development: Central and Eastern Europe between the Two World Wars* (Boulder, CO: Westview, 1997).

11. For the strong hold of economic autarchy in the national imagination of east-central Europe in the interwar period, see T. Ivan Berend, *Decades of Crisis: Central and Eastern Europe before World War II* (Berkeley: University of California Press, 1998), 234ff.

12. Of course, states do not label their own measures—such as those that have long impeded poor countries' access to the markets of rich

countries for agricultural products, textiles, and other goods—as "protectionist"; it is always *others'* policies that are so labeled. "Protectionism," like "crisis," is a category of practice, mobilized to do political work, not—in the first instance—a neutral category of socioeconomic analysis.

13. The first and third quotations are from Dani Rodrik, "Dani Rodrik Commentary: The Myth of Rising Protectionism," Harvard Kennedy School website, October 13, 2009, http://www.hks.harvard.edu/news-events/news/commentary/myth-of-rising-protectionism; the second is from Simon Lester, "Economic Nationalism," *International Economic Law and Policy Blog,* February 8, 2009, http://worldtradelaw.typepad.com/ielpblog/2009/02/economic-nationalism.html.

14. Baldwin and Evenett, "Introduction and Recommendations"; Simon Evenett, "This Is No Time for Complacency in the Fight against Protectionism," *VoxEU.org,* May 16, 2009, http://www.voxeu.org/index.php?q=node/3571; Simon Evenett, ed., *Broken Promises: A G-20 Summit Report by the Global Trade Alert* (London: Centre for Economic Policy Research, 2009); and Simon Evenett, ed., *Will Stabilisation Limit Protectionism? The 4th GTA Report* (London: Centre for Economic Policy Research, 2010), http://globaltradealert.org/gta-analysis/will-stabilisation-limit-protectionism-4th-gta-reporthttp://www.voxeu.org/reports/part_1_GTA_second_report.pdf.

15. For a rich and detailed study of public opinion toward foreigners in the 1930s, see Ralph Schor, *L'opinion francaise et les etrangers en France, 1919–1939* (Paris: Publication de la Sorbonne, 1985), 555–611.

16. For a comparative study of repatriation pressures in France and the United States in the interwar period, see Matthew Baltz, "Protecting Citizens in Times of Economic Distress: State Expansion, Citizenship, and Repatriation Pressures in the United States and France during the 1930s" (master's thesis, Department of Sociology, UCLA, 2010).

17. Jean-Marie Henckaerts and Louis B. Sohn, *Mass Expulsion in Modern International Law and Practice* (Cambridge, MA: Kluwer Law International, 1995), 63.

18. Manolo Abella and Geoffrey Ducanes, "The Effect of the Global Economic Crisis on Asian Migrant Workers and Governments' Responses" (paper presented at Responding to the Economic Crisis—Coherent Policies for Growth, Employment and Decent Work in Asia and Pacific conference, Manila, Philippines, February 18–20, 2009),

8–9, http://www.ilo.org/wcmsp5/groups/public/---asia/---ro-bangkok/documents/publication/wcms_101729.pdf.

19. Douglas S. Massey, Jorge Durand, and Nolan J. Malone, *Beyond Smoke and Mirrors: Mexican Immigration in an Era of Economic Integration* (New York: Russell Sage Foundation, 2002), chapter 6.

20. Jeffrey S. Passel and D'Vera Cohn, *Mexican Immigrants: How Many Come? How Many Leave?* (Washington, DC: Pew Hispanic Center, 2009), http://pewhispanic.org/files/reports/112.pdf (accessed May 26, 2010); and Michael Hoefer, Nancy Rytina, and Bryan Baker, "Estimates of the Unauthorized Immigrant Population Residing in the United States: January 2009," Department of Homeland Security, Office of Immigration Statistics, 2010, http://www.dhs.gov/xlibrary/assets/statistics/publications/ois_ill_pe_2009.pdf.

21. Gary Freeman, "Modes of Immigration Politics in Liberal Democratic States," *International Migration Review* 29, no. 4 (1995): 881–902.

22. "Other Border States Shun Arizona's Immigration Law," *Washington Post,* May 12, 2010, http://www.washingtonpost.com/wp-dyn/content/article/2010/05/12/AR2010051203919.html.

23. On limits on noncitizens' access to welfare benefits in the United States during the Great Depression, see Cybelle Fox, *The Boundaries of Social Citizenship: Race, Immigration and the American Welfare State, 1900–1950* (PhD diss., Harvard University, 2007), chapters 5 and 6. It is important to note, however, that the most substantial recent limitation of noncitizens' access to benefits in the United States—the 1996 Clinton-era welfare-reform legislation that, among other things, denied federal funding for Medicaid to legal immigrants during their first five years of residence—was not a response to economic distress. In the current crisis, liberal Massachusetts—one of the few states that had filled the gap created by the 1996 legislation—did scale back its program of subsidized insurance for new immigrants in response to a large budget deficit. See Abby Goodnough, "Massachusetts Cuts Back Immigrants' Health Care," *New York Times,* September 1, 2009, http://www.nytimes.com/2009/09/01/health/policy/01mass.html.

24. Ioannis Glinavos, "The Credit Crunch and the End of Neoliberalism," Social Science Research Network, December 7, 2008, http://ssrn.com/abstract=1312722.

25. Michael Mann, "Neoliberalism: Rise and Recession" (paper presented at the Comparative Analysis Seminar, Department of Sociology, UCLA, 2010).

26. David Harvey, "The Crisis and the Consolidation of Class Power: Is This *Really* the End of Neoliberalism?" *Counterpunch*, March 15, 2009, http://www.counterpunch.org/harvey03132009.html.

27. Daw Khin Yi, *The Dobama Movement in Burma (1930–1938)* (Ithaca, NY: Cornell University Southeast Asia Program, 1988), 4–5; and Michael Adas, "Immigrant Asians and the Economic Impact of European Imperialism: The Role of the South Indian Chettiars in British Burma," *Journal of Asian Studies* 33 (1974): 385–401.

28. On the distinctive urban ethnic demography of the region, see John Alexander Armstrong, *Nations before Nationalism* (Chapel Hill: University of North Carolina Press, 1982), 113–22.

29. Joseph Rothschild, *East Central Europe between the Two World Wars* (Seattle: University of Washington Press, 1974), 12–13.

30. Rogers Brubaker, Margit Feischmidt, Jon Fox, and Liana Grancea, *Nationalist Politics and Everyday Ethnicity in a Transylvanian Town* (Princeton, NJ: Princeton University Press, 2006), 50, 70ff.

31. Jemma Purdey, *Anti-Chinese Violence in Indonesia, 1996–1999* (Singapore: Singapore University Press, 2006), chapter 3.

32. Edna Bonacich, "A Theory of Middleman Minorities," *American Sociological Review* 38 (1973): 583–94.

33. Amy Chua, *World on Fire: How Exporting Free Market Democracy Breeds Ethnic Hatred and Global Instability* (New York: Anchor Books, 2003).

34. On Jews and Chinese in comparative perspective, see Daniel Chirot and Anthony Reid, eds., *Essential Outsiders: Chinese and Jews in the Modern Transformation of Southeast Asia and Central Europe* (Seattle: University of Washington Press, 1997).

35. Chua, *World on Fire*.

36. On anti-Semitism and the crash of 1873, see Albert Lindemann, *Esau's Tears: Modern Anti-Semitism and the Rise of the Jews* (Cambridge: Cambridge University Press, 1997), 118ff.

37. D. Chirot and C. Ragin, "The Market, Tradition and Peasant Rebellion: The Case of Romania," *American Sociological Review* 40 (1975): 428–44.

38. Although Max Weber did not address economic crises per se, he suggested that the "naked class situation" tends to predominate during periods of economic transformation, whereas status-group (*ständisch*) claims focused on social honor and shared style of life—a category that, for Weber, included ethnicity—predominate during periods of economic stability. Max Weber, *Economy and Society: An Outline of Interpretive Sociology*, ed. Guenther Roth and Claus Wittich (1922; repr., Berkeley: University of California Press, 1978), 938. And the distinguished historian Richard Hofstadter argued in a contribution to a collection on the radical Right that "interest politics" predominate in times of economic distress, whereas "status politics" or "cultural politics"—which Hofstadter associated with the radical Right—flourish in times of prosperity. Richard Hofstadter, "The Pseudo-Conservative Revolt," in *The Radical Right,* 3rd ed., ed. Daniel Bell, (1955; repr., New Brunswick, NJ: Transaction, 2002, 84–85); and Richard Hofstadter, "Pseudo-Conservatism Revisited: A Postscript," in ibid., 99.

39. See Kristina Rizga, "Latvia Moves Leftward in Recent Elections," Pulitzer Center on Crisis Reporting, June 8, 2009, http://pulitzercenter.org/blog/untold-stories/latvia-moves-leftward-recent-elections.html.

40. Darryl Fears and Carol D. Leonnig, "Activists Angered by Blame for Crisis," *Washington Post,* October 3, 2008, http://www.washington post.com/wp-dyn/content/article/2008/10/02/AR2008100204115. html; and Jonathan Wheatley, "Brazil's Leader Blames White People for Crisis," *Financial Times,* March 27, 2009, http://www.ft.com/cms/s/0/ae4957e8-1a5f-11de-9f91-0000779fd2ac.html?nclick_check=1.

41. The American survey reported (without details about the questions or sample) that nearly a quarter of non-Jewish respondents blamed "the Jews" at least "a moderate amount" for the financial crisis. Neil Malhotra and Yotam Margalit, "State of the Nation: Anti-Semitism and the Economic Crisis," *Boston Review,* May–June 2009, http://boston review.net/BR34.3/malhotra_margalit.php. The Anti-Defamation League reported a substantial upsurge in anti-Semitic postings on Internet discussion boards in September and October 2008: "Financial Crisis Sparks Wave of Internet Anti-Semitism," http://www.adl.org/main_internet/Anti-Semitism_Financial_Crisis.htm. The European survey, commissioned by the Anti-Defamation League, was based on telephone interviews

with five hundred persons in each of seven countries: Austria, France, Germany, Hungary, Poland, Spain, and the United Kingdom. The largest numbers assigning "a great deal," "a good amount," or "a little" blame for the crisis to "Jews in the financial industry" were recorded in Hungary (46 percent), followed by Austria (43 percent) and Poland (38 percent). The report, however, did not break down the results by degrees of blame. ADL, "Attitudes toward Jews in Seven European Countries," February 2009, http://www.adl.org/Public%20ADL%20Anti-Semitism%20Presentation %20February%202009%20_3_.pdf. Political anti-Semitism has been more central in Hungary since the collapse of Communism than it has been elsewhere in Europe, but it does not appear to have intensified in response to the crisis.

42. Jens Rydgren, "The Sociology of the Radical Right," *Annual Review of Sociology* 33 (2007): 249.

43. Some Islamist narratives of the crisis have been framed in broader civilizational terms rather than in nation-statist terms: in such accounts, the crisis resulted from the bankruptcy of the entire Western system of political economy and highlights the superiority of the compre- hensive moral economy required by Islam, including specifically the rap- idly growing Islamic banking and finance sector. See, for example, AFP, "Iran Hails World Financial Crisis as 'End of Capitalism,'" *Breitbart,* October 15, 2008, http://www.breitbart.com/article.php?id=0810151 52055.72llwkbo&show_article=1; and AFP, "Global Crisis a 'Golden Opportunity' for Islamic Banking: Malaysia," *Muslims.net,* January 12, 2009, http://www.muslims.net/news/newsfull.php?newid=282859.

44. Henry Chu, "In Debt-Plagued Greece, Immigrants Feel the Heat," *New York Times,* March 16, 2010; and Suzanne Daley, "Spain's Jobless Find It Hard to Go Back to Farm," *New York Times,* May 14, 2010.

Notes to Chapter 5

1. I am largely using the periodization developed by Carlota Perez, *Technological Revolutions and Financial Capital: The Dynamics of Bubbles and Golden Ages* (Cheltenham, UK: Elgar, 2002). I am very grateful to her for extensive discussion of and comments on this chapter.

2. Quincy Wright, *A Study of War* (Chicago: University of Chicago Press, 1942).

3. Nikolai Kondratieff, *The Long Wave Cycle* (1928; repr., New York: Richardson and Snyder, 1984), 95.

4. Joshua S. Goldstein, *Long Cycles: Prosperity and War in the Modern Age* (New Haven, CT: Yale University Press, 1988); and Paul Kennedy, *The Rise and Fall of the Great Powers: Economic Change and Military Conflict 1500 to 2000* (London: Unwin Hyman, 1988).

5. This is an argument I develop in my book *The Baroque Arsenal* (New York: Hill and Wang, 1982).

6. Mary Kaldor, Margaret Sharp, and William Walker, "Industrial Competitiveness and Britain's Defence Commitments," *Lloyds Bank Review* 162 (October 1986): 31–49.

7. Joseph E. Stiglitz, *Freefall: America, Free Markets, and the Sinking of the World Economy* (New York: Norton, 2010).

8. Perez, *Technological Revolutions and Financial Capital*, 75.

9. See José Gabriel Palma, "The Revenge of the Market on the Rentiers: Why Neo-liberal Reports of the End of History Turned Out to Be Premature," *Cambridge Journal of. Economics* 33, no. 4 (2009): 829–69.

10. See also Carlota Perez, "The Double Bubble at the Turn of the Century: Technological Roots and Structural Implications," *Cambridge Journal of Economics* 33 (2009): 779–805.

Notes to Chapter 6

1. Alan Milward, *The European Rescue of the Nation-State*, 2nd ed. (London: Routledge, 2000); and Andrew Moravcsik, *The Choice for Europe: Social Purpose and State Power from Messina to Maastricht* (Ithaca, NY: Cornell University Press, 1998).

2. Ernst Haas, *The Uniting of Europe: Political, Social, and Economic Forces, 1950–57* (Stanford, CA: Stanford University Press, 1958).

3. Simon J. Bulmer, "New Institutionalism and the Governance of the Single European Market," *Journal of European Public Policy* 5, no. 3 (1998): 365–86; and Alec Stone Sweet, Neil Fligstein, and Wayne Sandholtz, eds., *The Institutionalization of Europe* (Oxford: Oxford University Press, 2001).

4. Sam-Sang Jo, *European Myths: Resolving the Crises in the European Community/European Union* (Lanham, MD: University Press of America, 2007).

5. Kenneth Dyson and Kevin Featherstone, *The Road to Maastricht: Negotiating the Maastricht Treaty* (Oxford: Oxford University Press, 1999).

6. Jean Pisani-Ferry, "Monetary Union with Variable Geometry," in *The New Political Economy of EMU*, ed. J. Frieden, D. Gros, and E. Jones (Lanham, MD: Rowman and Littlefield, 1998).

7. Amy Verdun, "An 'Asymmetrical' Economic and Monetary Union in the EU: Perceptions of Monetary Authorities and Social Partners," *Journal of European Integration* 20, no. 1 (1996): 59–81.

8. Patrick Leblond, "The Political Stability and Growth Pact Is Dead: Long Live the Economic Stability and Growth Pact," *Journal of Common Market Studies* 44, no. 5 (2006): 969–90.

9. Jacques de Larosière, *Report of the High Level Group on Financial Supervision in the EU* (Brussels: Commission of the European Union, 2009), 41.

10. Otmar Issing, "Why a Common Eurozone Bond Isn't Such a Good Idea," *Europe's World* (Summer 2009): 76–79.

11. Wolfgang Münchau, "Germany and France Need to Sing in Tune," *Financial Times*, June 29, 2009.

12. Andrew Grice, "Sarkozy Claims Victory over Britain as EU Strikes Deal," *Independent*, June 24, 2007.

13. Joël Bourdin and Yvon Collin, *La coordination des politiques économiques en Europe: Le malaise avant la crise?* (Paris: Sénat, 2007).

14. Kathleen McNamara, *The Currency of Ideas: Monetary Politics in the European Union* (Ithaca, NY: Cornell University Press, 1998).

15. Leblond, "Political Stability and Growth Pact."

16. Otmar Issing, "On Macroeconomic Policy Co-ordination in EMU," *Journal of Common Market Studies* 40, no. 2 (2002): 345–58; and Jean Pisani-Ferry, "Only One Bed for Two Dreams: A Critical Retrospective on the Debate over the Economic Governance of the Euro Area," *Journal of Common Market Studies* 44, no. 4 (2006): 823–44.

17. Verdun, "'Asymmetrical' Economic and Monetary Union."

18. Jean Pisani-Ferry and André Sapir, foreword to *Europe's Economic Priorities 2010–2015: Memos to the New Commission*, ed. André Sapir (Brussels: Bruegel, 2009), 6.

19. R. Daniel Kelemen and Anand Menon, "You Thought We've Got an EU Single Market? Think Again!" *Europe's World*, Summer 2007.

20. George Ross, "Danger, One EU Crisis May Hide Another: Social Model Anxieties and Hard Cases," *Comparative European Politics* 4, no. 4 (2006): 309–30.

21. Andrew Martin and George Ross, eds., *Euros and Europeans. Monetary Integration and the European Model of Society* (Cambridge: Cambridge University Press, 2004).

22. André Sapir, "Globalization and the Reform of European Social Models," *Journal of Common Market Studies* 44, no. 2 (2006): 369–90.

23. Ian Manners, "Normative Power Europe: A Contradiction in Terms?" *Journal of Common Market Studies* 40, no. 2 (2002): 235–58.

24. Philip Stephens, "Four Things You Must Know about the Global Puzzle," *Financial Times,* September 25, 2009.

25. Richard Gowan and Franziska Brantner, "The EU and Human Rights at the UN—2009 Review," in *The European Union and Human Rights at the UN Annual Review* (London: European Council on Foreign Relations, 2009).

26. Alexander C.-G. Stubb, "A Categorization of Differentiated Integration," *Journal of Common Market Studies* 34, no. 2 (1996): 283–95.

27. Alberto Alesina and Vittorio Grilli, "On the Feasibility of a One-Speed or Multispeed European Monetary Union," *Economics and Politics* 5, no. 2 (1993): 145–65.

Notes to Chapter 7

1. On "secularization," see Harvey Cox, *The Secular City: Secularization and Urbanization in Theological Perspective,* rev. ed. (London: Penguin, 1968); Bryan Wilson, *Religion in Sociological Perspective* (Oxford: Oxford University Press, 1982); Steve Bruce, ed., *Religion and Modernization: Sociologists and Historians Debate the Secularization Thesis* (Oxford: Clarendon, 1992); Steve Bruce, ed., *God Is Dead: Secularization in the West* (Oxford: Blackwell, 2002); and the earlier work of Peter L. Berger: *The Sacred Canopy: Elements for a Sociology of Religion* (New York: Anchor Books, 1967); and *The Social Reality of Religion* (London: Faber, 1969). On "desecularization," see Peter Berger, ed., *The Desecularization of the World: Resurgent Religion and World Politics* (Grand Rapids, MI: Eerdmans, 1999); and Pippa Norris and Ronald Inglehart, *Sacred and Secular: Religion and Politics Worldwide* (Cambridge: Cambridge

University Press, 2004). Cf. the pioneering research of David Martin beyond the (false) divide between the two theses: "Towards Eliminating the Concept of Secularization," in *Penguin Survey of the Social Sciences*, ed. J. Gould (Harmondsworth, UK: Penguin, 1965), 169–82; *A General Theory of Secularization* (Oxford: Blackwell, 1978); and *On Secularization: Towards a Revised General Theory* (Aldershot, UK: Ashgate, 2005).

2. John Milbank, *Theology and Social Theory: Beyond Secular Reason*, 2nd ed. (Oxford: Blackwell, 2006); Charles Taylor, *A Secular Age* (Cambridge, MA: Harvard University Press, 2007); and Michael Allen Gillespie, *The Theological Origins of Modernity* (Chicago: University of Chicago Press, 2008).

3. Cf. Shmuel N. Eisenstadt, ed., *Multiple Modernities* (New Brunswick, NJ: Transaction, 2002).

4. Bruno Latour, *Nous n'avons jamais été modernes: Essai d'anthropologie symétrique* (Paris: La Découverte, 1991), translated by Catherine Porter as *We Have Never Been Modern* (London: Harvester Wheatsheaf, 1993).

5. Adrian Pabst, "Unholy War and Just Peace: Religious Alternatives to Secular Warfare," *Politics and Religion* 3 (2009): 209–31. Cf. Gilles Kepel, *The Revenge of God: The Resurgence of Islam, Christianity, and Judaism in the Modern World*, trans. A. Braley (University Park: Pennsylvania State University Press, 1994); Mark Juergensmeyer, *Terror in the Mind of God: The Global Rise of Religious Violence* (Berkeley: University of California Press, 2000); and Gabriel A. Almond, R. Scott Appleby, and Emmanuel Sivan, *Strong Religion: The Rise of Fundamentalisms around the World* (Chicago: University of Chicago Press, 2003).

6. Philip S. Gorski, "Historicizing the Secularization Debate: An Agenda for Research," in *Handbook of the Sociology of Religion*, ed. Michele Dillon (Cambridge: Cambridge University Press, 2003).

7. Martin, *On Secularization*, 17–25.

8. Peter L. Berger, "Desecularization of the World: A Global Overview," in Berger, *The Desecularization of the World*, 1–18.

9. The modern shift from objective revelation to subjective belief redefines religion as "a set of propositions to which believers gave assent, and which could therefore be judged and compared between different religions and as against natural science." Talal Asad, *Genealogies of Religion: Discipline and Reasons of Power in Christianity and Islam*

(Baltimore, MD: Johns Hopkins University Press, 1993), 41. Cf. Amos Funkenstein, *Theology and the Scientific Imagination from the Middle Ages to the Seventeenth Century* (Princeton, NJ: Princeton University Press, 1986), 25–63; and Peter Harrison, *"Religion" and the Religions in the English Enlightenment* (Cambridge: Cambridge University Press, 1990), 19–60, 130–72.

10. Andrew Wernick, *Auguste Comte and the Religion of Humanity: The Post-theistic Program of French Social Theory* (Cambridge: Cambridge University Press, 2001). Positivism shapes the dominant contemporary conceptions of religion, including the atheism of Russell and Dawkins but also the religious fundamentalism of Al Qaeda's intellectual fathers. See Aziz Al-Azmeh, *Islams and Modernities* (London: Verso, 1993); and John Gray, *Al Qaeda and What It Means to Be Modern* (London: Faber and Faber, 2003).

11. Milbank, *Theology and Social Theory*; Taylor, *A Secular Age*. Cf. Gillespie, *Theological Origins of Modernity*.

12. André de Muralt, "Kant, le dernier occamien: Une nouvelle définition de la philosophie moderne," *Revue de Métaphysique et de Morale* 80 (1975): 32–53; André de Muralt, *L'unité de la philosophie politique: De Scot, Occam et Suarez au libéralisme contemporain* (Paris: Vrin, 2002); and Pierre Manent, *Histoire intellectuelle du libéralisme: Dix leçons* (Paris: Calmann-Lévy, 1987).

13. Adrian Pabst, "Modern Sovereignty in Question: Theology, Democracy and Capitalism," *Modern Theology* 26 (2010): 570–602.

14. John Bossy, "The Mass as a Social Institution," *Past and Present* 100 (1983): 29–61; and John Bossy, *Christianity in the West, 1400–1700* (Oxford: Oxford University Press, 1985).

15. José Casanova, *Public Religions in the Modern World* (Chicago: University of Chicago Press, 1994); and José Casanova, "Rethinking Secularization: A Global Comparative Perspective," *Hedgehog Review* 8 (2006): 7–22.

16. On the contrary, Rémi Brague shows that notions such as "Abrahamic faiths" or "monotheism" overlook fundamental differences between Judaism, Christianity, and Islam. See Rémi Brague, *Du Dieu des chrétiens: Et d'un ou deux autres* (Paris: Flammarion, 2008).

17. Émile Durkheim, *Elementary Forms of the Religious Life*, trans. J. S. Swain (London: Allen and Unwin, 1915), 37.

18. Asad, *Genealogies of Religion*; and Talal Asad, *Formations of the Secular: Christianity, Islam, Modernity* (Stanford, CA: Stanford University Press, 2003).

19. Cf. William T. Cavanaugh, "'A Fire Strong Enough to Consume the House': The Wars of Religion and the Rise of the State," *Modern Theology* 11 (1995): 397–420; and William T. Cavanaugh, "Killing for the Telephone Company: Why the Nation-State Is Not the Keeper of the Common Good," *Modern Theology* 20 (2004): 243–74.

20. Michel Foucault, *Surveiller et punir: Naissance de la prison* (Paris: Gallimard, 1975); and Michel Foucault, *Naissance de la biopolitique: Cours au Collège de France, 1978–1979* (Paris: Seuil, 2004). Cf. Pabst, "Modern Sovereignty in Question."

21. Cf. John Robertson, *The Case for the Enlightenment: Scotland and Naples 1680–1760* (Cambridge: Cambridge University Press, 2005). Cf. Adrian Pabst, *Metaphysics: The Creation of Hierarchy* (Grand Rapids, MI: Eerdmans, 2011).

22. Adam Smith, *An Inquiry into the Nature and Causes of the Wealth of Nations*, intro. D. D. Raphael (London: Random, 1991), Book I, chapter ii, 1.

23. See Janet Coleman, "Ockham's Right Reason and the Genesis of the Political as 'Absolutist,'" *History of Political Thought* 20 (1999): 35–64; C. B. MacPherson, *The Political Theory of Possessive Individualism: Hobbes to Locke* (Oxford: Clarendon, 1962); John Milbank, Catherine Pickstock, and Graham Ward, eds., *Radical Orthodoxy: A New Theology* (London: Routledge, 1999); Steven Shapin and Simon Schaffer, *Leviathan and the Air-Pump: Hobbes, Boyle, and the Experimental Life* (Princeton, NJ: Princeton University Press, 1985); and Quentin Skinner, *Hobbes and Republican Liberty* (Cambridge: Cambridge University Press, 2008).

24. Jon Butler, *Awash in a Sea of Faith: Christianizing the American People* (Cambridge, MA: Harvard University Press, 1990); and Michael Young, *Bearing Witness against Sin: The Evangelical Birth of the American Social Movement* (Chicago: University of Chicago Press, 2006).

25. E. P. Thompson, "The Moral Economy of the English Crowd in the 18th Century," *Past and Present* 50 (1971): 76–136; and E. P. Thompson, *Customs in Common: Studies in Traditional Popular Culture* (London: Merlin, 1991). Cf. David Hempton, *The Religion of the People: Methodism and Popular Religion, c. 1750–1900* (London: Routledge,

1996); and David Hempton, *Methodism: Empire of the Spirit* (New Haven, CT: Yale University Press, 2006).

26. The Protestant powers of England, Holland, and the United States rejected the overarching ecclesial and social unity of their Catholic rivals, in terms of national self-conception and as a principle of social organization. This led to successive waves of secular modernization of religion and later culture (c. 1590s–1660s; c. 1790s–1850s; after 1900), culminating in Pentecostal awakenings, "themselves harbingers of global society," and "their spread corresponded to the movement of lay people around the globe, to South Africa, Norway, Sicily, Korea or the Southern Cone of Latin America." Martin, *On Secularization*, 27. Cf. John Micklethwait and Adrian Wooldridge, *God Is Back: How the Global Rise of Faith Is Changing the World* (London: Allen Lane, 2009), 213–42.

27. Wolfram Kaiser, *Christian Democracy and the Origins of European Union* (Cambridge: Cambridge University Press, 2007).

28. Benedict XVI, *Caritas in Veritate* (Dublin: Veritas, 2009). Cf. Adrian Pabst, ed., *The Crisis of Global Capitalism: Caritas in Veritate and the Future of Political Economy* (Eugene, OR: Wipf and Stock, 2011).

29. The episcopal churches differ on important issues, such as church-state relations, but are united in their opposition to modern secularism, as evinced by their agreement on moral and social teaching. See, for instance, the forewords by the Metropolitan Kirill (now Patriarch of the Russian Orthodox Church) to the book on the common good by Cardinal Bertone and to the Russian translation of Pope Benedict's *Introduction to Christianity*. Tarcisio Bertone, *The Ethics of the Common Good in Catholic Social Doctrine* (Vatican City: Libreria Editrice Vaticana, 2008).

30. See Martin, *On Secularization*, 47–74, for a survey of supporting evidence. See Paul Froese, *The Plot to Kill God: Findings from the Soviet Experiment in Secularization* (Berkeley: University of California Press, 2008), on the endurance of religious faith in the Soviet Union despite violent campaigns of atheism and persecution.

31. In addition to Berger, *Desecularization of the World*, see Steve Bruce, ed., *Religion and Politics* (Oxford: Blackwell, 2003); and Martin, *On Secularization*; see Norris and Inglehart, *Sacred and Secular*, for a global overview of contemporary patterns of secularization and religious resurgence.

32. For example, see Geoffrey Hosking, *Rulers and Victims: The Russians in the Soviet Union* (Cambridge, MA: Harvard University Press, 2006), 3–35, for evidence of the secular messianism of Soviet Communism.

33. Pavlos Hatzopoulos and Fabio Petito, eds., *Religion in International Relations: The Return from Exile* (London: Palgrave, 2003); and Scott M. Thomas, *The Global Resurgence of Religion and the Transformation of International Relations: The Struggle for the Soul of the Twenty-First Century* (London: Palgrave, 2005).

34. Despite violent clashes between state and church in France up to separation in 1905, the population remained predominantly Catholic until the late 1950s, when "French Christendom" (*chrétienté*) began to disappear from the regions and countryside, as depicted in the writings of George Bernanos. In Britain, the "de-christianization" of the public sphere and social life did not take off until the late 1960s. Cf. Callum Brown, *The Death of Christian Britain* (London: Routledge, 2001); and Callum Brown, *Religion and Society in Twentieth-Century Britain* (Harlow, UK: Pearson, 2006). Scandinavia and the Mediterranean countries only became markedly more secular from the mid-1970s onward. After decades of atheist rule, central/eastern Europe and Eurasia are characterized by profound contrasts between a strong and sustained religious revival in countries such as Poland and Russia and a growing tendency toward agnosticism and atheism in countries such as the Czech Republic. See Norris and Inglehart, *Sacred and Secular*; Martin, *On Secularization*, 47–90; and Peter L. Berger, Grace Davie, and Effie Fokas, eds., *Religious America, Secular Europe? A Theme and Variations* (Aldershot, UK: Ashgate, 2008), 23–122.

35. Cf. William E. Connolly, *Capitalism and Christianity, American Style* (Durham, NC: Duke University Press, 2008), 17–68.

36. Will Herbert, *Protestant, Catholic, Jew: An Essay in American Religious Sociology*, rev. ed. (New York: Doubleday, 1960); Thomas Luckmann, *The Invisible Religion: The Problem of Religion in Modern Society* (New York: Macmillan, 1967); Harold Bloom, *The American Religion* (New York: Simon and Schuster, 1992); and Nancy Ammerman, *Congregation and Community* (New Brunswick, NJ: Rutgers University Press, 1997).

37. Cf. Mark A. Noll, *America's God: From Jonathan Edwards to Abraham Lincoln* (New York: Oxford University Press, 2002), 227–367.

38. On Catholicism: George Weigel, "Roman Catholicism in the Age of John Paul II," in Berger, *Desecularization of the World*, 19–35; and Philip Jenkins, *The Next Christendom: The Coming of Global Christianity* (Oxford: Oxford University Press, 2002). On Islam: Kepel, *Revenge of God*; Fazlur Rahman, *Revival and Reform in Islam: A Study of Islamic Fundamentalism*, ed. Ebrahim Moosa (Oxford: Oneworld, 2000); and Olivier Roy, *Globalised Islam: The Search for a New Ummah* (London: Hurst, 2004). On Buddhism: Charles S. Prebish and Martin Baumann, eds., *Westward Dharma: Buddhism beyond Asia* (Berkeley: University of California Press, 2002).

39. Grace Davie, *Religion in Britain since 1945: Believing without Belonging* (Oxford: Blackwell, 1994); Norris and Inglehart, *Sacred and Secular*; and Eric Kaufmann, "Breeding for God," *Prospect* 128 (November 2006), http://www.sneps.net/RD/uploads/06prospect-Kaufmann.pdf. In recent research, Grace Davie has qualified the distinction between believing and belonging by theorizing the idea of "vicarious religion." See Grace Davie, "Vicarious Religion: A Methodological Challenge," in *Everyday Religion: Observing Modern Religious Lives*, ed. Nancy Ammerman (New York: Oxford University Press, 2007), 21–36; and Grace Davie, "Vicarious Religion: A Response," *Journal of Contemporary Religion* 2 (2010): 261–67.

40. Christopher Caldwell, *Reflection on the Revolution in Europe: Immigration, Islam and the West* (London: Allen Lane, 2009); and Eric Kaufmann, *Shall the Religious Inherit the Earth? Demography and Politics in the Twenty-First Century* (London: Profile Books, 2010).

41. David Martin, *The World Their Parish: Pentecostalism as Cultural Revolution and Global Option* (Oxford: Blackwell, 2001); and Martin, *On Secularization*, 26–43, 141–54.

42. Jenkins, *The Next Christendom*; David Aikman, *Jesus in Beijing: How Christianity Is Changing the Global Balance of Power* (Washington, DC: Regnery, 2003).

43. James Noyes, *The Politics of Iconoclasm: Religion, Violence and the Culture of Image-Breaking in Christianity and Islam* (London: I. B. Tauris, 2012).

44. Martin, *On Secularization*, 142.

45. Walter Benjamin, "Capitalism as Religion," in *Walter Benjamin: Selected Writings—Volume 1 (1913–1926)*, ed. Marcus Bullock and Michael W. Jennings (Cambridge, MA: Harvard University Press, 1996), 288–91.

46. For example, Jürgen Habermas and Joseph Ratzinger, *Dialektik der Säkularisierung: Über Vernunft und Religion* (Freiburg: Herder, 2004), translated by Brian McNeil as *The Dialectics of Secularization: On Reason and Religion* (San Francisco: Ignatius, 2007).

47. Jürgen Habermas, *Zwischen Naturalismus und Religion: Philosophische Aufsätze* (Frankfurt: Suhrkamp, 2005), translated by Ciaran Cronin as *Between Naturalism and Religion: Philosophical Essays* (Cambridge, UK: Polity, 2008).

48. For Schmitt's account of sovereign power, see Carl Schmitt, *Politische Theologie: Vier Kapitel zur Lehre von der Souveränität* (Munich/ Leipzig: Duncker und Humbolt, 1922); Foucault, *Naissance de la biopolitique.*

49. De Muralt, "Kant, le dernier occamien"; and de Muralt, *L'unité de la philosophie politique.*

50. Joseph Ratzinger, "Homily during the Mass *pro eligendo romano pontifice,*" Vatican, April 18, 2005, http://www.vatican.va/gpII/ documents/homily-pro-eligendo-pontifice_20050418_en.html.

51. For compelling critiques of the new militant atheism, see Terry Eagleton, *Reason, Faith, and Revolution: Reflections on the God Debate* (New Haven, CT: Yale University Press, 2009); and David Bentley Hart, *Atheist Delusions: The Christian Revolution and Its Fashionable Enemies* (New Haven, CT: Yale University Press, 2009).

52. Stephen Jay Gould, *Ever since Darwin: Reflections in Natural History,* rev. ed. (London: Penguin, 1991); Stephen Jay Gould, *The Structure of Evolutionary Theory,* rev. ed. (Cambridge, MA: Harvard University Press, 2002); and Stephen Jay Gould, *Punctuated Equilibrium* (London: Belknap, 2007).

53. Simon Conway Morris, *The Crucible of Creation: The Burgess Shale and the Rise of Animals* (Oxford: Oxford University Press, 1998); Simon Conway Morris, *Life's Solution: Inevitable Humans in a Lonely Universe,* new ed. (Cambridge: Cambridge University Press, 2004); and Simon Conway Morris, ed., *The Deep Structure of Biology: Is Convergence Sufficiently Ubiquitous to Give a Directional Signal?* (West Conshohocken, PA: Templeton Foundation Press, 2008).

54. Nidhal Guessoum, *Réconcilier l'islam et la science moderne: L'esprit d'Averroès* (Paris: Presses de la Renaissance, 2009), translated by Alessia Weil as *Islam's Quantum Question: Reconciling Muslim Tradition and*

Modern Science (London: I. B. Tauris, 2011); and Conor Cunningham, *Darwin's Pious Idea: Why the Ultra-Darwinists and Creationists Both Get It Wrong* (Grand Rapids, MI: Eerdmans, 2010).

Notes to Chapter 8

1. Even in a country such as India, a growing number of Internet users are on social-networking sites. Comscore, "Facebook Captures Top Spot among Social Networking Sites in India," August 25, 2010, http://www.comscore.com/Press_Events/Press_Releases/2010/8/Facebook_Captures_Top_Spot_among_Social_Networking_Sites_in_India.

2. Brian Larkin, *Signal and Noise: Media, Infrastructure, and Urban Culture in Nigeria* (Durham, NC: Duke University Press, 2008).

3. Elizabeth Eisenstein, *The Printing Press as an Agent of Change: Communications and Cultural Transformations in Early Modern Europe* (Cambridge: Cambridge University Press, 1979), 470.

4. For a critique of Eisenstein's book, see Adrian Johns, *The Nature of the Book: Print and Knowledge in the Making* (Chicago: University of Chicago Press, 1998).

5. Siegfried Kracauer, *The Mass Ornament: Weimar Essays,* trans. and ed. Thomas Y. Levin (Princeton, NJ: Princeton University Press, 1995).

6. Yochai Benkler, *The Wealth of Networks: How Social Production Transforms Markets and Freedom* (New Haven, CT: Yale University Press, 2006).

7. Johns, *Nature of the Book.*

8. D. N. Rodowick, *The Virtual Life of Film* (Cambridge, MA: Harvard University Press, 2007).

9. Ibid., 93.

10. Ibid., 94.

11. For the simplest of technical introductions to the differences between analog and digital media, see Marshall Brain, "How Analog and Digital Recording Works," *HowStuffWorks,* http://communication.how stuffworks.com/analog-digital.htm.

12. Lev Manovich summarizes this process as the variability of the digital: "Old media involved a human creator who manually assembled textual, visual and/or audio elements into a particular composition or a sequence. This sequence was stored in some material, its order determined

once and for all. Numerous copies could be run off from the master, and, in perfect correspondence with the logic of an industrial society, they were all identical. New media, in contrast, is characterized by variability. Instead of identical copies a new media object typically gives rise to many different versions. And rather than being created completely by a human author, these versions are often in part automatically assembled by a computer." Lev Manovich, *The Language of New Media* (Cambridge, MA: MIT Press, 2002), 56.

13. Friedrich Kittler, *Gramophone, Film, Typewriter* (Stanford, CA: Stanford University Press, 1999), 2.

14. Jonathan Crary, *Techniques of the Observer: On Vision and Modernity in the 19th Century* (Cambridge, CA: MIT Press, 1992), 2.

15. See http://wikileaks.org/ for a good selection of the hacker–transparency activist combination.

16. Walter Benjamin, *Illuminations* (New York: Schocken, 1969).

17. Larkin, *Signal and Noise*; and Ravi Sundaram, *Pirate Modernity: Delhi's Media Urbanism* (London: Routledge, 2009).

18. Toby Miller, with Nitin Govil, John McMurria, and Richard Maxwell, *Global Hollywood* (London: BFI, 2005).

19. Wendy Ellen Everett, ed., *European Identity in Cinema* (London: Intellect Books, 2005).

20. Miller et al., *Global Hollywood*, 24, also see 27–28.

21. David Bordwell, Janet Staiger, and Kristin Thompson, *The Classical Hollywood Cinema. Film Style and Mode of Production to 1960* (New York: Columbia University Press, 1985).

22. Victoria de Grazia, *Irresistible Empire: America's Advance through 20th-Century Europe* (Cambridge, MA: Harvard University Press, 2005).

23. John Tomlinson, *Cultural Imperialism: A Critical Introduction* (London: Continuum, 1991).

24. Jane Gaines, "Early Cinema's Heyday of Copying," *Cultural Studies* 20, nos. 2–3 (2006): 227–44.

25. Guy Debord, *The Society of the Spectacle* (Brooklyn, NY: Zone Books, 1994).

26. Martin Heidegger, "The Question Concerning Technology," in *Basic Writings*, ed. David Krell (New York: HarperCollins, 1993).

27. Giovanni Arrighi, *The Long Twentieth Century: Money, Power, and the Origins of Our Times* (London: Verso, 1994), 27–84.

28. Tom O'Regan, "From Piracy to Sovereignty: International VCR Trends," *Continuum: Australian Journal of Media and Culture* 4, no. 2 (1991), http://wwwmcc.murdoch.edu.au/ReadingRoom/4.2/oregan.html.

29. This was the age before the Internet and widespread use of digital technology.

30. See Miller et al., *Global Hollywood*.

31. Néstor García Canclini, *Consumers and Citizens: Globalization and Multicultural Conflicts* (Minneapolis: University of Minnesota Press, 2001).

32. Ibid., 116.

33. Déborah Holtz, quoted in Canclini, *Consumers and Citizens.*

34. Sundaram, *Pirate Modernity.*

35. Jonathan Haynes and Onookome Okome, "Evolving Popular Media: Nigerian Video Films," *Research in African Literatures* 29, no. 3 (Autumn 1998): 117.

36. *Sony Corporation of America v. Universal City Studios, Inc.,* 464 U.S. 417 (1984), http://www.law.cornell.edu/copyright/cases/464_US_417.htm.

37. The literature on this period is vast. For lucid summaries, see Mark Rose, *Authors and Owners: The Invention of Copyright* (Cambridge, MA: Harvard University Press, 1993), particularly chapters 2 and 3; and for a comprehensive account, see Johns, *Nature of the Book.*

38. This act was followed by a long struggle in England (expressed in court cases) between the idea of the author's perpetual right (i.e., that of the publishers to whom it was assigned) in common law and the more limited right that was set up in the Statute of Anne. The matter was finally resolved in 1774 in the celebrated case of *Donaldson vs. Becket,* in which the statute of limitations was upheld in a majority decision of the House of Lords.

39. Peter Jaszi argues that the statute had nothing to do with working writers: "The Statute of Anne of 1710 was the result of lobbying by London-based publishers and booksellers seeking new legal weapons against down-market competition spawned by the proliferation of print technology." Peter Jaszi, "On the Author Effect: Contemporary Copyright and Collective Creativity," in *The Construction of Authorship: Textual Appropriation in Law and Literature,* ed. Martha Woodmansee and Peter Jaszi (Durham, NC: Duke University Press, 1994), 32. Mark

Rose presents a more complex story of debates on property and personhood—involving, among other personalities, John Locke and Daniel Defoe—that led to the Statute of Anne. Rose, *Authors and Owners.*

40. Locke's "labor" theory of property argued that "everyman has a property in his person" and that man has a right to that which he has mixed with his labor, converted into a "private dominion." See John Locke, *Two Treatises of Government and A Letter Concerning Toleration* (New Haven, CT: Yale University Press, 2003). In this theory of appropriation, Locke argued that one can appropriate but also "leave enough for others." Thus, property was a natural right but was based on physical possession of property. Lockean theory had to be significantly amended for modern copyright doctrine, but the rhetoric of natural rights and protections has often crept into contemporary enforcement.

41. Quoted in Simon Frith and Lee Marshall, *Music and Copyright* (Edinburgh: Edinburgh University Press, 2004), 30. For a fascinating history of nineteenth-century US government encouragement of piracy, see Doron Ben Atar, *Intellectual Piracy and the Origins of American Power* (New Haven, CT: Yale University Press, 2004).

42. For a greater discussion, see Rose, *Authors and Owners,* chapter 7.

43. Woodmansee and Jaszi, *Construction of Authorship*; James Boyle, *Shamans, Software, and Spleens: Law and the Construction of the Information Society* (Cambridge, MA: Harvard University Press, 1997).

44. Jessica Litman, "The Demonization of Piracy" (address to the Tenth Conference on Computers, Freedom, and Privacy, April 6, 2000), http://www-personal.umich.edu/~jdlitman/. For an extensive analysis of the Digital Millennium Copyright Act, see ibid.

45. See its website: www.iipa.com. Along with the IIPA's industry-advocacy model, WIPO (the World Intellectual Property Organization) is a significant intergovernmental body established by the United Nations.

46. For a useful survey of Hollywood's international campaigns, see Miller et al., *Global Hollywood.*

47. See IIPA, "The Copyright Industries Note USTR Decisions in Its Annual Special 301 Report," press release, April 30, 2007, http://www.iipa.com/pdf/IIPA2007PressReleaseonUSTRSpecial 301decisionsFINAL04302007.pdf.

48. Fair use in the United States follows the three-step test laid down in Berne, of which creative reuse is one but not the only one.

49. Boyle, *Shamans, Software, and Spleens*, 139.

50. Litman, "Demonization of Piracy," 8.

51. For a summary of all the bizarre cases pursued by the US RIAA against individuals, see the webpage maintained by the Electronic Frontier Foundation, http://w2.eff.org/IP/P2P/riaa-v-thepeople.php.

52. The statistics are available on the websites of the IIPA and the MPA. Loss statistics are based on cost projections of media costs, assuming, of course, that every person who bought pirated media would have also bought a legal copy. For arguments that piracy is actually beneficial to industry, see Bin Gu and Vijay Mahajan, "How Much Antipiracy Effort Is Too Much? A Study of the Global Software Industry" (McCombs Research Paper, SSRN, February 2005), http://ssrn.com/abstract=825165.

53. Govil Nitin, "War in the Age of Pirate Reproduction," *Sarai Reader 04: Crisis Media* (Delhi: CSDS, 2004).

54. P2P networks are a significant part of rising internet usage. In 2004, P2P networks accounted for up to 60 percent of global traffic. See Morgan Stanley, "The State of the Internet, Part 3," November 8, 2006, http://www.morganstanley.com/institutional/techresearch/pdfs/Webtwopto2006.pdf.

55. This section expands on a fragment from Ravi Sundaram, "Revisiting the Pirate Kingdom," *Third Text* 23, no. 3 (2008): 335–45.

56. Boyle, *Shamans, Software, and Spleens*; Lawrence Lessig, *Free Culture: How Big Media Uses Technology and the Law to Lock Down Culture and Control Creativity* (New York: Penguin, 2004).

57. "Social media" is a typically twenty-first-century term, which exposes the limits of the twentieth-century divisions of social and leisure space.

58. Miller et al., *Global Hollywood*, summarizes and even agrees with this trend.

59. The former CEO of AOL–Time Warner recently apologized for the "worst deal of the century." See Natalie Erlich, "My Fault for 'Worst Deal of Century': Gerald Levin," CNBC, http://www.cnbc.com/id/34687639.

60. TorrentFreak, "Cisco Expects P2P Traffic to Double by 2014," June 10, 2010, http://torrentfreak.com/cisco-expects-p2p-traffic-to-double-by-2014-100611/). Video is seen as surpassing P2P traffic by 2014.

61. Organized international media pirate networks have also attracted organized crime, though this remains a small part of the local and regional story.

62. Gaines, "Early Cinema's Heyday," 237–38.

63. This is in remarkable contrast to the continuation of vast pirate cultures for a good four hundred years after the onset of print culture. See Johns, *Nature of the Book.*

64. James Boyle, "The Second Enclosure Movement and the Construction of the Public Domain," *Law and Contemporary Problems* 66 (2003): 33; Lawrence Lessig, *Free Culture: How Big Media Uses Technology and the Law to Lock Down Culture and Control Creativity* (New York: Penguin, 2004).

65. Bruno Latour, *Reassembling the Social: An Introduction to Actor Network Theory* (Oxford: Oxford University Press, 2005).

Notes to Chapter 9

1. Georg Simmel, "The Sociology of Secrecy and of Secret Societies," *American Journal of Sociology* 11 (1906): 462.

2. Ibid., 463.

3. Ronen Palan, *The Offshore World: Sovereign Markets, Virtual Places, and Nomad Millionaires* (Ithaca, NY: Cornell University Press, 2003), 104–6.

4. Susan Roberts, "Small Place, Big Money: The Cayman Islands and the International Financial System," *Economic Geography* 71, no. 3 (1995): 237–56. For more detailed stories, see William Brittain-Catlin, *Offshore: The Dark Side of the Global Economy* (New York: Picador, 2006).

5. Nand Bardouille, "The Offshore Services Industry in the Caribbean: A Conceptual and Sub-regional Analysis," *Economic Analysis and Policy* 31, no. 2 (2001): 112.

6. X. L. Ding, "Informal Privatization through Internationalization: The Rise of Nomenklatura Capitalism in China's Offshore Business," *British Journal of Political Science* 30, no. 1 (January 2000): 121–46.

7. Milton Friedman, correspondence with the Center for Freedom and Prosperity, May 15, 2001, http://www.freedomandprosperity.org/update/u05-15-01/u05-15-01.shtml#3.

8. Sixth Offshore Alert Due Diligence Financial Conference, "Offshore Financial Centers: The Big Debate," February 7, 2008, http://www.offshorealertconference.com/OAC2008/OFCDebate.asp.

9. Anthony Maingot, "Offshore Secrecy Centers and the Necessary Role of States: Bucking the Trend," *Journal of Interamerican Studies and World Affairs* 37, no. 4 (1995): 1–24.

10. Ahmed Zoromé, "Concept of Offshore Financial Centers: In Search of an Operational Definition" (working paper, IMF, April 2007). In that same review, the IMF's Statistics Department, in an effort to define the perimeter of its data collection, called an OFC "a jurisdiction in which international investment position assets, including as resident all entities that have legal domicile in that jurisdiction, are close to or more than 50 percent of GDP and in absolute terms more than $1 billion."

11. Zorome, "Concept of Offshore Financial."

12. Antilles, Bahamas, Bahrain, Barbados, Bermuda, Cayman Islands, Cyprus, Guernsey, Hong Kong, Ireland, Isle of Man, Jersey, Latvia, Luxembourg, Malta, Mauritius, Netherlands, Panama, Singapore, Switzerland, United Kingdom, Uruguay, and Vanuatu.

13. Palan, *Offshore World,* 50–56.

14. Ibid., 46.

15. Tax Justice Network, "The Price of Offshore" (briefing paper, March 14, 2005), http://www.taxjustice.net/cms/upload/pdf/Price_of_Offshore.pdf.

16. Quoted in Lucy Komisar, "Tax Havens in Spotlight at G20 Meet," IPS, March 29, 2009, http://ipsnews.net/news.asp?idnews=46308.

17. Mahathir Mohamad, "The Currency Crisis Past and Present," *American Homeowners Resource Center,* January 29, 2010, http://www.ahrc.se/new/index.php/src/news/sub/article/action/ShowMedia/id/5416.

18. Tax Justice Network, "Economic Crisis + Offshore," n.d., www.taxjustice.net/cms/front_content.php?idcat=136&client=1&lang=1m.

19. SwissInfo, "UBS Agrees on Tax Fraud Settlement in US," February 19, 2009, www.swissinfo.ch/eng/index/UBS_agrees_on_tax_fraud_settlement_in_US.html?cid=7346.

20. G20, "Global Plan for Recovery and Reform," communiqué, G20 London Summit, April 2, 2009, www.g20.org/Documents/final-communique.pdf.

21. For details, see OECD, "Overview of OECD's Work on Countering International Tax Evasion: A Background Information Brief," August 11, 2009, http://www98.griffith.edu.au/dspace/bitstream/10072/30882/1/61506_1.pdf.

22. Palan, *Offshore World,* 148.

23. James Scott, *Seeing like a State: How Certain Schemes to Improve the Human Condition Have Failed* (New Haven, CT: Yale University Press, 1999)

24. *Hedge Funds Review,* Cayman Islands Supplement, April 2009, 4–5, http://www.incisivemedia.com/hfr/specialreport/cayman_islands09.pdf.

25. Cited in Philip Aldrick, "G20 Summit: Sun Setting on Tax Havens," *Telegraph,* April 2, 2009, www.telegraph.co.uk/finance/finance topics/g20-summit/5090593/G20-summit-Sun-setting-on-tax-havens.html.

26. Quoted in "Switzerland, Austria, Luxembourg to Ease Bank Secrecy Laws," *Dawn.com,* March 14, 2009, http://www.dawn.com/wps/wcm/connect/dawn-content-library/dawn/the-newspaper/front-page/switzerland,-austria,-luxembourg-to-ease-bank-secrecy-laws.

27. Mohamad, "Currency Crisis Past and Present."

About the Contributors

William Barnes holds a PhD in political science from the University of Michigan and a law degree from Boalt Hall, University of California, Berkeley. He has practiced as a plaintiff's-side tort litigator in the San Francisco Bay Area for the past twenty-five years while also becoming an authority on public-opinion polling, election campaigns, and the evolution of the Left in Nicaragua and El Salvador. His current work represents a return to the issues taken up in his PhD dissertation, issues that have come back into fashion in recent times.

Rogers Brubaker is Professor of Sociology at UCLA. He has written widely on social theory, immigration, citizenship, nationalism, and ethnicity. His books include *The Limits of Rationality: An Essay on the Social and Moral Thought of Max Weber* (1984), *Citizenship and Nationhood in France and Germany* (1992), *Nationalism Reframed: Nationhood and the National Question in the New Europe* (1996), *Ethnicity without Groups* (2004), and *Nationalist Politics and Everyday Ethnicity in a Transylvanian Town* (with Margit Feischmidt, Jon Fox, and Liana Grancea, 2006).

Craig Calhoun is President of the Social Science Research Council and University Professor of Social Sciences at NYU. His most recent book is *Nations Matter: Culture, History, and the Cosmopolitan Dream* (2007). He has also edited *Lessons of Empire: Historical Contexts for Understanding America's Global Power* (with F. Cooper and K. Moore, 2006), *Sociology in America* (2007), *Robert K. Merton: Sociology of Science and Sociology as Science* (2010), and *Knowledge Matters: The Public Mission of the Research University* (with Diana Rhoten, forthcoming).

Vincent Della Sala teaches at the University of Trento and is also Adjunct Professor of Political Science at the Bologna Center of the Johns Hopkins School of Advanced International Studies. His recent work includes *Governance and Civil Society in the European Union: Exploring Policy Issues* (coauthored, 2007) and *Governance and Civil Society in the EU: Normative Perspectives* (coauthored, 2007). His current work focuses on the role of narratives and myths in the construction of the European Union.

Georgi Derluguian is a historical sociologist. His last monograph, *Bourdieu's Secret Admirer in the Caucasus* (2005), won numerous awards including the Norbert Elias Prize and was recognized by the American Sociological Association as among the best books in political sociology and political economy for the year 2005.

Nils Gilman is a consultant with Monitor 360, where he focuses on emerging geostrategic issues. He is the author of *Mandarins of the Future* (2004), an intellectual history of modernization theory, and *Deviant Globalization* (forthcoming 2011), an anthology that explores how globalized black-market economies are challenging traditional state authority. He is also the coeditor of *Humanity,* an international journal of human rights, humanitarianism, and development, published by the University of Pennsylvania Press.

David Held is the Graham Wallas Chair in Political Science and Co-director of LSE Global Governance at the London School of Economics. Among his most recent publications are *Cosmopolitanism: Ideals and Realities* (2010), *Globalisation/Anti-globalisation* (2007), *Models of Democracy* (2006), *Global Covenant* (2004), *Global Transformations: Politics, Economics and Culture* (1999), and *Democracy and the Global Order: From the Modern State to Cosmopolitan Governance* (1995). His main research interests include the study of globalization, changing forms of democracy, and the prospects of regional and global governance. He is a Director of Polity Press, which he cofounded in 1984, and General Editor of *Global Policy*.

Mary Kaldor is Professor and Director of the Centre for the Study of Global Governance, London School of Economics. She is the author of many books, including *The Ultimate Weapon Is No Weapon: Human Security and the Changing Rules of War and Peace* (coauthored, 2010), *New and Old Wars: Organised Violence in a Global Era* (2007), and *Global Civil Society: An Answer to War* (2003). Professor Kaldor was a founding member of European Nuclear Disarmament and of the Helsinki Citizen's Assembly. She is the convenor of the Human Security Study Group, which reported to Javier Solana, the High Representative for Common Foreign and Security Policy of the European Union, and now reports to his successor, Cathy Ashton.

Adrian Pabst is a lecturer in politics at the University of Kent, UK, and a visiting professor at the Institut d'Etudes Politiques de Lille (Sciences Po), where he teaches political theory and political economy. He is the editor of several books, including *The Crisis of Global Capitalism: Pope Benedict's Social Encyclical and the Future of Political Economy* (2011). His first monograph is entitled *Metaphysics: The Creation of Hierarchy* and will be published in 2011. He is currently writing *The Politics of Paradox*, a book on alternatives to the logic of left/right and state/market that has been dominant since the secular settlement of the French Revolution. His main research interests include the links between democracy and capitalism and the role of religion in the economy and the intermediary institutions of civil society.

Ravi Sundaram is a Fellow at the Centre for the Study of Developing Societies and one of the founders of Sarai, the CSDS's program on media and urban life. He recently published *Pirate Modernity: Media Urbanism in Delhi* (2009) and has just completed an edited volume, *No Limits: Media Studies of India*, due out next year.

Vadim Volkov is Vice Rector for International Affairs and Professor of Sociology in the Department of Political Science and Sociology at the European University in St. Petersburg. He is the author of *Violent Entrepreneurs: The Use of Force in the Making of Russian Capitalism* (2002) and of articles in *Social Research, Politics and Society* and *Europe-Asia Studies*. His research interests include economic sociology, problems of state and violence, public and private security, comparative mafia, and sociology of everyday life.

Michael J. Watts is Class of '63 and Chancellor's Professor of Geography and Development Studies at UC Berkeley, where he has taught for thirty-two years. He is currently completing a book on the political economy of oil in Nigeria, a companion to his book *Curse of the Black Gold* (with Ed Kashi), which recently appeared in a second edition (2010).

Kevin Young holds a PhD from the London School of Economics and is currently LSE Fellow in Global Politics within the Department of Government at the London School of Economics and Political Science. His research focuses on the politics of financial regulation and the operation of lobbying communities within the financial sector. He teaches classes on globalization and international political economy and is currently working on a book that documents how private-sector groups organize coalitions to lobby for regulatory change at the national and global levels.

Index

Information in figures and tables is denoted by *f* and *t*. Information in footnotes is denoted by "n" following the page number and preceding the note number.

in, 69; postcolonial, 74–81; Sahel region of, 74, 75–76, 245n35; sustainable development in, 69; tragedy of the commons in, 76

Africa as a Living Laboratory (Tilley), 71–72

African sleeping sickness, 244n21

Agriculture: colonialism and, 73; grain-livestock complex in, 68; indigenous knowledge and, 73–74; oil prices and, 67, 68; tragedy of the commons and, 76

AIG (insurance company), 142

Albert, Michael, 63

Amnesty International, 22

Amsterdam, as offshore gateway, 206

Analog technology, media and, 186

Andorra, 212

Anselm of Canterbury, 177

Anthropology, religion *vs.*, 160–161

Anti-Semitism, 255n41

AOL-Time Warner merger, 198

Arab-Israeli war, 113

Argentina, on copyright watch list, 195

Arizona, immigration legislation in, 100

Arkwright's Mill, 111

Association for Financial Markets in Europe (AFME), 38

Association of American Publishers (AAP), 195

Atheism, science and, 177–179

Augsburg peace, 166

Augustine of Hippo, 166

Australia, on Basel Committee, 35

Austria, banking crisis in, 143

Austro-Prussian War, 116, 119*t*

Autarkic nationalism, 96

Author, copyright and, 194–195

Automobile Age, 111–112, 111*t*, 115*f*

Automobile sector stimulus, in European Union, 146

Bacevich, Andrew, 43

Bacon, Francis, 161

Bahamas, secrecy in, 206

Bahrain, as offshore insurance center, 210

Bank for International Settlements, 25–26, 223n16

Ban Ki-moon, 93

Barnes, William, 275

Basel Capital Accord, 26

Basel Committee on Banking Supervision (BCBS), 35; in fragmented global financial governance system, 25; membership exclusivity in, 27; private sector privilege with, 38; regulatory standards of, 35–36

Basel Concordat, 26

Basel II Capital Accord, 26, 35

Basel III Accord, 36

BCBS. *See* Basel Committee on Banking Supervision (BCBS)

Belgium, 212

Bell, Daniel, 43

Benedict XVI, Pope, 176, 177

Benjamin, Walter, 175, 187

Benkler, Yochai, 195

Berg, Elliot, 77, 79

Berg Report, 76–77

Bermuda, as offshore insurance center, 210

Berne Convention, 194–195

Biofuels: African land and, 68; short-comings of, 49

Birth of Biopolitics, The (Foucault), 67

Blair, Tony, 56

BNP Paribas, 141

Bonds, joint European, 144

Bottom Billion, The (Collier), 69

Boulding, Kenneth, 51

Boyle, James, 195

Branson, Richard, 81, 82*f*

Brazil: on Basel Committee, 35; carbon emissions and growth of, 47; ethnopolitics in, 105; in Financial Stability Forum, 34; offshore sector as investment source for, 213

Break Through: Why We Can't Leave Saving the Planet to Environmentalists (Nordhaus & Shellenberger), 56

Bretton Woods conference, 33, 113, 190–191

Brown, Gordon, 145

Brubaker, Rogers, 275

Brundtland Report, 83

BSA. *See* Business Software Alliance (BSA)

Bukharin, Nikolai, 61

Burma, ethnopolitics in, 102

Bush doctrine, 31–32

Business Software Alliance (BSA), 195

Calhoun, Craig, 275–276

Canada: registered enterprises in, 216*f;* "social economy" model in, 63–64

Canclini, Néstor Garcia, 192

Capacity problem: Afghanistan and, 31; in environmental governance, 28–30; in financial governance, 25; of global governance, 23; Iraq War and, 31; in security governance, 30–31

Cap-and-trade, 49–50

Capital: Basel Committee standards on, 35–36; neoliberalism and, 122

Capitalism: in European Union, competing models of, 135; ex-territorial, 204, 212–217; "managed," 83; as model, 236n26; in neo-Schumpeterian theory, 110–121; petty-bourgeois culture of, 60–61; "producerist," 61; war and, 116; as world ecology, 70–71

Carbon levels, 47, 48, 82, 234n11. *See also* Climate change; Greenhouse gas (GHG) emissions

Carbon prices, 50

Carnegie Commission, 32

Carter, Jimmy, 51

Cato Institute, 208

Cayman Islands, 206, 211, 215

CDOs. *See* Collateralized debt obligations (CDOs)

CFSP. *See* Common Foreign and Security Policy (CFSP)

Chance, science and, 178

Chang Mai Initiative, 36

Channel Islands, secrecy in, 206

Chechnya conflict, 128, 131

Chile, on copyright watch list, 195

China: on Basel Committee, 35; carbon emissions and growth of, 47; Catholics in, 172; Christianity in,

168; Copenhagen Summit failure and, 46; on copyright watch list, 195; in Financial Stability Forum, 34; Muslims in, 172; national bank of, as rising power, 37; offshore sector as investment source for, 213; Protestantism in, 172; "Yenan Way" in, 61

Chinese, as market-dominant minorities, 103

Christian Democrats, 168

Cinema, 186, 187, 188–189, 188–190

Cité Soleil, Port au Prince, 126

Civilization, climate change and fundamental aspects of, 47

"Civil religion," 169–170

Civil society, in neoliberalism, 87

Civil War, American, 116, 119*t*

Climate change. *See also* Environment; Greenhouse gas (GHG) emissions: adaptation to, 87–88; Africa as disproportionately affected by, 68; carbon prices and, 50; civilization and, 47; concomitant crises with, 44; consensus on, 45; consumption and, 51–55; Copenhagen Summit on, 29, 46–48; disasters and, 44; Dyer on, 46–47; as emergency, 85; energy requirements and, 48; evolutionary gradualism and, 84; geoengineering to counter, 236n21; human carrying capacity of planet and, 44; impact of, 43–44, 84–85, 230n1; importance of, 84–85; lopsided responsibilities in, 46–47; as market governance stage, 84; negative

effects of, 30; positive feedback in, 230n1; problem of, 29; realism in approach to, 45–46; refugee problems and, 44; renewable energy as insufficient to address, 48–49; resiliency and, 86; scientific debate on, 230n1; scope of changes needed to address, 45; sea levels and, 44, 231n1; technological inability to address, 45, 48–51, 233n10, 234n15; temperature increases in, 82; United Nations Framework Convention on, 82; unpalatability of solutions to, 47; as vehicle for new discourses, 82–83

Club of Rome, 74–75, 86, 89

Cohesiveness, of systems, 88

Collateralized debt obligations (CDOs), Basel Committee and, 36

Collier, Paul, 69

Colonialism: in Africa, 71–72; agriculture and, 73; ethnopolitics and, 102–103; famine and, 78; green governmentality and, 71–74; modernity and, 71–72; secularism and, 168

Commission for Sustainable Development, 29

Common Foreign and Security Policy (CFSP), 137

Commons, global, 24

Communication, in financial governance, 25–26

Competition, in Lisbon Treaty, 146

Complex adaptive systems, 86–87

Complexity science, 88

Doria, Paolo Mattia, 166

Drought: in Africa, 74, 75–76; mediation of, 80

Durkheim, Émile, 160

Dussel, Enrique, 71

Dyer, Gwynne, 46–47

Easterly, William, 69

ECB. *See* European Central Bank (ECB)

Ecological modernization theory, 55–59, 237n31

"Economics of the Coming Spaceship Earth, The" (Boulding), 51

ECOSOC. *See* United Nations Economic and Social Council (ECOSOC)

EFSF. *See* European Financial Stabilization Facility (EFSF)

Egypt, on copyright watch list, 195

Eisenstein, Elizabeth, 184

Electricity Age, 111, 111*t*

Emergency, climate change as, 85

Emissions Trading Scheme (ETS), 247n61

Empiricism, 166

Employment, consumption reduction and, 52

End of Faith, The (Harris), 178

Endogamy, 170–171

Energy, renewable, shortcomings of, 48–49

Energy requirements, in climate change problem, 48

Entertainment Software Association (ESA), 195

Environmental Chamber of the

International Court of Justice, 29

Environment and environmentalism. *See also* Climate change; Greenhouse gas (GHG) emissions: accountability and, 29; Africa as laboratory for ideas on, 69–70, 90–91; capacity problem and, 28–30; Copenhagen Summit on, 29, 46–48; ecological modernization theory and, 55–59; factions in, 238n34; fragmentation of global governance in, 28–29; in global commons, 24; global governance of, 28–30; inclusion and, 29; indigenous knowledge of, 73–74; inefficiency of agreements on, 29; international regime of, 83; ISO management standards, 84; neo-Malthusian, 75–77, 77*f*; power disparity and, 29–30; resiliency and, 86; security and, 85, 86–91

Environment Directorate, 29

Environment Management Group, 28–29

Episcopalianism, 263n29

ESA. *See* Entertainment Software Association (ESA)

Ethiopia, scramble for land in, 68

Ethnic exclusion, 105–106

Ethnicity, politicized, 94–96

Ethnic outsiders, 95

"Ethno-botany," 73

Ethnopolitics: colonialism and, 102–103; division of labor and, 102; economically empowered minorities in, 103–104; economic crisis and, 102–106; nationalism

Fides et Ratio (Pope John Paul II), 177

Film, 186, 187, 188–189, 188–190

Finance: accountability problems in, 27; capacity problem and, 25; communication in, institutions facilitating, 25–26; developing countries' inclusion in governance of, 34; fragmentation of global governance in, 25; in global commons, 24; global governance deficiencies in, 24–28; inclusion problems in, 27; inertia and reforms in, 37; lack of central authority in, 26–27; reforms since crisis, 33–34; responsibility problem and, 27; risk dispersal in, 24–25; skewed representation in, 27

Financial Action Task Force (FATF), 25, 208, 212

Financial centers, offshore, 204, 209, 273n10

Financial Stability Board (FSB): expanded role of, 34; risk and, 34; supervisory colleges of, 34

Financial Stability Forum, 25–26, 34

Financial transactions tax, 36, 40

Flags of convenience, 210

Flickr, 184

Food security, in Africa, 67

Fordism, 111–112, 113

Foreign workers: economic crisis and, 99; in labor market, 100; nation-statism and, 101; unemployment and, 95; vulnerability of, 99

Fortis, 142

Foucault, Michel, 67, 70, 77, 85, 87, 91, 175

Fragmentation: in environmental governance, 28–29; in financial governance, 25

France, 119*t*; European Financial Stabilization Facility and, 149; Germany *vs.*, in response to financial crisis, 145–146; in Great Depression, immigration and, 99; nationalism in, 105–106; push for regulation by, 146; registered enterprises in, 216*f*; rejection of European constitution by, 140; religion in, 264n34; Stability and Growth Pact and, 147; stimulus package by, 146; unemployment in, 151

Franco-Prussian War, 116

Freeman, Chris, 110

"French Christendom," 264n34

Friedman, Milton, 207

Frow, John, 195

FSB. *See* Financial Stability Board (FSB)

Fundamentalism, secularism *vs.*, 157

G20: in Basel Committee, 35; Financial Stability Board and, 34; reform call by, 34–35; summits, after crisis, 33–34

Gaines, Jane, 199

Gakkai, Soka, 171

Gelasius I, Pope, 166

General Theory (Keynes), 52

Genovesi, Antonio, 166

Geoengineering, 236n21

Geothermal energy, shortcomings of, 49

required in, 46, 48, 50–51, 234n11, 234n13; increasing, 44; in International Panel on Climate Change Report, 48; political difficulty of reduction in, 53; stalling political will on, 45; technology as unable to address, 48–49

Griffith, Saul, 48, 234n15

Grove, Richard, 69, 81

Growth: Bell on, 43; consumption and, 51–52; as goal, 43; limits and, 124; military spending and, 118; as normative assumption, 52–53; as political promise, 53; predication of economy on, 52–53; success and, 53; sustainable, 55–59; sustainable development and, 74–75

Guernsey, 212

Hardin, Garrett, 78

Harris, Sam, 178

Harvey, David, 102

Hayek, Friedrich, 89

Health care reform, 53–54

Hedge funds, 211

Hegemonic wars, 116, 125

Held, David, 276–277

Helleiner, Eric, 38

Holling, C. S., 87, 88, 89

Hollywood, 188–190

Hong Kong: on Basel Committee, 35; as export-processing zone, 210

"Human security," 130

"Human security forces," 132

Hume, David, 166

Hungary, ethnopolitics in, 105

Hypo Realty Estate, 142

IBC. *See* International Business Company (IBC)

IBRD. *See* International Bank for Reconstruction and Development (IBRD)

Iceland, in European Union, 152

IFTA. *See* Independent Film and Television Alliance (IFTA)

IIF. *See* Institute of International Finance (IIF)

IIPA. *See* International Intellectual Property Alliance (IIPA)

IMF. *See* International Monetary Fund (IMF)

Immigration, economic crisis and, 99

Imperialism, famine and, 78

Inclusion: environmental governance and, 29; in financial governance institutions, 27; global governance and, 23–24

Independent Film and Television Alliance (IFTA), 195

India: alternative to materialism in, 59, 61; on Basel Committee, 35; carbon emissions and growth of, 47; on copyright watch list, 195; ethnopolitics in, 102; films in, 192; in Financial Stability Forum, 34; offshore sector as investment source for, 213; video in, 192

Indigenous knowledge, 73–74

Indonesia: attacks on Chinese in, 93, 103, 104–105; ethnopolitics in, 103

Industrial Revolution: Catholic Church and, 168; as technological cycle, 111, 111*t*, 115*f*

Industry, consumption reduction and

Locke, John, 160, 161, 270n40
London, as offshore gateway, 206
Lovelock, James, 44
Luxembourg, secrecy in, 206, 212

Macao, 207, 212
Madagascar, 68
Malthusianism, 74–81
"Managed capitalism," 83
Manhattan Project, 50, 235n19
Manovich, Lev, 268n12
Maritime registration, low-cost, 210
Market governance, climate change as theater for, 84
Marshall Islands, 212
Marx, Karl, 116
Mass Production Age, 111–112, 111*t*, 115*f*
Materialism: alternative to, in India, 59; environmentalism and, 56–58
Materiality, media and, 187–188
Mbembe, Achille, 79
McChrystal, Stanley, 129
McNamara, Robert, 75
MDG. *See* Millennium Development Goals (MDG)
Meadows, Dennis, 75
Media: consumer production of, 185; digital technology and, 186–187; fair-use doctrine and, 195–196; geographical stability of, 183; institutional regulation of, 183; materiality and, 187–188; population participation in, 185; public domain and, 195; recent changes in, 184; sharing, 184; social-networking and, 186–187; spectacle

and, 190; traditional forms of, 183; video and, 190–193
Media piracy: control and, 185; copyright and, 193–198; examples of, 185; laws for, 197; materiality and, 188; peer-to-peer networks and, 199; rise in, 185; video and, 193
Medicalization, of social structure, 70
Merkl, Angela, 147, 150
Mexico: on Basel Committee, 35; as export-processing zone, 210
Military Keynesianism, 123–124
Military spending: on anachronistic projects, 124; economic growth and, 118; financial crisis and, 226n32; global, 31; hegemony and, 117; innovation and, 120; "spin-offs" from, 121; trade deficit and, 120; in United States, 120–121, 123
Mill, John Stuart, 79
Millennium Development Goals (MDG), 23, 69, 242n6
Mitchell, Daniel, 208
MIT Systems Dynamics Group, 74–75
Modernity: colonialism and, 71–72; as dialectical process, 158; dialectic of, 164–171; religion and, 157; sacred in, 165; secularism and, 159; theism and, 161; universalization of, 236n26
Modernization theory, ecological, 55–59, 237n31
Mohamad, Mahathir, 211, 219
Monaco, secrecy in, 206
Monbiot, George, 84

Monterrey Consensus, 27

Moore, Jason, 71

Morris, Simon Conway, 179

Motion Picture Association of America (MPAA), 189, 195, 271n52

MPAA. *See* Motion Picture Association of America (MPAA)

Nally, David, 78

Napoleonic Wars, 116, 118, 119*t*, 128

Nationalism: autarkic, 96; economic, 93; ethnopolitics and, 95; European debt crisis and, 94; in France, 105–106; IMF assistance and, 97; narratives of current crisis in, 106; nation-statism and, 94–95; protectionism and, 97; "resource," 97

National Music Publishers' Association (NMPA), 195

Nation-statism: credit crisis in, 106; economic crisis in, 97–102; foreign workers and, 101; nationalism and, 94–95; privilege in, 95–96; protectionism in, 98–99

Natural selection, religion and, 178

Neoliberalism: Berg Report and, 76–77; under Bush, 123–124; capital and, 122; civil society in, 87; democratization and, 127; disenchantment with, 98, 101; financial reform and, 39; Global South and, 101; innovations and, 123; institution building and, 123; military Keynesianism and, 123–124; in post-war period, 123; protectionism and, 98; under Reagan, 123; resilience of, 101–102; shift away

from, 217; technology cycles and, 122, 123

Neo-Malthusian environmentalism, 75–77, 77*f*

Neo-Platonism, 166

Neo-Schumpeterianism, 110–121

Netherlands, rejection of European constitution by, 140

New Jersey, incorporation in, 205

New Labor, 56

New Right, 58

Nigeria: protectionism and, 99; video in, 192

NMPA. *See* National Music Publishers' Association (NMPA)

Nordhaus, Ted, 56–57

Northern Rock bank, 142

Nuclear energy, shortcomings of, 49

Obama, Barack, 211

OECD. *See* Organisation for Economic Co-operation and Development (OECD)

OFCs. *See* Offshore financial centers (OFCs)

Offshore financial centers (OFCs), 204, 209, 273n10

Offshore insurance centers, 210

Offshore sector: climate and, 214–215; conceptions of, 205–207; democracy and, 208; entities in, 210; ex-territorial capitalism and, 212–217; features of, 209; geography and, 214; growth of, 206–207; hedge funds in, 211; ideology of, 207–209; as investment source for developing countries, 213; legal entity element of, 215–216; liberal vision of, 207–208; moves against, 210–212; origins of, 205; registered enterprises in, 216f; as shadow economy, 208; size of, 209–210; tax losses due to, 211; transparency and, 217–218; wealth held in, 210, 214; in welfare-state view, 208

Oil Age, 111–112, 111t, 112, 115f

Oil prices: agriculture and, 67, 68; trade deficit and, 113

O'Regan, Tom, 191

Organisation for Economic Co-operation and Development (OECD): in environmental governance, 29; Global Forum on Transparency and Exchange of Information, 212; Global Tax Justice Network, 208; transparency push by, 217–218

Orkut, 184, 186–187

Ostrom, Elinor, 80

Ottoman Empire, 168

Our Common Future (United Nations World Commission on Environment and Development), 83

Outsiders, insiders *vs.*, 94–95

Overpopulation, in Foucault, 78–79

Oxfam, 22

Pabst, Adrian, 277

Palan, Ronen, 205, 213

Palestinian conflict, 128

Panama, as flag of convenience, 210

Panitchpakdi, Supachai, 28

Paterson, Matthew, 83–84

Peccei, Aurelio, 74

Peer-to-peer networks, 199, 271n54

Pentecostalism, 172, 173

People's Bank of China, rising power of, 37

Perez, Carlotta, 110, 112, 115, 119, 122

Petraeus, David, 129

Petroleum, waning supply of, 44

Petty-bourgeois culture, 60–61

"PIGS" group, in Europe, 144

Piore, Michael, 63

Piracy, media: control and, 185; copyright and, 193–198; examples of, 185; laws for, 197; materiality and, 188; peer-to-peer networks and, 199; rise in, 185; video and, 193

Polanyi, Karl, 77

Politics of Climate Change, The (Giddens), 232n6

Pope Benedict XVI, 176

Pope Gelasius I, 166

Pope John Paul II, 177

Populism, democratic, 61–62

Port au Prince, Haiti, 126

Porter, Tony, 38

Portugal, debt crisis in, 144

Positive feedback, in climate change, 230n1

Positivism, 161

Postcolonialism: in Africa, 74–81; ethnopolitics and, 102–103

"Post-materialism," 57–58

Postmodernity, religion and, 157–158

Poverty: in Global South, 68–69; as humanitarian arena, 69

Poverty and Famines (Sen), 79–80

Prevention of Deadly Conflict: Final Report (Carnegie Commission), 32

161; postmodernity and, 157–158; science and, 177–179; shift from revelation to belief, 261n9

Renewable energy, shortcomings of, 48–49

Republicanism, producerist, 61, 231n1

Rerum Novarum, 168

Reserve currency, dollar *vs.* euro as, 144

Resilience, 86–91

Resilience Alliance, 88

Resilience Center, 88

"Resource nationalism," 97

Responsibility problem: climate change and, 46–47; in financial governance, 27; of global governance, 23–24; in security governance, 32

RIAA. *See* Recording Industry Association of America (RIAA)

Risk: calculation of, 86–87; Financial Stability Board and, 34; interconnectedness and dispersal of, 24–25; resiliency and, 86–87; shifting concept of, 86–87; systemic inability to track, 26

Rodowick, D. N., 186

Rodrik, Dani, 98

Romania, ethnopolitics in, 103

Romm, Joseph, 231n1

Roosevelt, Teddy, 53

Roots of Resilience, 89, 90

Rostow, Walt, 54

Roy, Ananya, 68

Russia. *See also* Soviet Union: on Basel Committee, 35; on copyright watch list, 195; offshore sector

as investment source for, 213; produceris republicanism in, 61; registered enterprises in, 216f; Soviet collapse and, 32

Sabel, Charles, 63

Sachs, Jeffrey, 69

Sahel region, of Africa, 74, 75–76, 245n35

Saint John Chrysostom, 166

São Paulo G20 summit, 33–34

Sarkozy, Nicolas, 145, 146

Save the Children, 22

Scarcity, in Foucault, 77–78

Schmitt, Carl, 175

Schumpeteriansim, 110

Science: atheism and, 177–179; chance and, 178; colonialism and, 72; complexity, 88; religion and, 177–179

Scott, James, 80

Scott, John, 214

Sea levels, global warming and, 44, 231n1

Secrecy: history and, 203; institutionalization of, 203–204; security and, 203; selective, 218; specialization in, 204; as special service of states, 204; in Switzerland, 205

Secularism: alternative account of, 162–164; chance and, 178; colonialism and, 168; deconstruction of, 159; dualism in, 161; extreme, 169; fundamentalism *vs.,* 157; hegemony of, 170; industrialization and, 160; at level of ideas, 165–167; at level of practice,

167–171; modernization and, 159; in philosophy, 167; premodern *vs.* modern, 166; "programmatic," 180; Protestantism and, 167; religious embrace of, 180; resistance to, 168–169; in United States, 169–170; universalism and, 180; violence in 20th century and, 169

Security: capacity problem and, 30–31; crisis of, 125–128; development and, 132; environmentalism and, 85, 86–91; food, in Africa, 67; in Foucault, 77, 85; in global commons, 24; global governance of, 30–32; "human," 130; institutional adaptation and, 128; in neo-Schumpeterianism, 127–129; privatization and, 127; resilience and, 87; responsibility problem and, 32; secrecy and, 203

Security Council, United Nations, 32

Selective secrecy, 218

Self-interpretation, 107

Selfishness, 122

Self-segregation, 170–171

Sen, Amartya, 79–80

Seoul G20 summit, 36

September 11, 2001: effects of, 31–32; as indicative of global shift, 183

Seven Years' War, 116

SGP. *See* Stability and Growth Pact (SGP)

Shadow economy, 208–209

Shapin, Steven, 74

Sharing, of media, 184

Shellenberger, Michael, 56–57

Simmel, Georg, 203

Singapore: on Basel Committee, 35; offshore sector in, 212

Sleeping sickness, 244n21

Slovakia, European Financial Stabilization Facility and, 149

Smith, Adam, 79, 167

"Social economy" model, 63–64

Social-networking, 186–187, 267n1

Society of the Spectacle (Debord), 190

Socioecological resilience, 87

Soil moisture, 231n1

Solar energy, shortcomings of, 49

Sonny Bono Copyright Extension Act, 195

Sony Corporation of America v. Universal City Studios, 193

South Korea, on Basel Committee, 35

Sovereignty: global governance and, 22; international governmental organizations and, 22

Soviet National Accounts, 52

Soviet Union. *See also* Russia: collapse of, 32; military spending in, 120

Spain: debt crisis in, 144, 148; deficit levels in, 145; housing bubble in, 150; unemployment in, 94

Spectacle, media and, 190

Stability and Growth Pact (SGP), 138, 145, 147

Stalin, Joseph, 52

Standard of living, rise in, as goal, 53

State governance, global governance *vs.,* 21

Stationers Company, 193–194

Statute of Anne, 193, 269n38, 270n39

Steam Age, 111, 111*t,* 115*f*

Steel Age, 111, 111*t,* 115*f*

Steinbrueck, Peter, 211
Stern, Nick, 49
Stiglitz, Joseph, 121
Stimulus packages, in European Union, 146
Stockholm Conference, 74, 75, 81
Stockholm Resilience Center, 87, 89
Stop Tax Haven Abuse Act, 211–212
Style, technological, 111
Success, consumption and, 53
Sudan, scramble for land in, 68
Sundaram, Ravi, 277
Sun Yat-sen, 168
Sustainable development: in Africa, 69; history of concept, 74–75
Sustainable growth, 55–59
Sutterlin, James, 32
Swift, Jeremy, 80
Switzerland: moves against offshore sector in, 212; secrecy in, 205
System cohesiveness, 88
Systems Dynamics Group, 74, 75

Taiwan, as export-processing zone, 210
Tax, on financial transactions, 36, 40
Tax-exempt trusts, 206
Tax havens, 204, 210, 211–212. *See also* Offshore sector
Tax Justice Network, 210, 211
Taylor, Peter, 75
Tea Party movement, as producerist, 65
"Techno-economic paradigm," 111, 117
Technology: adaptation and, 112; analog, media and, 186; colonialism and, 72; digital, media and, 186–187; geoengineering, 236n21; inability of, to address climate change, 48–51, 233n10, 234n15; neoliberalism and, 122, 123; in neo-Schumpeterian theory, 110–111; post-materialism and, 58; revolutions in, 111*t*; transition of styles in, current period as, 110; war and, 117
Techno-military paradigm, 117
Telecommunications Age, 111*t*, 114, 115*f*
Territory, jurisdiction and, 213–214
Terrorism, security governance and, 31–32
TEU. *See* Treaty on European Union (TEU)
Thailand, on copyright watch list, 195
Thatcher, Margaret, 53, 58
Theism, modernity and, 161
Third Way, 56, 58, 239n36
Thomas Aquinas, 161
Tilley, Helen, 69, 71–72, 74
Time Warner-AOL merger, 198
Trade regimes, 97, 98
"Trading diasporas," 103–104
Tragedy of the commons, 76
Transactional reality, 87
Transcendentalism, 161, 163
"Transition town" model, 63–64
Transparency, demands for, 217–218
Treaty of Maastricht, 137
Treaty of Rome, 136
Treaty of Westphalia, 166
Treaty on European Union (TEU), 137–138
Trotsky, Leon, 116

undocumented workers in, 100; welfare benefit access in, by non-citizens, 253n23; World Wars and, outcome of, 119, 119t
Universalism, secularism and, 180
Universal principles, 22–23
US Agency for International Development (USAID), 76

VCRs. *See* Video cassette recorders (VCRs)
Venezuela, on copyright watch list, 195
VHS, 191
Vico, Giambattista, 166
Video, 187–188, 190–193
Video cassette recorders (VCRs), 191
Video clubs, 192
Vietnam War, 109, 120, 190
Virgin Islands, 206
Volkov, Vadim, 277–278

Walker, J., 89
War(s): business analogy of, 117; capitalism and, 116; decrease in major, 125; economic crises and, 109; hegemonic, 116, 125; insecurity *vs.*, 126; interstate, decrease in, 125, 226n31; in neo-Schumpeterian theory, 116–117; peripheral, increasing visibility of, 126; technology and, 117; upswings and, 116
War on Terror, security governance and, 31
Wars of Spanish Succession, 116
Washington, D.C. G20 summit, 33–34

Water, waning supply of, 44
Watts, Michael J., 278
Wealth, in offshore sector, 210, 214
Wealth of Nations (Smith), 167
Weather-related disasters, 44
Weber, Max, 40, 160, 255n38
Weinberg, Alvin, 50
Welfare benefits, noncitizen access to, 253n23
WHO. *See* World Health Organization (WHO)
WikiLeaks, 200
Wind energy, shortcomings of, 49
Windward Islands, 206
World Bank: accountability of, 34; on agriculture business, 50; Berg Report by, 77; financial governance role of, 25; resilience in policy document of, 89; voting rules of, 27
World Health Organization (WHO), founding principles of, 22
World order, as dysfunctional, 40
World Resources Institute, 89
World Trade Organization (WTO): Committee on Trade and the Environment, 224n22; trade regimes and, 98
World War I, geopolitical outcome of, 119t
World War II: geopolitical outcome of, 119t; Great Depression and, 113; mass production and, 118; multilateral order after, 22; neo-liberalism after, 123; UN Security Council and, 32; U.S. assistance after, 113; U.S. hegemony and, 119, 119t